EVERYTHING
YOU NEED TO KNOW ABOUT...

EVERYTHING

YOU NEED TO KNOW ABOUT...

Paganism

SELENE SILVERWIND

D&C
David and Charles

A DAVID & CHARLES BOOK

Updates and amendments copyright © David & Charles Limited 2006

Copyright © 2004 F+W Publications Inc.

David & Charles is an F+W Publications Inc.
4700 East Galbraith Road
Cincinnati, OH 45236

First published in the UK in 2006
First published in the USA as *The Everything® Paganism Book*,
by Adams Media in 2004

A catalogue record for this book is available from the British Library.

ISBN-13: 978-0-7153-2486-8 paperback
ISBN-10: 0-7153-2486-1 paperback

Printed in Great Britain by CPI Bath
for David & Charles
Brunel House   Newton Abbot   Devon

Visit our website at www.davidandcharles.co.uk

David & Charles books are available from all good bookshops;
alternatively you can contact our Orderline on 0870 9908222 or
write to us at FREEPOST EX2 110, D&C Direct, Newton Abbot,
TQ12 4ZZ (no stamp required UK only); US customers call
800-289-0963 and Canadian customers call 800-840-5220.

Everything You Need to Know About Paganism is intended as a reference
book only. While author and publisher have made every attempt
to offer accurate and reliable information to the best of their
knowledge and belief, it is presented without any guarantee.
The author and publisher therefore disclaim any liability incurred
in connection with the information contained in this book.

Contents

Acknowledgments

I would like to thank the following people for their valuable advice and support during the writing of this book: Brian Ewing for advising on the legal chapter and understanding when I couldn't go out to dinner because I had to write, and Ed and Dorothy Kennedy for reviewing the early chapters. Michael Gorman, Druid Founder of the Sacramento Grove of the Oak, Inc., and Lisa Tonner both generously offered to review the chapters on Druidry and Asatru. Their corrections helped me better understand both faiths, and will benefit your understanding as well. Sheela Ardrian's editing and advice greatly improved the chapter on alternative sexuality. Special thanks also to Karen Tate for her help with Egyptian history. I'd also like to thank those who chose not to be named. I couldn't have done it without you.

The Top Ten Myths
about Pagans

1. Pagans worship the devil.
2. Pagans can fly on a broomstick and have special magical powers.
3. Pagan women are nymphomaniacs and all Pagans have wild orgies every night.
4. Pagans lack a code of ethics and are amoral.
5. Pagans worship outdated gods and goddesses.
6. Pagans were all raised by hippie nomads.
7. Pagans practice animal sacrifice.
8. Pagans live in wooden huts outside of society.
9. Pagans are a very small minority of the population.
10. Pagans don't have the same legal rights as members of other religions.

Introduction

PAGANISM IS SOMETIMES DEFINED as any non-Judeo-Christian or Muslim religion. By this definition, Buddhism, Hinduism, and many other faiths are Pagan, but for purposes of this book, Paganism refers to a group of religions that promote reverence for the earth and/or the deities of pre-Christian religions. The term *Neo-Paganism* applies specifically to Wicca and other religions that were created during the last century or two. Some Druids call themselves Neo-Pagans, but others dislike the term because they associate their beliefs with older traditions. Asatruars and other reconstructionists sometimes balk at the term Neo-Pagan because they attempt to reconstruct the original beliefs and practices of a specific people rather than creating new beliefs. Santerians, Native Americans, and Vodouns are not Neo-Pagan because they practice older religions with a direct heritage of worship and belief. When talking about themselves, many Neo-Pagans shorten the term to Pagan, and Santerians, Native Americans, and Vodouns don't usually call themselves Pagan at all.

Collectively, Paganism is one of the most rapidly growing religions in the world. It is a beautiful, life-affirming faith that honors the land and all its creatures. Because it has revived the old gods, it is sometimes called the Old Religion. Whatever the name, many people have found that the faith fills a void they've long carried.

Have you ever wondered what happened to the ancient gods you learned about in grade school? Have you ever felt the need to sit beside a tree and listen to it speak? Do lights twinkle at the corners of your eyes and you wonder if they might be faeries? Do animals visit you in your dreams, carrying powerful messages? Do you notice the cycles of the moon and feel a special significance on the solstices and equinoxes? Do you believe Viking lore has much to offer today's society? Do you feel a call to the sacred sites of Ireland and England? If the answer to any of these questions is "yes," you just might be Pagan!

This book has several goals. The first is to educate people who feel drawn to an alternative faith, but aren't quite sure what that means. You might have researched many beliefs, and maybe tried a few practices. This book gives an overview of several of the major Pagan faiths and some of the minor ones. It also offers insights on how many aspects of human life tie into Paganism and how to incorporate Paganism into your life.

Paganism can't be learned in a day, and you could spend decades researching every branch and every facet. *The Everything® Paganism Book* aims to give you an overview so you can decide how to start your life as a Pagan and research more specifically from there. It will also give you the tools you need to get started. And if you are a Pagan who wants to know more about another branch of Paganism you are not familiar with, this book can serve as a light refresher on the most important aspects of each faith.

If you need help explaining your Pagan beliefs to someone close to you, this book is a handy tool for conveying your message, and it offers a few tips on just how to do it. As you'll see, being Pagan is a daily experience and a constant learning process. Even after ten, twenty, or thirty years as a Pagan, you'll discover new information or wander down a new road to wisdom.

So grab your knapsack, pick up your walking stick, and step out on the path to Paganism. The spirits and the gods will guide you, if you let them. You might stumble over a twig or be carried along by the wind, but don't be afraid, for many good things lie ahead. When you come to a fork in the road, listen to your heart and it will help you follow the right path. And regardless of how long or how far you travel, you'll come out the other side a whole new person.

Chapter 1

The Roots of Paganism

Scholars date polytheism, or belief in multiple deities, to prehistoric times, when it took the form of goddess worship. As cultures and societies became more complex, and as people began to gather in large urban communities, their beliefs also expanded to meet new needs. Although religious practices varied widely from region to region, these societies largely remained polytheistic until the rise of monotheism.

Prehistoric Beliefs

Early humans venerated nature, the cycle of the sun, and the hunt. They honored fertility goddesses for their ability to create life. The oldest image of a goddess dates back to 35,000 B.C.E., and hundreds of goddess figures from this era have been found. They are usually pregnant women with pendulous breasts and broad hips, although some feature only the pubic triangle. Male figures, developed later, were generally depicted by the phallus.

The Willendorf Venus, one of the most famous of the early goddess figures, dates back to 25,000 B.C.E. and was discovered in Willendorf, Austria. She has no facial features, but wears an ornate hairstyle. The figure, carved from limestone, was painted with red ochre.

Early humans were nomads, and their survival was contingent on the hunt and the vegetative gifts of nature. Around 10,000 B.C.E., as tribes settled in permanent villages, people began attempting to control nature. Village hunters conducted rituals to symbolically re-create the hunt to ensure that it would be successful, and then wore the skins of the beasts they hunted to become one with the animal. Women were the keepers of the medicine and were responsible for developing agriculture.

The shift away from the goddess culture began around 4000 B.C.E., coincident with the rise of militarism and hierarchal societies. As these societies developed, beliefs became more aligned with where people lived. Male deities acquired greater importance in people's lives, in many cases superseding the roles once held by female deities. The last surviving goddess culture came to an end around 1500 B.C.E.

Ancient Greece

The Minoan society existed from about 2800 to 1500 B.C.E. and is one of the oldest cultures that would later merge with other cultures to form the Greek society. Ancient Minoans lived on the island of Crete and worshipped a goddess associated with animals and a young god, either

her son or her consort, who symbolized the cycle of nature. Minoans may have also worshipped Poseidon, although he is never pictured in temple artwork.

The Mycenaeans, another pre-Greek culture, occupied much of mainland Greece. In 1100 B.C.E., the Dorians, who arrived from northern Greece, invaded their lands. Little is known about this period, but by 800 B.C.E., the beliefs of Minoans, Mycenaeans, and Dorians merged to form the myths of the twelve Olympian Gods. Their veneration became the centerpiece of life in ancient Greek culture.

What is the origin of the word *Pagan*?
The term is derived from the Latin *paganus* (or *pagani* in plural) and was originally used by the urban Romans to refer to people who preferred the faith of their local ruling body. It was later applied to people who worshipped local deities, or people who practiced polytheism.

Worship centered around a sacred tree or spring inside a sanctuary; later, people would construct temples on these sites. Greek rituals involved burnt offerings, including animal sacrifices, as well as offerings of wool, oil, honey, and milk. People also made sacrifices on the home hearth and attended festivals to honor agricultural events, the birth of a new city, a hero's death, or life passages. Oracles, or shrines for the purpose of prophecy, were important to people's way of life. The most famous oracle was located at Delphi.

The Greek Creation Story

Part of the Greek mythology was a story of how the world was created. At the beginning, there was nothing (Chaos). From that came Gaea (the earth), and Tartarus (the underworld). Next came Eros (love). Night and Erebus (darkness) emerged together. From their mating came Day and Ether (air). Gaea then created Ouranos (heaven) and the mountains and the sea. Gaea took Ouranos as her consort, and Oceanus was born as a great river that surrounded the flat disk of the earth. They also gave birth to the six Titans, the Furies, nymphs, giants, and monsters. Aphrodite emerged from the foam of the sea, and Love and Desire joined her.

The Titans mated and gave birth to Isis, the Harpies, and the Gorgons. One of the Titans, Kronos, married his sister, Rhea, who gave birth to Hestia, Demeter, Hera, Hades, Poseidon, and Zeus. To avoid the prophecy that his son would overthrow him, Kronos ate each of his sons at birth. But when Zeus was born, Rhea hid the baby until he grew up. Rhea then convinced Kronos to regurgitate their other children, and Zeus returned to kill his father.

Zeus and his siblings took up residence on Mount Olympus and waged war against the Titans. After winning the Cyclopes over to his side, and receiving from them the thunderbolt and lightning, Zeus led the Olympians to victory. The Titans were imprisoned in Tartarus. Aphrodite, Ares, Hephaestus, Hermes, Athena, Apollo, and Artemis joined the Olympians, and Hades took up residence in the underworld.

Prominent Greek Deities

Among the male deities are Zeus, Poseidon, Hermes, Hephaestus, Ares, Apollo, Hades, and Dionysus:

- **Zeus** is the king of the Olympian gods and is the god of the sky. He is also the father of many of the other gods.
- **Poseidon,** Zeus's brother, is ruler of the sea.
- **Hades** is the god of the underworld, who kidnapped his sister Demeter's daughter, Kore, to be his queen.
- **Hermes** is the son of Zeus and the messenger of the gods.
- **Hephaestus** is the husband of Aphrodite and the god of fire and smithcraft. He made the first woman, Pandora, from clay.
- **Ares** is the god of war and is disliked by the other gods.
- **Apollo** is the god of music and poetry. The oracle to Gaea at Delphi was rededicated to him, and later to Dionysus.
- **Dionysus** is the god of wine, and is not one of the original Olympians.

The female deities include Hera, Demeter, Aphrodite, Athena, Artemis, and Hestia:

- **Hera** is the wife and sister of Zeus and is the goddess of marriage.
- **Demeter** is the earth goddess, the goddess of the harvest, and is associated with winter and spring.
- **Athena** sprang fully formed from the head of Zeus. She is a virgin warrior goddess and is of Mycenaean descent.
- **Artemis** is the virgin goddess of the hunt and animals, and may be descended from the Minoan goddess, although she is Apollo's twin.
- **Aphrodite** is the goddess of love. She is known for her many sexual escapades, especially her affair with Ares.
- **Hestia** is the goddess of the hearth and her worship was central to ancient Greek home life.

The Greek gods are also frequently referred to by their Roman names because the two pantheons were merged following the Roman invasion of Greece. Some of these Greek assimilations were less appropriate than others, but the associations have survived to modern times.

Ancient Rome

According to legend, Rome was established in 753 B.C.E. by Romulus, but archaeological evidence tells us that the technological advancements of the Romans followed the emigration of the more advanced Etruscans from northern Italy over 100 years later. The Romans responded to the invasion by conquering the Etruscans, and they continued to expand their territory, eventually amassing the Roman Empire. Their reign of power lasted until 476 C.E. and was partly responsible for the advent of Christianity throughout Europe.

Etruscan Beliefs

Etruscans were among the first peoples of the Italian region. They were masters of engineering and their cities were aligned with the four cardinal points of the compass. Professionally trained priests and seers oversaw religious ceremonies, led by the high priest, who was also their king. The three main Etruscan deities took the form of a triad, and accordingly, the temple was divided into three parts.

Roman Beliefs

Among the ancient Romans, the first gods were guardians of the land, called *Lares,* and did not have icons or other forms of personification. Each Lare had its own shrine and sacrificial altar, and crossroads were marked with shrines where people made offerings in December. Families also worshipped two household deities, but rather than being highly developed figures like the Greek Olympians, these gods resided in the object being honored. For example, Vesta, the goddess of the hearth, was the flame itself. The doorway to the home was the god Janus.

As the Roman society developed, so did their religion. Etruscan deities and practices merged with Roman ones. Eventually, thirty-three deities came to prominence, and twelve priests were responsible for performing sacrifices and rituals in order to keep the peace between the gods and the people. Jupiter, Mars, Quirinus, and Janus were seen as animals or natural objects. As the Roman Empire grew, local deities were accepted and venerated because it was believed that different deities protected different peoples.

Eventually, the Romans adopted a solar calendar, comprised of ten months, and the festivals followed the cycle of the year. Laws were based on logic, but also on omen, and divination was common. Preferred divination methods involved interpreting bird flight or the entrails of a ritually sacrificed animal.

Ancient Egypt

Like the Greek and Roman cultures, the Egyptian society and its accompanying beliefs evolved over time.

According to legend, Osiris was the first king. He was murdered by his brother Set, and his son Horus took his place on the throne. Each pharaoh was Horus incarnate, who became Osiris at his death. This meant the pharaoh ruled by divine right and was divine himself (or herself in the case of the few Egyptian queens). The pharaoh was the source of all law and justice, charged with maintaining right and harmony with the gods.

Egyptian View of Death

Egyptians viewed time as cyclical rather than linear. To them, the world was essentially unchanging. Recurring events were part of the natural order. Singular events were given little attention. The death of the pharaoh was a transition, not a time of upheaval.

Despite this outlook, death was of great concern. At death, it was believed that each person's *ka*, the portion of the spirit that was human nature, was taken to Osiris. He weighed each heart against a feather to determine whether or not the person should be blessed and join the *akh*, the blessed dead, or be damned. Another portion of the spirit, the *ba*, enabled movement, and remained connected to the body after death. The *ba* was represented in the form of a bird. Mummification was required to preserve the body so that the *ka* could take its rightful place. Food and other gifts were included because life continued after death, and the next phase of life required the same necessities as the former life on Earth.

Egyptian Deities

Egyptian mythology includes countless numbers of deities. Ra, Atum, Amun-Ra, and Aten (the disk of the sun) are all personifications of the sun. According to the Egyptian creation story, Atum created the world, either through speech, spitting, or masturbation. Ptah, the creator according to the Memphite people of Egypt, thought the world into being.

Several deities were linked to each other, and those connections helped explain the cycle of life. For example, Osiris was murdered by Set, then Isis revivified Osiris and became pregnant by him, resulting in the birth of Horus. All four were necessary for the cycle of birth, death, and rebirth.

For a brief period, Egyptians adopted monotheism (belief in one god), after a pharaoh named Akhenaten declared that Aten, the sun, was the only god. Tutankhamun, his successor, restored the other gods, but the sun god, in the form of Ra, maintained his newfound importance.

Egyptians venerated certain animals, not as divine beings but as manifestations of the divine. Anubis, the god of cemeteries and funerals, is connected to the jackal. Hathor is connected to the cow in her role as the goddess of motherhood, but is depicted as woman when honored for her role in love and sex. Ra, the god of the sun, is connected to the bull. The divine also existed within certain phenomenon, such as the rising of the sun or the flooding of the Nile.

Norse/Germanic People

Originating in Scandinavia, the Norse/Germanic people were actually several groups of people whose beliefs varied, but had some similarities. Over time, these groups spread out throughout much of Europe, moving south, west, and east.

The ancient Scandinavians thought that the trees and bodies of water were sacred. The trees linked humans to the gods, and most especially to the Yggdrasil, the World Tree. It was believed that the Yggdrasil stands at the center of a disk of land surrounded by the ocean, which is occupied by a giant serpent, and its roots reach into the underworld. Below the tree lies the spring of fate, and the tree provides nourishment and healing. The gods live in the sky above the tree and meet under its shade to hold council.

Scandinavians worshipped in sacred groves and sometimes in wooden temples. The dead were buried in mounds, which also served as meeting places. Animal sacrifices and feasts were conducted at major festivals, but also at other times of the year. These feasts and sacrifices were necessary to show respect for the gods or ensure a desired result, especially in battle, because the Germanic peoples were a warring people.

Divination was very important. In some regions, women were considered prophetic, and some were believed to be divine. In other areas, a priest or the father of the family performed divination via symbols carved on sticks, the flight of birds, or the movement of horses. In still other regions, shamanic trances were the primary method of soothsaying.

tips

Some of the Germanic peoples had formal priests who also made the laws, while others had no formal priesthood. In those regions, the king generally performed religious duties.

Ancient Celts

One of the groups that branched off from the Norse/Germanic people was the Celts. The term *Celtic* does not imply a genetic race of people. The Greeks and Romans referred to all peoples north of their region as Keltoi. As the Celts spread to various regions and separated from their Germanic counterparts, the Celtic belief system evolved into a more cohesive whole that centered on their warrior culture and interaction with deities and other spirits.

The ancient Celts worshipped in *temenos* and *nemetons*. Temenos were outdoor enclosures surrounded by a bank of earth and a ditch. Nemetons were clearings occupied by sacred trees. Trees played an important role in Celtic worship: People believed the trees were occupied by land spirits and decorated them with carvings of rudimentary images of the spirits.

Springs, wells, rivers, and other bodies of water also had their own deities and some were places of healing. Caves were seen as entrances to the underworld, which could be visited, and there were rules governing the use of the knowledge people received in other realms. *Gaes*, or taboos, were very prevalent in Celtic society, and they were seen as necessary for the protection of the people.

Did the Celts and Germanic peoples share the same deities and beliefs?

Although some similarities can be detected, these people did not worship the same deities. While the Germanic peoples had a creation story and an end-of-the world scenario, the Celts had no similar beliefs.

Celtic Holy People

The Celts had three classes of holy people: the Druids, vates, and bards:

- **Druids:** A class of priests, judges, and philosophers. The Druid role was hereditary, passed on from generation to generation. The Druids learned by memory, and their training could last up to eighteen years. With some exception, the Druids were male.
- **Bards:** A class of poets and singers. During the summer months, the bards traveled the land, relating the tales of the people. Like the Druids, they wrote nothing down and received several years of training, during which time they memorized traditional lore.
- **Vates:** A class of seers skilled in interpreting dreams and reading omens. The vates received less training than either the Druids or the bards. Their acceptance into the order rested largely on their psychic abilities. The vates employed several methods of divination, including bird flight, animal movement, water movement, tides, and clouds. They also interpreted the patterns of thrown stones and special sticks.

Celtic Calendar

The Coligny Calendar, discovered in 1897 in Coligny, France, is the oldest known Celtic calendar and dates back to the first century B.C.E. It spanned thirty years, with five divisions of sixty-two lunar months, and a sixth division of sixty-one months. The calendar indicated which days were good or bad. The single lunar year had two extra months to realign it with the solar year. The year was divided into dark and light halves, with the dark half coming first, and had three seasons: summer, winter, and spring. Summer was the longest, spring the shortest.

The Celts had no written language, so what is known about their practices today is based on the writings of Julius Caesar and other outside observers, and the archaeological discoveries of the last two centuries.

Introduction of Monotheism

Monotheistic faiths (faiths that accept only one god) did not arise all at once, but rather evolved over time, just as other ancient faiths. The marked difference, however, lay in the intolerance of the monotheistic god toward other gods. When monotheism gained the upper hand, pagan faiths were extinguished, surfacing again in the last few hundred years.

Rise of Judaism

Monotheism emerged in the land of Canaan, now modern Israel. The ancient Canaanites were initially polytheists who worshipped gods of the hunt, war, fertility, and death. Their faith allowed for direct contact with the gods and they believed, as did most other peoples of the time, that their deities had local jurisdiction and did not influence life in other regions.

The Canaanites' slow transition to monotheism began around 2000 B.C.E., when the first Jewish patriarch, Abraham, adopted the local god, El, as his main deity. He had direct contact with this god, and made sacrifices to him. The episode from the Bible in which El requested the sacrifice of Abraham's son Isaac is notable as the last time a human would be prepared for sacrifice, and it was an important turning point for the faith.

With the patriarch Jacob came another transition. Canaanites believed that knowing the true name of a god gave humans power over it. When Jacob encountered Abraham's god, the god refused to reveal his name, thereby establishing that humans cannot have power over god. The all-powerful god later told the Canaanites that his name was "Yahweh," roughly translated to mean "I am what I am." A non-name.

At Mount Sinai, Yahweh gave Moses the Ten Commandments and ordered that no other gods be worshipped, but the shift was not immediate. Over the course of the next 700 years, belief in Yahweh as the sole god solidified through a series of events. The final turning point came in 586 B.C.E. when the Babylonians conquered Jerusalem and the people who served him, now known as the Hebrews, were exiled. Because the Hebrews took Yahweh with them into exile, he became more than just a local god and was established as the sole, universal deity.

Jesus and Christianity

Judaism continued as a monotheistic faith for some 600 years, even after the Jews came under Roman rule. Then came Jesus, preaching at a critical time when the Jewish people sought to free their nation from the Romans. After his death, a Jewish sect came to believe that he was the messiah. At first, they did not believe that Jesus was the literal son of God, but rather a human who was closer to God than others.

Paul took up the message that Jesus was the messiah and carried it not just to fellow Jews, but to all people. Christ's worship grew among the slaves and the poor because of his egalitarian message of salvation. They believed that if he could reach such closeness to God, so could they. As the sect grew, so did its persecution under Roman rule. This persecution lasted 300 years.

The Roman Emperor Constantine was a Christian who is credited with first establishing Christianity as the official religion of Rome. In 325 B.C.E., he called the Council of Nicaea, which declared that Christ was divine. In 346 B.C.E. Paganism was banned in the Roman Empire, was briefly restored, and then banned again.

As Christianity spread through the empire, local practices, festivals, gods, and worship sites were Christianized, with many of the gods being recast as Christian saints. The Celtic lands became Christian, although their Pagan traditions continued as folk customs. The Saxons and Vikings were the last to convert. In 1000 B.C.E., Christianity became the official religion of Iceland. Paganism continued in Norway until the 1120s, when it also became Christian.

Islam emerged in what is now Saudi Arabia in 610 C.E. when Muhammad received the words of the Koran. He carried the message to Mecca, but the people rejected him and sent him to Medina. There, he gathered followers and raised an army to bring Islam to the entire Arab world. After his death in 632 C.E., four of his caliphs continued the war. By 641 C.E., Iran, Iraq, Egypt, Syria, and Jerusalem had been conquered and converted. In Northern Africa, the Mandinka people were brought into the faith and continued to spread the Islamic faith.

European Witch Craze

The European Witch Craze, known among Pagans as the Burning Times, spanned from the fourteenth to the eighteenth century, with most of the trials taking place between 1550 and 1650. The majority of trials occurred in Western European nations: France, England, Scotland, Switzerland, and Germany.

Witches became the main target of the Catholic Inquisition in 1484, following Pope Innocent VIII's "Bull of the Witches," which made belief in witchcraft a heresy. *Malleus Maleficarum* (Hammer of the Witches), published in 1486, provided detailed instructions on the practices and prosecution of suspected witches.

Accusations of witchcraft tended to flare up during times of famine, plague, social unrest, and other afflictions. Witches were blamed for changes in weather, sudden illness, the death of children, poor crops, and sick or dying animals. Once an accusation of witchcraft was leveled, it was the witch's duty to prove his or her innocence rather than the duty of the accuser to prove guilt.

Usually, a confession was extracted by means of torture. During torture, the examiner asked a series of leading questions intended to produce confessions and details of the accused's experiences with the devil. The accused were also asked to name other witches, and some would name their accuser.

Because the accused had to pay for their own trial and imprisonment, trials became big business for judges, jailers, prosecutors, and executioners. As a result, corruption was rampant. Specialists in examination by torture developed special instruments such as retractable blades to give the impression that the accused didn't bleed when pricked, when in fact they hadn't been pricked at all.

A death sentence was not the final result of all trials, but nearly half of the accused were sentenced to burning or hanging. The final count of the executed is not known, but scholars place it somewhere between 50,000 and 100,000 victims. Of these, only 25 to 35 percent were men.

The witch trials were a dark period in human history. Finally, when Europe entered a period known as the Enlightenment, logic and reason overcame superstition, and the witch trials were brought to an end.

Salem Witch Trials

The Salem witch trials in Salem, Massachusetts, were the result of a confluence of factors, including a smallpox outbreak, the constant danger of attacks from Native Americans, the revocation of the colonial charter, the deep-seated Puritan fear of sin and punishment from God, and feuding between the farming community and the more fortunate citizens who earned their livelihood from the harbor.

Life in Salem was difficult, and children had little entertainment. When the Reverend Parris and his family moved to Salem from Barbados, they brought their slave, Tituba, who entertained the girls of Salem with fortune telling. The Parris girls received disturbing fortunes in January of 1692, and panicked. Perhaps fearful of being caught or of receiving damnation for their sins, the girls exhibited violent symptoms of hysteria, and they were diagnosed as being bewitched. When questioned, the girls named Tituba and two other women. One was an elderly woman and the other one very poor; both had already been under suspicion of witchcraft.

The hysteria of the two girls soon spread to six others. All eight served as witnesses against the accused, and their evidence took the form of screaming, stamping their feet, and falling to the floor in convulsions. Of those accused, only Tituba confessed. The accusations continued for several months, with several townspeople standing trial and their convictions resting largely on spectral evidence provided by the girls.

The Salem Witch Museum in Salem, Massachusetts, offers a great deal of information about the Witch Trials, including a dioramic presentation of the sequence of events. A memorial to the victims has also been erected in the town.

As the number of accused increased, the townspeople began to doubt the veracity of the accusations and their faith in the evidence waned. In October 1692, the governor of Massachusetts suspended arrests for witchcraft, issued an order protecting current prisoners, and dissolved the court. The last trial was held in January 1693, and Governor Phipps pardoned those still imprisoned in May 1693.

In total, more than 200 people were accused and jailed. Fourteen women and five men were hanged, seventeen others died in prison, and one man was pressed to death for refusing to stand trial. It is unlikely that any of the accused, with the possible exception of Tituba, practiced witchcraft.

The beliefs of ancient peoples form the basis of modern Pagan worship. Interest in the ancient people was first sparked over four hundred years ago in the Renaissance. This interest still exists today, and although some of the practices of these societies are shrouded in mystery, enough is known to allow for a rich and vibrant religious life for modern Pagans.

Chapter 2

The Advance of Neo-Paganism

Modern Paganism, also known as Neo-Paganism, is rapidly growing troughout the world. As with other religions, there are several sects within Neo-Paganism, in much the same way there are various branches like Catholicism and Protestantism within the Christian faith. Evolved over the course of the last 200 years, it is the product of archaeological discovery and theory as well as the human imagination and a longing to return to a simpler age in order to recover what was lost.

Dispelling the Myths

As the various faiths within Neo-Paganism have developed, so have misunderstandings about what its adherents believe and how they practice. Controversy has also swirled about the history of Paganism and how it evolved into its modern forms. The most common myths surrounding Neo-Paganism are the myths that it has a direct line of descent from the ancient religions, that the ancient peoples worshipped a single goddess, and that Neo-Pagans worship Satan.

Myth 1: Direct Line of Descent

Neo-Paganism first emerged as a new religion in an age when lineage was very important. People wanted to be able to say that their faith or practices had continued underground from the ancient times. Some came to believe that Paganism had continuously existed from the ancient times to the modern, and that even when Christians dominated the religious landscape and witchcraft was actively persecuted, an organized system of covens still practiced Paganism in secret. Neo-Pagans proudly proclaimed that they had inherited their beliefs from a long line of witches and Pagans.

The term *Neo-Paganism* refers to most earth-based or polytheistic faiths that emerged in the last century, but most who follow these faiths refer to themselves simply as Pagans.

History does not bear out the myth. There is no evidence that covens of witches survived underground, or that their beliefs flourished amidst oppression. While some of the early Pagan practices persisted as folk customs and folk magic, and indeed even some of their festivals were supplanted with Christian holidays, the ancient religions as a whole did not survive. And even if certain pockets of Pagan practices and beliefs did persist, they were not organized in any way.

Myth 2: Worship of the Great Mother

Some writers have asserted that prehistoric peoples worshipped a single, universal goddess called the Great Mother, and this theory was widely accepted in the feminist movement of the 1970s, but it's difficult to prove or disprove because the worshippers were prehistoric and had no written records.

The theory is based on archaeological evidence, but the interpretation of the evidence is tinged with personal ideology. In light of the knowledge that later Pagan gods were local to their regions and that the people could deal with them directly, scholars now think it more likely that prehistoric people worshipped local goddesses rather than a single, universal goddess.

Myth 3: Neo-Pagans Worship Satan

Many non-Pagans believe that Neo-Pagans are Satan worshippers. Accompanying that belief are claims that Neo-Pagans (witches and Wiccans specifically) hold Satanic rituals that include human sacrifice, grave desecration, and child molestation. These claims are often made by those who are intolerant of all faiths other than their own.

Are Satanists Neo-Pagans?
Some Satanists worship Lucifer (or other figures closely connected to Satan) as a deity. These worshippers might consider themselves Neo-Pagans. Other Satanists do not worship any specific deity, and are less likely to call themselves Neo-Pagans. There are also Satanists who consider Wiccans and other Neo-Pagans light and fluffy people who fear the dark side. These Satanists never refer to themselves as Neo-Pagans.

While Satanism does exist as a religion, neither Satanists nor Neo-Pagans worship Satan, because they don't believe in Satan. It's important to understand that Satan is a Christian construct. Satanists honor the human characteristics Satan represents, but not the figure of Satan. Some

Neo-Pagans honor gods who wear horns or take the form of horned animals, but these gods predate the Christian Satan. It is believed that the modern image of Satan stems from attempts by the Catholic Church to recast the Pagan deities as demons when Pagan lands were conquered and converted.

Needless to say, neither Satanists nor Neo-Pagans practice any form of human sacrifice. They do not worship in cemeteries or desecrate the dead. They do not molest children; the flurry of accusations of Satanic child molesters in the 1980s were later proven false by authorities. News reports of satanic crimes persist, but usually the perpetrators of those crimes have no actual connection to the Church of Satan or any Neo-Pagan group. Instead their actions are based on "satanic" practices they may have discovered in movies and on television, and may only have been used to add a touch of sensationalism or excitement to the crime.

Major Branches of Neo-Paganism

Neo-Paganism today consists of three main branches and several smaller sects. The major branches consist of three divergent faiths: Wicca, Druidry, and Asatru. The sects, described in greater detail in Chapter 15, include Hellenism (Greek Reconstructionist Paganism), Senistrognata (Celtic Reconstructionist Paganism), Kemeticism (Egyptian Reconstructionist Paganism), and Thelema.

Wicca, a modern blend of polytheism and occult practices, is the largest of the faiths within Neo-Paganism and has several offshoots within it. Druidry, which is based on ancient Celtic Druidism, is more closely aligned with ancient practices and beliefs than Wicca. Asatru is the smallest of the three, but it is growing rapidly. Its beliefs and practices are based on Norse Paganism of Iceland, Germany, and Scandinavia.

All three faiths developed independently and each flourishes today. Druidry and Wicca are more prevalent in the United Kingdom and Asatru is most popular in northern Europe. All three are actively practiced in the United States, and they are also growing in popularity in South America, Australia, and parts of Asia.

The Roots of Wicca

Wicca does not have an unbroken line of practice stemming from ancient times, but it didn't emerge overnight either. Rather, its beliefs and practices evolved over the course of about 200 years. Its modern roots lie in folk magic, the romantic movement, magical organizations, and archaeological discoveries.

Family Traditions

Family Traditions, or Fam-Trads for short, are comprised of practices that are inherited and passed down through generations of a family, sometimes dating back several hundred years. Modern descendants of Fam-Trads generally explain their practices as just "the way it was."

Their ancestors, and even their parents, didn't call these traditions witchcraft or Paganism. Before the emergence of Neo-Paganism, most Fam-Trad families were Christian, sometimes avowedly so. They may also have been members of the various magical societies that arose in the last 200 years, but with a focus on magic, not religion. As Neo-Paganism came into the limelight, members of Fam-Trad families found the new beliefs similar or well suited to their own heritage and so became Neo-Pagans.

Romantic Longing

The romantic movement of the eighteenth and nineteenth centuries stirred up longings for a return to the ancient Pagan ways, which were viewed as joyous and life-affirming, qualities the modern age seemed to lack. To the romantics, Paganism meant freedom from oppression, poverty, and political upheaval. The goddess figure represented nature and the moon. The Greek god Pan served as a symbol of liberated sexuality and homosexuality.

Romantic sentiments are evident in the following passage from a poem by William Wordsworth, who wrote, "Great God! I'd rather be / a Pagan suckled in a creed outworn; / So might I, standing on this pleasant lea / Have glimpses that would make me less forlorn" ("The World Is Too Much with Us").

Magical Organizations

Magical organizations began to emerge in Europe as early as the seventeenth century. Freemasonry was originally an order for masons that was not magical in nature. However, initiation and oaths of secrecy were required for membership and as the order grew, so did the degrees of initiations and the elaborate ceremonial structure that surrounded them. The Theosophical Society was formed to explore Hindu beliefs, Buddhism, and Gnostic texts by those who considered these teachings to be superior to Christian doctrine. From the Theosophical Society sprang the Hermetic Society, which had an interest in Kabbalah (Jewish mysticism) and European magic. Although members of the Hermetic Society studied methods for performing magic, they did not actually use it.

The Rosicrucians, an organization of ceremonial magicians, emerged in the eighteenth century as an offshoot of Freemasonry. In 1888, this organization gave birth to the Hermetic Order of the Golden Dawn. The Order of the Golden Dawn was the first group to allow members with higher degrees of initiation to use ceremonial magic. It also established several of the magical tools used in modern Wiccan practices. Aleister Crowley, a member of the Order of the Golden Dawn, established his own offshoot organization, known as the Ordo Templis Orientis, which was specifically based on Pagan deities. He also added tools to the craft of magic, and some of his writings were later adapted by Wiccans.

Archaeological Discoveries

The last three centuries spawned great interest in archaeology and theories about the beliefs and practices of ancient faiths. Archaeologists and antiquarians explored the ruins and relics of most of Europe's ancient cultures. While some of their theories were largely unfounded, others have withstood the tests of time.

Margaret Murray, Charles Leland, and Sir James Frazer had a great influence on the development of Neo-Paganism. Margaret Murray's 1921 work, *The Witch-Cult in Western Europe,* put forth the idea that Paganism had continued unbroken since ancient times. Basing her theories on the transcripts of the witch trials, she declared that these underground covens were fertility cults with thirteen members celebrating eight seasonal festivals.

According to journalist Margot Adler, the work of Margaret Murray may have inspired several modern covens that based their practices on her claims. Covens claiming to have an ancient heritage may actually stem from this period.

Sir James Frazer's book, *The Golden Bough* (1890), introduced the concept of the ancient sacrificial king and the god known as the Green Man, who is still honored in Wicca today. Charles Leland purported to find evidence of the Old Religion in Italy, where he claimed to have found an unbroken witchcraft religion.

All of these theories have since been disproved, but they sparked a resurgence of interest in Neo-Pagan faiths and many groups were formed as a result of their findings.

Emergence of the Wiccan Faith

Although Wicca is based on what are believed to be the practices and beliefs of the ancient peoples, it was born of modern desires to return to the ancient ways, and so it is a very modern religion. Wicca's modernity does not make it any less valid, but it is important to be aware of how Wicca emerged in order to fully understand it.

Dion Fortune

Dion Fortune was not herself a Wiccan, but her work contributed greatly to its development. She was a member of the Golden Dawn and studied the Kabbalah and psychic abilities extensively. In the 1930s her focus shifted to Isis, whom she saw as the one goddess. She stressed the polarity of the universe, a feature important to Wiccan magical and ritual practice.

Gerald Gardner

Gerald Gardner is known as the Father of Wicca. According to his own testimony, in 1939 he contacted a coven of witches that also included Rosicrucians and was subsequently initiated into Wicca. By 1947, he had also been initiated into Crowley's Ordo Templis Orientis (OTO), becoming its European leader in 1948. In 1949, he published *High Magic's Aid,* a novel about magic that contained accurate information about the modern practice of magic. Following the repeal of British anti-witchcraft laws in 1951, Gardner became more public with his coven's activities. In 1954 he published *Witchcraft and Today*, which was followed by *The Meaning of Witchcraft* in 1959.

While Gardner said he had been initiated into a coven in 1939, it was not Wiccan, and reports of that coven's activities and members have been difficult to confirm. But the veracity of his claim is less important than the contributions Gardner made to Wicca. Drawing on the best of several sources, including the OTO, the practices of his coven, and Freemasonry, he developed a workable system, much of which is still presentin Wicca today.

Among the ideas Gardner introduced was the term *Wicca* itself, and the way the religion was first practiced. He added the solstices and equinoxes to the festival calendar of his original coven, and he stressed gender equality, although the triple goddess was worshipped above the god. A priestess led his Wiccan coven and performed rituals skyclad (in the nude). The rites practiced by his coven were based on fragments of rites he said he'd received from his coven and the work of Aleister Crowley.

Doreen Valiente

In 1953, Gerald Gardner initiated Doreen Valiente into his coven, and she served as his high priestess for some years. During that time, she contributed and improved the rituals, chants, and poems used by

Gardner's covens, and by current covens. Two of her most famous works are "The Charge of the Goddess" and "The Charge of the God," which are partly based on Charles Leland's *Aradia*.

Valiente and Gardner disagreed on the public nature of Wicca. While he actively sought publicity, Valiente preferred to practice in secret. Following her break with Gardner, she became involved with a second tradition and later contributed to the 1970s movement toward acceptance of the solitary practice of Wicca. She is also the author of several influential books on the faith.

In 1948, the poet Robert Graves published *The White Goddess,* which he claimed was a true history of the worship of the Great Mother, the purported prehistoric goddess. His claims were an accepted belief for many years and helped fuel feminist Neo-Paganism. Today his claims are widely considered untrue.

Wicca in the United States

Except for Long Island's Church of Aphrodite, which has been around since 1938, Wicca did not really appear in the United States until the 1960s and 1970s. Many credit author Raymond Buckland with bringing Wicca to the United States, but it was American authors, especially Z. Budapest and Starhawk, who helped it become popular and made it more accessible to the general public. Their Wiccan gatherings produced many of the popular chants used at festivals and rituals today. Starhawk and Budapest also injected feminism and political activism into their branches of Wicca.

The 1980s saw an increase in the number of books published on the topic, which attracted yet more adherents. That era also saw the growth of Wiccan organizations and gatherings. In the 1990s, there was a resurgence in political activism, especially with regard to religious tolerance and public understanding of Wicca. While Wicca is popular in other countries, it has its greatest number of practitioners in the United States.

The Roots of Asatru

Asatru developed separately from Wicca. Its resurgence may have started earlier, but its current form emerged later. Unlike Wicca, it is largely based on archaeological findings and historic record. The Asatru faith possesses a rich mythology dating back hundreds of years.

Icelandic History

Many of the modern Asatru practices are based on Icelandic lore recorded in two thirteenth-century books called the *Poetic Edda* and *Prose Edda* (sagas). The Eddas relate the history of the kings, gods, and other matters of importance to the Icelanders. As time went on, Icelanders converted to Christianity and stopped following the ancient Pagan ways, but they did preserve the Eddas until modern times as works of literature and folklore (see Chapter 7 for more on the Eddas).

The Romantic Movement

Around the same time that romanticism swept through Britain, it also sparked an interest in the classics in the regions formerly inhabited by the Norse. The Brothers Grimm studied Germanic fairy tales and mythology. Richard Wagner based the four operas of his Ring Cycle on the Volsunga saga, an Icelandic saga of the thirteenth century based on poems in the *Poetic Edda*. This Germanic romanticism, accompanied by increased nationalism in German and Scandinavian countries, fostered the resurgence of interest in ancient lore that flourished into the early twentieth century.

Modern History of Asatru

The word *Asatru* is translated as "true to the Æsir," one branch of the Norse pantheon. The ancient people did not call themselves Asatruar; the religion gained this title sometime in the 1830s. In 1874, when Iceland was granted freedom of religion, Asatru re-emerged as a practiced faith. The following year, the cathedral of Reykjavik began offering Asatru religious services.

Other Asatru groups appeared in Germany and other areas, but the movement was not organized in any fashion. When Germany was under Hitler's control, Asatruar were persecuted and the practice of Asatru was forbidden. After the fall of Nazi Germany, Asatru groups began to meet again.

Although the Asatru faith was never a facet of Nazism, the Nazis used Asatru beliefs and symbols to stir up German nationalism. Today, the Asatruar may still be unfairly accused of being Nazis and racists.

In 1972, Asatru was reintroduced in Iceland, and in that same year, Sveinbjorn Beinteinsson convinced the Icelandic government to formally recognize the faith. At about the same time, an English Asatru group was formed. Asatruar adherents also appeared in Australia.

In the United States, Stephen McNallen established the Viking Brotherhood, which later became the Asatru Folk Assembly, but this was dissolved in 1987. The Ring of Troth and the Asatru Alliance were then formed, and a few years later McNallen created the Asatru Free Assembly. In 1989, the first U.S.–published book on Asatru appeared.

Brief History of Druidry

Modern Druidry is based on what are believed to be the practices of the ancient Druids. It has its roots in the era that also created Freemasonry. In the seventeenth century, John Aubrey, an antiquarian, researched the megalithic sites in the United Kingdom and developed the theory that they were built by the Druids. William Stukeley adopted the theory in the eighteenth century and developed additional theories based on Druidic lore.

In 1717, members of several Druidic orders met with John Toland and created the Ancient Druid Order. In 1781, Henry Hurle established the Ancient Order of Druids, but its focus was social rather than religious. In 1833, the latter group split and those interested in the religious aspects of Druidry formed the Albion Lodge of the Ancient Order of Druids of Oxford. French Druidism was reborn in 1869.

The romantic movement of the eighteenth and nineteenth centuries also affected modern Druidry. The romantic poet William Blake had an interest in Druidry and created fanciful myths about it. Other poets and writers also took a literary interest in the Druids and created fantastical pictures of their practices. These literary treatments of Druids launched them into greater popularity, which resulted in the construction of Druidic temples and the publication of Druidic magazines.

The gatherings of the Welsh bardic orders were called eisteddfods, meaning "sitting together" or "gathering." The first gathering was held in 1176, and subsequent meetings were sporadic until the nineteenth century. There are now annual eisteddfod events in many locales.

Druidry waxed and waned in small groups for several decades, then modern Druid organizations were re-established or newly founded in the 1960s and 1980s. These groups included the Order of Bards, Ovates, and Druids; the British Druid Order; Ár nDraíocht Féin; and the Henge of Keltria. These groups continue to flourish as more people turn to Druidry as a system of belief and a way of life.

Wicca, Asatru, and Druidry emerged from the ashes of the old ways to create new religions for modern people. Some are more strongly rooted in the past than others, but regardless of their heritage, they are viable today. The largest Neo-Paganist group is Wicca, and its beliefs appeal to many.

Chapter 3

Wiccan Beliefs

The Wiccan belief system is both struc-tured and unstructured. Wiccans don't follow a strict dogma or doctrine and there is no holy book equivalent to the Christian Bible, but certain common beliefs have developed over time. It is fairly safe to make a few generalities about Wiccan beliefs, but bear in mind that different groups and indi-viduals may interpret them in a different manner and add their own modifications. As the common saying goes, "Ask five Pagans a question and you'll get six answers."

Prevalence of Wicca

Wicca is among the fastest-growing religions in the United States, and it is seeing an explosion of popularity in other countries as well. It is difficult to determine the precise number of adherents to the faith, but several estimates have been made.

In 2001, the City University of New York conducted the American Religious Identification Survey. It found that 134,000 adults professed to be Wiccan; in 1990 there were merely 8,000 people who identified themselves as Wiccan. Today, the Ontario Consultants on Religious Tolerance estimate the actual number of Wiccan adults at 408,000.

People who practice witchcraft call themselves witches, whether they are male or female. These people may or may not be Wiccan. Some Wiccans do not practice witchcraft. And some witchcraft practitioners do not adhere to the Wiccan faith.

In 1999, the Covenant of the Goddess conducted a voluntary poll through the Internet and mail-in responses. Based on the results, they estimate that there are 768,000 Wiccans and Pagans in the United States, with the ratio of women to men being two to one. The faith seems to be most popular among people between the ages of eighteen and thirty-nine, which could account for the rapid growth as new seekers come of age and begin to explore alternative religions.

Organization and Structure

Unlike most traditional religions, Wicca does not have a single governing body that dictates dogma and behavior for the religion as a whole. There is no Wiccan pope. Certain community leaders or elders have emerged and are treated with respect appropriate to those who possess great knowledge, but they have no special powers over the direction the faith takes.

Covens and Other Groups

Wicca isn't completely without structure. Some Wiccans operate within covens, circles, groves, lodges, or working groups. Covens are generally highly ordered. They have up to thirteen members and are usually led by a high priestess or priest. Generally, this person is elected to this post by the rest of the group, or she may be the coven's founder. If elected, the post is held for a year and a day.

Once a coven exceeds thirteen members, some of the more experienced members may "hive off" and create a new, autonomous coven, although the two covens may join together for sabbats or other major workings. Some of the oldest covens in the United States have hived off many covens that have spread across several states. A coven generally has rules governing the initiation of new members and the use of magic. Some covens only work magic as a group, while others allow for magic to be performed alone by individual members.

Initiation is a formal statement of a person's dedication to the Wiccan path and follows a period of study, most commonly a year and a day. The initiation is a formal welcoming of new members into the coven as a full member. Completing another level of training may also be celebrated with an initiation.

Other Wiccans prefer to work with a group, often called a circle, but not in a formal coven structure. They usually refer to their group by some other name and operate on a consensus basis. Such a group may or may not have a leader. Sometimes the leader is the person who came up with the idea to meet, the person who holds the meetings at her or his house, or a teacher who has collected a group of students to work together. Again, hiving off into new groups is common if the group swells to an unwieldy size. A circle may be composed of coven-initiated members as well as self-initiated members.

Not all Wiccans work in groups; there is also a strong solitary contingent in the Wiccan community. Solitaries are largely self-taught and self-initiated, and they work alone for magic and sabbats, although they may attend public sabbats as well. There has been some debate in the past about the legitimacy of solitary practitioners, but this seems to have subsided.

Wiccan Organizations

There are also a few Wiccan organizations dedicated to facilitating communication among Wiccans and with those outside the Wiccan community. The Covenant of the Goddess (CoG) is a collective of covens and solitaries. CoG has chapters around the world and any coven or solitary who adheres to its code can join. The members of CoG act as public spokespeople for the Wiccan community, offer ministerial credentials, and host public events and rituals. Witches Against Religious Discrimination is another group that seeks to correct public misconceptions about Wiccans, as well as to secure the legal rights of Pagans.

If you choose to become a solitary practitioner, you may wish to seek guidance from a teacher. While you can learn the basics in books, sabbats and magic are best learned through practice and experience.

Pantheism: All Is Divine

Pantheism is the belief that divinity is in everything, that every plant, rock, animal, and person is divine and is inhabited by the divine energy of the universe. This is not to say that every plant, rock, animal, and person is a god. Rather, the gods created these objects and they still harbor the divine energy of the creator.

Pantheism sees everything in the universe as sacred, but that doesn't mean you should approach every object with complete awe and sanctity. The tree is sacred, but its purpose is to create oxygen and wood, and therefore it is not necessarily a violation to take a branch, or even chop it down, if that is part of its purpose, or it has become diseased.

Wiccans vary in their acceptance of pantheism. Some Wiccans do see each object as inhabited by a divine spirit with which they can communicate. This is why you will often hear admonitions to ask a plant for permission before cutting it, and to thank it afterward. Others view living plants as the homes of spirits such as dryads, faeries, gnomes, and other nature creatures.

The system can become rather complicated, even more so when animals are considered. Out of reverence for the sacredness of animals, some Wiccans follow a vegetarian diet. Other Wiccans do not, and see little distinction between killing an animal for food and killing a plant for food. The choice is up to the individual. There is no Wiccan doctrine stating which one is correct.

Acceptance of Multiple Deities

Polytheism, or the belief in many gods, is common to almost all branches of Wicca, but the gender and cultural derivation of the gods varies according to the believer. These beliefs generally depend on an individual's personal views and the views of his or her teacher or group.

Some Wiccans see a family tree that begins with the One, the Source, or the Universe. From the universe come the god and goddess, who have many faces, or perhaps only the goddess. The god and goddess have many aspects. Calling to the aspect of Aphrodite, for example, will cause the goddess will turn that aspect of herself toward the worshipper. Wiccans may call on a specific deity, but someone else (someone more appropriate) may sometimes arrive. When in doubt, it is possible to simply call the goddess and allow her to decide the personality she may choose for communication.

In other Wiccan traditions, the gods and goddesses are finite beings. Aphrodite is an individual goddess, not just one face of a multifaceted divine being. When a specific deity is called, that is the one who arrives, but many deities have multiple sides even within themselves. For instance, Kali is a goddess of creation and destruction, so it may also be necessary to specify which aspect of that deity you are inviting.

Wiccan Traditions

Just as Christianity encompasses a variety of faiths such as Protestantism and Catholicism, Wicca also has several denominations, which are called traditions. In recent years there has been an explosion of new traditions within the Wiccan community, too many to list here. The following is a brief overview of some of the more common traditions practiced today.

Gardnerian Tradition

The oldest of all the Wiccan traditions, the Gardnerian tradition was established in the 1940s by Gerald Gardner, who is considered the Father of Wicca. Founded in England, where witchcraft was still illegal, the tradition is secretive, involves a strict hierarchy and dogma, and includes extensive training. Gardnerian covens are difficult to locate because they tend to keep to themselves and do not advertise their presence.

Gardnerians honor the god and goddess equally and gender equality is of supreme importance. Most Gardnerian rituals are practiced skyclad, meaning ritually nude, and they operate in autonomous covens.

Gardnerians offer three degrees of training and initiation. Those who reach the third degree are ready to become high priests and priestesses. Doreen Valiente, a prominent Wiccan author, was Gerald Gardner's first high priestess and played an important role in shaping the beliefs and practices of Wiccans.

Alexandrian Tradition

Alex Sanders established this tradition in the 1960s. The rituals are modified versions of Gardnerian rituals, and much of the belief system is the same, but Alexandrians place a stronger focus on ceremonial magic.

The covens have the option of working skyclad, but it is not a requirement. Some of the other rules are more liberal as well.

Alexandrians tend to be less secretive about their practices and will occasionally allow noninitiates to attend their gatherings. They may also allow students to attend rituals before they have completed their first-degree initiation. Janet and Stewart Farrar are perhaps the most well known initiates into the tradition and have written several influential books on Wicca.

Dianic Tradition

Most of the practitioners of the Dianic tradition are women, although some men do follow it as well. That's because Dianic rituals are frequently closed to men as well as male-to-female transsexuals, although men have gained admittance to some Dianic groups. Dianics welcome lesbians, but being gay is not a requirement to join the group.

The tradition is based on the teachings of Margaret Murray's 1921 work *The Witch-Cult in Western Europe*. Many within the Craft consider it to be "Feminist Wicca," and it has been the subject of some undeserved scorn. The movement has become political in recent years, and one of its main proponents is Z. Budapest, another prominent author.

Dianic covens tend to work on a consensus basis with no hierarchical structure. They worship the goddess alone, and exclude all male deities. As such, they have modified the sabbat cycle to relate to the female cycle of life: the cycle of maiden, mother, and crone. The menstrual cycle and the close relation of women to the phases of the moon are honored and considered the source of women's power.

Feri Tradition

The Feri (pronounced fairy) tradition began its evolution in the 1930s when Victor Anderson began working with an Oregon coven whose tradition included American folk magic as well as African-American and Native American beliefs and practices. The tradition was expanded to include southern folk magic when Victor married Cora in 1944. Later students would incorporate Hawaiian Huna and Celtic magic into the tradition. The goddess is central to the Feri faith, which is quite complex.

Feri covens are autonomous and unstructured. Students receive only one initiation, but study is quite lengthy and arduous. Purification is of extreme importance. The Feri tradition is considered to be continuously evolving, and current offshoots of the tradition include Starhawk's Reclaiming tradition and Francesca De Grandis's Third Road.

Faery Tradition

The Faery tradition is completely different from the Feri tradition. This tradition has no direct lineage or known date of founding, but it has become very popular among Wiccans. In Faery covens or circles, the members base their practices on Celtic faerie lore, legends, and beliefs; to them, reverence for the earth is very important. Wiccans who adhere to the Faery tradition work with the wee folk in ritual.

The word *fairy* is used to refer to tales like "Cinderella," as in "fairy tales." *Faery* or *faerie* are words used to describe the creatures of Celtic legend, who take on a wide variety of shapes and sizes.

There are a few books on the subject of Faery Wicca, as well as Internet correspondence courses, but the tradition is largely self-taught and there are no formal rules regarding the formation or management of covens and working groups.

One subgroup of the Faery tradition is known as the Faerie Faith. The Faith is based out of Georgia and it is Dianic in nature, although men are allowed to participate. The Faery Faith involves extensive training that lasts for several years, degreed initiations, and a hierarchical coven structure. It is not strictly Wiccan and incorporates many shamanic elements.

Strega Tradition

According to legend, a woman named Aradia established Stregheria (also known as Italian witchcraft) in the fourteenth century. The tradition came to public knowledge in 1890 with the publication of Charles Leland's *Aradia: Gospel of the Witches* and is enjoying a modern resurgence. Strega incorporates both Roman and Etruscan deities and has a modified Wheel of the Year to match more closely with their practices.

Strega Wiccans operate in covens, which they call *boschettos,* but they allow solitary study as well. In their tradition, Wiccan practices are combined with other practices and beliefs that differ from traditional Wicca. Moreover, Strega in Italy practice the faith differently from those residing in the United States. The leading figure to emerge from Stregheria is author Raven Grimassi, who has written several books on the topic.

Popular Pantheons

Each ancient culture had a pantheon of deities, which is essentially a collection of gods and goddesses. In the pantheon, each deity has a defined role, mythology, and place within the hierarchy of gods. Wiccans have a variety of pantheons to choose from. Some of the cultures in which these deities originated survive today and their legends have been passed on to modern generations, although the original religions associated with them were extinguished long ago. Worship of some deities also extended to other cultures or areas, and there the deities were given additional duties or aspects.

Greco/Roman Pantheon

One of the most well known pantheons is the Greco-Roman pantheon, made up of gods and goddesses honored in ancient Greece and ancient Rome. Over time, the deities of these two pantheons have been merged into one. For example, Zeus (Greek) and Jupiter (Roman) share many similar characteristics, as do Aries and Mars. Due to historical interest in Greco-Roman antiquity and culture, we know a lot about their deities, and many schoolchildren learn about them as part of a section on mythology. The stories of Apollo, Demeter, Persephone, and others are recognizable to most people. Some of the sabbat observances are based on Greco-Roman myths, as well.

While many Wiccans use Greek or Roman gods in their rituals, there are some covens that limit themselves to worship of the gods. It is considered polite to match a Roman goddess with a Roman god in ritual, even though their names are largely interchangeable. For example, the Greek god Zeus and his wife Hera are connected to the Roman god Jupiter and his wife Juno, but it is inappropriate to invoke Zeus and Juno together. This is to show a respect for, and an awareness of, their origins.

How can I choose a pantheon for myself?
Look to your blood heritage or consider a culture that may interest you. Wiccans believe in reincarnation, so you may have been a part of that culture in another life. Choosing a pantheon is not a requirement. You can work with whichever gods feel most appropriate at a given time.

Celtic Pantheon

The Celtic pantheon is one of the most popular. This is in part due to the British origins of the Wiccan faith. Furthermore, many Americans of Celtic descent that have adopted the Wiccan faith choose this pantheon as the one to worship. There are well over 300 Celtic deities. A few deities were considered universal among the Celtic people, while many others were associated with a specific locality. Some Roman deities also had a following in the British Isles due to the long occupation by the Roman Empire, and these were incorporated into the Celtic pantheon.

Much of what is known about Celtic beliefs is based on oral legends that have survived in the British Isles and what archaeologists have been able to piece together. Unlike the Greeks, Romans, or Egyptians, the Celts did not leave behind a written record of their culture and beliefs. However, Christianity came to Ireland relatively late, so much of the lore has survived to this day.

Egyptian Pantheon

The Egyptian pantheon has recently become very popular, and a wealth of information about Egyptian deities is available thanks to detailed archaeological study and the ancient Egyptian practice of recording their legends in writing. The Egyptians had a large pantheon, and many of those same gods are well suited to modern concerns.

Some Wiccans do choose to abandon their practices in favor of Celtic Reconstructionism (see Chapter 15), but more prevalent is the adoption of Celtic deities into Wiccan practices. A third alternative for worshipping Celtic deities is to become a Druid, which is a different practice from Wicca altogether, and will be discussed in later chapters.

Followers of the Egyptian pantheon take two approaches. The first is to adopt the Wiccan Wheel of the Year, beliefs, and framework, but to use the Egyptian deities in ritual. The second method is a re-creation of the ancient Egyptian faith. Most Pagans involved with Egyptian re-creations began as Wiccans who leaned toward the Egyptian pantheon. As they delved deeper, they decided to forgo the Wiccan cycle and use Egyptian rituals re-created from archaeological documents. Some continue to also honor the Wiccan sabbats and to use magic in the Wiccan way, but some others do not.

Germanic/Norse Pantheon

Some Wiccans choose to use Germanic/Norse deities as part of their Wiccan practices, while others prefer a more reconstructionist method, and leave their traditional Wiccan practices behind. Those who leave Wicca are most likely to adopt the Asatru faith. However, there are those who feel called to the Wiccan belief system, but because of their cultural heritage or bloodlines, they would also like to adopt the deities of northern Europe. In this case, they would practice traditional Wicca using Norse deities, or perhaps other deities from the north, such as Finnish deities.

To many, the legends of the Norse deities seem foreign, or at least less widely known, but the Norse gods are a part of daily life for those residing in English-speaking countries. For instance, several days of the week are named in honor of Norse deities: Tuesday is the day of Tiw/Tyr, Wednesday is the day of Woden, Thursday honors Thor, and Friday Freya.

> During their 300 years of prominence, the Vikings explored a good portion of the Northern Hemisphere. Lands as far away as western Russia, Newfoundland, Canada, Spain, Iraq, and Greenland were all influenced by the Viking conquerors.

Hindu Pantheon

Hinduism is a religion dating back millennia, and as such has its own set of practices and beliefs unique to the culture of India. Very few modern Wiccans are of Indian descent, but the Hindu gods have become quite well known in Western culture, and so the influence of these deities is felt among some practitioners of Wicca. They choose to invoke deities such as Kali, Shakti, and Shiva in ritual, but still maintain the rest of the Wiccan ritual and seasonal framework.

The Hindu deities can be very tempting because they seem exotic, and because Indian clothing is beautiful and enticing. However, use caution when calling these deities. The Hindu gods are very complicated beings with multiple aspects, and calling the wrong one may result in a jarring or unwelcome surprise.

Nonetheless, the Hindu deities can offer wonderful opportunities for healing and removing outdated modes of being. Some people who honor the Hindu deities do so for a short time and then move on to other pantheons after they no longer need the healing Hindu deities offer.

Matron/Patron Deities

Many Wiccans have been "claimed" by specific deities. If a goddess chooses someone to worship her, she becomes that person's matron. If a god chooses someone, he becomes that person's patron. The chosen person is still free to call on other deities if the need arises or the occasion is appropriate, but when working magic, it is best to invite the matron or patron as well.

Some people discover the deity who has claimed them in meditation; others study the various pantheons and then discover the influence of specific deities in their lives. Still others discover the deities they are called to during research or ritual, or are simply struck by a deity's name and meditate on it. Being chosen is both a gift and a challenge, but one worth seeking.

A person may have more than one matron or patron over time. A goddess may choose someone in order to instill a lesson or conduct a healing, and when she is done, she leaves so that another goddess may claim that person. It is also possible for a person to have the same matron or patron for his or her entire life; it is best to leave the decision to the deities, who know what is best. Worshippers should not try to cling to a matron or patron who has decided it's time to move on. The choice is always theirs to make.

Chapter 4

Wiccan Celebrations

Wiccans celebrate many special days of the year. They have eight major holidays, called sabbats. The sabbats take place on fixed dates based on the solar calendar, and follow a cycle called the Wheel of the Year. Wiccans also honor the phases of the moon with esbats, which fall on new and full moons. Because the esbats are based on the lunar calendar, their dates change from year to year.

Wheel of the Year

The Wiccan calendar begins with Samhain, celebrated on October 31. The calendar is often represented with the Wheel of the Year, which is depicted as a circle with eight spokes, with Yule as the top spoke. The placement of Yule corresponds with the beginning of the god's mythological cycle, his birth. Samhain marks the end of his cycle.

Four of the sabbats, the Lesser Sabbats, take place at what are called the quarters: winter solstice, spring equinox, summer solstice, and fall equinox. The other four, the Greater Sabbats, take place on the cross-quarters (days halfway between the solstices and equinoxes) and are associated with ancient Celtic feast days and fire festivals. The sabbats fall roughly 6.5 weeks apart, and are evenly spaced throughout the year to coincide with the cycle of the seasons.

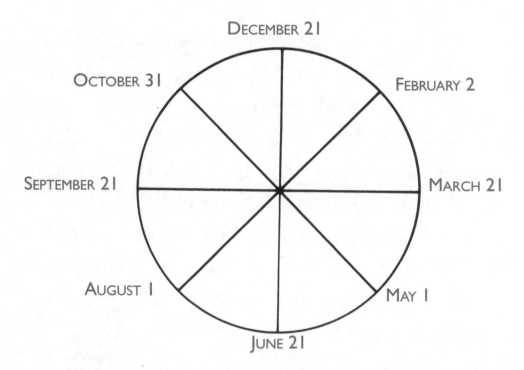

▲ The Wheel of the Year represents the Wiccan calendar. October 31: Samhain. December 20–23: Yule. February 2: Imbolc. March 20–23: Ostara. May 1: Beltane. June 20–23: Litha. August 1: Lammas. September 20–23: Mabon.

The Year Begins on Samhain

Samhain (pronounced *sow-en*) is honored on October 31. An alternative date for this sabbat is approximately November 6, when the sun is at fifteen degrees of Scorpio.

Samhain is one of the ancient Celtic fire festivals, and perhaps the most important day in the Pagan year. It is known by many other names, including Shadowfest, Hallowmas, Halloween, and the Day of the Dead, to name a few. Samhain marks the beginning of the time to study the dark mysteries, to banish weaknesses, and begin important inner work.

According to the mythological cycle, the god is dead. Some say the goddess is in mourning and enters the crone stage. For most Wiccans, she is in the mother stage, for although she mourns, she is pregnant with the god's child and due to give birth at Yule.

The goddess goes through three stages of life during the year. She begins as the maiden at Imbolc, then becomes the mother when she conceives the god at Beltane, and finally she becomes the crone after giving birth to the god at Yule. Her cycle mimics that of the earth, the moon, and the woman.

Traditionally, Samhain was the time of the final harvest, the blood harvest, when any animals that would not survive the winter on fallow were slaughtered. It was considered unwise to eat any fruit or grain not harvested by this day. The Celts also considered it the start of the dark half of the year, which also coincided with the start of the new year.

Samhain Traditions

It is said that on Samhain, the veil between the worlds is at its thinnest point and the spirits of the dead can most easily pass through it. It is a time for Wiccans to contact their ancestors and honor them, as well as to speak to those who have recently passed on and relate messages to them.

The dumb supper is one way to honor the dead. Each participant brings a favorite food of the dead person and a token of remembrance. In one variation, small bits of each dish are put on a plate and placed outside overnight. In the other variation, an actual meal is celebrated in silence, with seats at the table for the dead and offerings of their favorite foods on their plates.

Wiccans celebrate Samhain as their New Year's Eve because the Celts believed it was a day *between* the days. Samhain was not a day on the calendar, but the day in between the end of the old year and beginning of the new.

It is customary to cast the circle just before midnight and then those gathered go around the circle, taking turns saying what needs to be said to the deceased, and then placing offerings to them on the altar. The deceased can either be from the past year, or can be long-dead ancestors. Animals can also be honored. This ritual is very emotional and can last hours. After the ritual, a champagne toast is appropriate, and divination for the coming year is a popular post-ritual activity.

Samhain Deities

Crone goddesses such as Hecate (guardian of the crossroads), Inanna (aka, Ishtar; both underwent underworld journeys), Macha (mother of death), Cerridwen (keeper of the cauldron of the underworld), Lilith (protector of pregnant women and a death goddess), and Morrigan (goddess of death) are appropriate goddesses to invite to ritual, because the wisdom of the crone is honored at this time.

Because the god is dead at this time of year, there are very few gods associated with Samhain, but among the few options are Herne (god of the hunt) and the Horned God, a figure who represents the forest, the hunt, and the wild, fertile nature. He is sometimes associated with Cernunnos, but is often considered a god in his own right. Both are appropriate because Samhain was known as the "blood harvest," a time when animals that would not survive the winter were slaughtered to provide meat for the people.

Other Samhain Associations

Appropriate colors are orange and black. Altar candles are usually black and white, and most witches wear black. A few significant herbs are belladonna, thyme (associated with dead souls), rosemary for remembrance, and mugwort to aid second sight. Commonly seen animals are nocturnal beasts such as the owl, cat, and bat. The jack-o'-lantern is a very popular symbol in America because the pumpkin is an American fruit that ripens in the fall. The candle inside it is a symbol of the white, pure energy through which spirits and faeries are commonly seen. The candle guides these spirits to believers. The besom, or broom, is also associated with Samhain. Stones associated with the holiday are obsidian, onyx, and carnelian.

In old Ireland, townspeople had a practice similar to making jack-o'-lanterns. They carved turnips and put candles inside them, then set them on roads and doorsteps to guide the spirits home.

Yule: The Winter Solstice

Yule is celebrated on the winter solstice, which falls between December 20 and 23. The traditional Yule season is thirteen nights long, the Weihnachten, observed from December 20 to 31.

Yule is the longest night of the year, and it marks the astrological start of the sign Capricorn. The god is reborn on this day and fires are lit to welcome him and the strengthening sun. Following the god's birth, the goddess goes into a deep slumber and becomes crone while she recovers. This is a night to honor the goddess for her gift.

A second traditional myth is the battle between the Holly King and Oak King. At Yule, the Oak King wins and will rule until Midsummer. The tradition of re-enacting the battle may also be observed at Samhain and Beltane.

Yule Traditions

Many of the traditional Judeo-Christian winter holiday activities have Pagan roots, and this is particularly true of Christmas, which coincides with Yule. Traditions like decorating a wintergreen tree with fruit and flowers, burning the Yule log, and hanging wreaths are now Christmas traditions, but they had other, pagan meanings. Decorating the tree meant looking forward to spring and the fruit it would bring; burning the Yule log was done to give strength to the sun, and a wreath served as a symbol of the Wheel of the Year and the sun's passage through the sky. Tradition states that the ashes of a burned Yule log should be saved for a year as a protection amulet, and a piece of this year's log should be kept to start the next year's log.

> The date of Christmas is based on the European celebration of the birth of the god Mithras. The Mithraic faith of Iran, Syria, Persia, and Egypt observed the birth of Mithras on December 25, the date of the solstice on the Roman Julian calendar.

Gift giving comes from the Roman celebration of Saturnalia, which was a weeklong event at the end of the year honoring the god of death. Friends and family members give each other tokens as expressions of love.

Yule Associations

Yule is associated with reindeer, mistletoe, pine, holly, and the fox. Its colors are red, green, silver, and gold. Gold is the color of the god and silver is the color of the goddess. Mithras, the Sun King, the Baby Sun-God, Apollo, or the Great Mother can be invited. Usually the deities invoked are limited to two: a god and a goddess. Those who best suit the worshipper's purposes should be called. The altar can be decorated with rubies, garnets, or other reddish stones, and surrounded by poinsettias. A bowl of pinecones, a stag symbol, and a sun symbol are all appropriate additions to the altar.

Imbolc: Festival of Lights

Celebrated on February 2, Imbolc is one of the four fire festivals, and another Greater Sabbat. An alternative date is approximately February 4, when the sun is at fifteen degrees of Aquarius. On this day the goddess has recovered from childbirth and is maiden once more. She awakens from her slumber and the earth reawakens with her. The god is a young, growing boy, but not yet at the peak of his power.

Imbolc is literally translated as "in the belly," because spring is in the belly of the mother. It is also known as the festival of lights because on this day it is traditional to burn candles in every window from sundown to sunup to welcome the sun, although some people now choose to light every lamp in the house for a short time. It is also known as Oimelc, meaning "in milk" or "ewe's milk," because at this time of year, lambs are born. In the old days, the milk produced by sheep was used to sustain people through the rest of winter. Finally, this holiday is also known as Candlemas.

Imbolc Traditions

A corn dolly is a common symbol at this time of year. It represents the maiden as she prepares to become the bride. Traditionally, the one made at Lammas is now dressed as a bride, but a new one can be made specifically for Imbolc. The dolly is said to protect crops and is a symbol of fertility. While she is called a corn dolly, she is actually made out of wheat or other types of grain, although some Wiccans use cornhusks.

A candle blessing is usually included in any Imbolc ritual. To do this, candles in a variety of sizes and colors are placed in a basket. During the ritual, Brighid is called on to bless the candles for the coming year. Unused candles from the previous year can be reblessed for the next year. Some people save their candle drippings throughout the year, and then melt them into one large candle to be burned at Imbolc.

Because Imbolc honors new life and the return of life in its earliest stages, candles to be used over the course of the following year are blessed and many Wiccans choose to be initiated or to dedicate or re-dedicate themselves on this day. Imbolc is one of the few sabbats that is rarely open to outsiders. Most covens or working groups choose to keep this celebration a private one.

Imbolc Associations

White is the most common color associated with Imbolc. It is a symbol of innocence and purity, and represents the state of the goddess as maiden at this time of year. White is also the color of snow, and in many areas the earth is still covered with snow, although the land is showing signs of reawakening. White cloth, sheafs of wheat, and stones known as fairy crosses are often used to decorate altars. Warm foods are often consumed, because during Imbolc, it is still very cold in most places.

The most common goddess to be honored on Imbolc is Brighid (February 1 is her Catholic saint's day). In some places they still burn fires to honor her on this day. The god's role is usually quite small at Imbolc, if he is honored at all.

Ostara: The Spring Equinox

Ostara (pronounced *Oh-star-ah*) marks the official start of spring. Lady Day, as it is also called, falls sometime between March 20 and 23. It marks the astrological start of the sign Aries. It is honored on the day when night and day are of equal length. It is a day for lightheartedness and joy.

The goddess is still maiden. Whether or not she has had any physical relations with the god, she remains free and unencumbered. She holds no ties to any man or child. (This is the true meaning of "maiden," not simply *virgin*.) Popular goddesses to invite to ritual would be Kore (or Persephone), Hathor, Flora (goddess of flowers), or Inanna. Or the goddess can simply be welcomed as Lady of the Earth.

At this point in the cycle, the god is still growing. He is the laughing Lord of the Greenwood, young, carefree, still coming fully into his power. He maintains the wild spirit of youth and nature. He is often represented by Pan, Cernunnos, Ra, or Osiris.

Ostara Practices

The name Ostara comes from Eostre, an Eastern European moon goddess whose power peaks at this time of year. This is also where the word Easter comes from, and there are many similarities between the symbolism of Easter and Ostara, including decorating and hunting eggs. According to legend, Eostre is closely connected to rabbits. Ostara colors are pastels, especially blue, yellow, pink, and green. Popular flowers are daffodil and hyacinth, both of which bloom early in this season.

The tradition of decorating eggs comes from the ancient Egyptians and Persians who dyed them in pastel colors and exchanged them as gifts. In ancient Rome, eggs were given as prizes during spring races. The bunny was first associated with eggs in Germany in the 1500s, and Eostre sometimes takes the shape of an egg-laying bunny.

Other Ostara practices include lighting a fire during ritual or planting a seed in a pot. Because Ostara was one of the last sabbats added to the Pagan calendar, there are very few strict observances for the day. Instead, it is often celebrated as a carefree, fun, frolicking sort of day and the rituals are usually quite lighthearted.

Beltane: A Fertility Festival

Falling on May 1, Beltane (pronounced *Bell-tain* or *Bell-teen*) is the lustiest holiday on the Wheel of the Year. Beltane can also be celebrated on approximately May 4, when the sun is at fifteen degrees of Taurus. At this time, the god is a man and his courtship of the goddess has begun. It is a fertility festival as this is the day when the Lord and Lady consummate their courtship in the Great Rite and she conceives of him. All forms of creativity and fertility are renewed and celebrated at this time.

Traditional practices include dancing the Maypole, which is a phallic symbol topped by a flowered wreath to symbolize the womb of the goddess. It also honors the interconnectedness of life. In addition to making a flower wreath to top the Maypole, and flower crowns for the May Queen and King (who stand in for the god and goddess), some Wiccans make flower baskets to give as gifts. The colors of Beltane are red and white, but other bright colors are equally appropriate. Fresh flowers and mead should adorn the altar, along with phallic and yoni (female genital) symbols.

May Day is still celebrated in many European countries. Some nations have adopted May 1 as Labor Day. Many German cities still erect large Maypoles in their city centers and host Maypole dances.

On Beltane, many Wiccan rituals include leaping over a small fire to stimulate health and fertility. Couples may physically re-enact the Great Rite, which is the sexual union of Lord and Lady. It is also a popular day for handfastings, or traditional Wiccan wedding ceremonies. A handfasting lasts anywhere from a year and a day, for binding commitments that are nonlegal, to a lifetime, for those unions recognized by the state. (Pagan marriage customs are covered in Chapter 18.)

Beltane is the balance of Samhain and marks the beginning of the Celtic light half of the year. Gods that deal with sex, frivolity, or fertility are appropriate at this time, as are Celtic fire deities such as Belenos. Other gods to consider are Eros, the Green Man, and Pan. Goddesses associated with the day include Aphrodite, Astarte, Maia (goddess of plants), and Flora (goddess of spring).

Midsummer: The Summer Solstice

Midsummer (also known as Litha) falls on the summer solstice, sometime between June 20 to 23, and it marks the start of the astrological sign Cancer. On this day, the god has reached the peak of his power, signified by the fact that it is the longest day of the year. After the summer solstice, his power begins to weaken until he dies (in some traditions, he dies at Midsummer). The second battle between the Oak King and the Holly

King takes place on Midsummer, but this time the Holly King wins, and he rules until Yule.

Midsummer is a fire festival in honor of the great power of the sun, and even today some northern nations like Sweden feature all-night parties on the night when the sun never sets. To celebrate this day, it is traditional to drink mead, a wine made of honey. The colors of this festival are yellows, reds, oranges, and golds, and the appropriate flowers for decorating the altar are Saint John's wort, rose, angelica, and yarrow.

A popular practice for Midsummer is to burn the wickerman (a symbol of the god) with wishes for the coming year tucked inside it. The burning of the wickerman is not a symbolic sacrifice, as some outside the Pagan community wish to view it, but rather a way to transmit the wishes to the gods. The smoke carries the requests to them. Midsummer is another traditional day for bonfire leaping and handfastings. Making contact with faeries is easier on this day than on many others. Goddesses such as Freya, the Mother Goddess, Arianrhod, Flora, and Amaterasu (Japanese sun goddess), are appropriate. Gods to consider include Apollo, Bel, Lug, and Helios.

Even though it is referred to as Midsummer, the summer solstice is actually the first day of summer. The term derives from European farming because the date marks the midway point of the growing season.

Lammas: First Harvest

Lammas falls on August 1, or around August 6 if it is honored when the sun is at fifteen degrees of Leo. Lammas is known as the first harvest, or grain harvest; its name is derived from "loaf mass" because it was the day when the ancient people were again able to eat fresh bread. It is a time to honor the abundance of the earth.

Lammas is also known as Lughnasadh (pronounced *Loo-nah-sah*), the wake of the god Lug's mother, or in some circles, the wake of the god who died at Midsummer (although in some traditions he dies at Samhain). Celtic Lughnasadh celebrations were marked by fire festivals and the Tailltean games, which featured contests, races, and feasts. Couples were joined in "trial marriages," which would then be renewed a year later or dissolved, depending on the wishes of the couple and whether or not they had conceived a child during that year.

The colors of Lughnasadh are browns, reds, and oranges—the colors of late summer and early fall. Grains such as barley and wheat, and offerings of baked goods are appropriate for the altar. In addition to invoking Lug, it would be appropriate to call Inanna. This sabbat is fairly god-centric; however, the Great Mother or the Goddess can be invited to the celebration in lieu of a specific goddess.

Mabon: The Fall Equinox

Mabon occurs sometime between September 20 and 23. The astrological sign Libra begins on this day. Like Ostara, the day and night are of equal length. At this time, the season of harvest is coming to a conclusion as the earth begins to prepare for winter.

In most traditions, the god's funeral continues. In a few, he is still preparing for his death. Mythologically, this is when Persephone must return to the underworld. Demeter, saddened by this, brings winter to the land until her daughter returns at Ostara. The day is named after Mabon, who was born on the equinox, then kidnapped from his mother Modron when he was only three days old.

Mabon is also known as Harvest Home. Traditional activities include honoring fruit (formerly harvested in September) and gathering with family and friends for a witches' Thanksgiving feast. It is a time to give thanks for the abundance of the past year. The color of the sabbat is brown. Yarrow, wheat, apples, amber, acorns, and pomegranates are all appropriate altar decorations and offerings. Animals associated with Mabon include the owl and the stag. In place of Mabon, the legend of Demeter and Persephone can be retold or Dionysus can be invited. Cerridwen is sometimes called the barley goddess, and the god Frey is associated with the harvest.

Cycles of the Moon

Esbats are celebrated on the thirteen full and new moons of the year. Covens traditionally choose these nights to meet and honor the goddess. Esbats are deeply personal experiences, and many choose to work alone on these occasions. Full moons and new moons are highly magical nights and are generally the best times for spellwork.

Full Moon

During a full moon esbat, it is common to call only the goddess to honor her power. The full moon is the most magical night of the year, and all workings are appropriate, including healing, attraction, and divination. Love spells are especially powerful when performed on the full moon. Banishing spells can be cast on the day after the full moon to allow for the energy to drain away until the dark moon.

Lunar eclipses occur at full moon, and are excellent times for releasing or banishing magic. There are usually two total eclipses in a year, but they are not all visible in every locale.

The power lasts from the day before the moon reaches fullness to the day after, for a total of three days. To determine the date of the full moon, consult an astrological calendar. The period between the full moon and the new moon is best for releasing negativity, healing that involves the removal of pain or injury, and banishing unwanted people and emotions.

New Moon

The new moon is the second most powerful day of the month. Like the full moon, its energy lasts a full three days and is preceded by the dark moon. Almost any type of spell is appropriate for the new moon. Some people like to cast spells on the new moon so the energy released is fueled by the waxing moon, which is a time of increasing lunar power. The time between the new moon and the full moon is best for attraction, growth, prosperity, and love. It is also good for healings that involve drawing in positive energy or the creation of something new.

Draw Down the Moon

Esbats are the traditional time to Draw Down the Moon. Drawing Down the Moon is the practice of entering a trance and pulling the energy of the moon into the body. By doing this, the practitioner unites herself with the power of the moon and the goddess. Goddesses associated with the moon include Selene, Hecate, and Diana.

According to Hindu beliefs, the body has seven main energy centers known as chakras. They are located at the base of the spine, the sex organs, the solar plexus, the heart, the throat, the middle of the forehead (which is called the third eye), and the crown of the head. They are often pictured as lotus flowers or spinning disks in the colors red, orange, yellow, green, blue, indigo, and violet.

To Draw Down the Moon, the practitioner first opens her chakras and stands in the Goddess position (legs spread, arms held up and outward). She raises her arms over her head and points her wand or athame (ritual knife) at the moon and pulls the power down into her. As the practitioner feels it come down into her, she lowers the wand until the point is directed toward her heart. When the energy fades, she lowers her arms to her sides. The practitioner may now go deeper into meditation to learn the message that awaits her. To ground the energy at the end of the ritual, she places her hands on the ground and sends it into the earth.

Moon Names

Each lunar cycle has twenty-eight days, which means there are roughly thirteen moons in a year. Because the position and phase of the moon is sometimes easier to determine than the position of the sun during the course of a year, many early societies had lunar calendars. Each lunar month had a name, and several of those names have survived to this day.

Moon Names			
January	Wolf Moon	Old Moon	Winter Moon
February	Storm Moon	Hunger Moon	Ice Moon
March	Chaste Moon	Crow Moon	Windy Moon
April	Seed Moon	Pink Moon	Growing Moon
May	Hare Moon	Flower Moon	Milk Moon
June	Dyad Moon	Strawberry Moon	Hot Moon
July	Mead Moon	Thunder Moon	Summer Moon
August	Wyrt Moon	Red Moon	Fruit Moon
September	Barley Moon	Harvest Moon	Corn Moon
October	Blood Moon	Hunter's Moon	Travel Moon
November	Snow Moon	Beaver Moon	Frosty Moon
December	Oak Moon	Cold Moon	Snow Moon

The full moon that falls closest to the fall equinox is known as the Harvest Moon. The second full moon in a month is the blue moon and has no other name unless it's the Harvest Moon.

What is a blue moon?
Due to an error in the March 1946 issue of *Sky & Telescope* magazine, a blue moon is currently defined as the second full moon in any month. Prior to then it was the third full moon in any season with four. It is not known whether a blue moon has more magical significance than a regular full moon.

The Wiccan sabbats are usually days of merriment for Wiccans, a time of gathering for worship, feasting, and togetherness. Because they occur roughly every six and a half weeks, Wiccans have plenty of opportunities to celebrate. But these celebrations are not the only rituals performed by Wiccans. Wiccans lead lives filled with magic, and a set of tools has been developed to assist in creating this magic.

Chapter 5

Wiccan Tools

The practice of the Wiccan religion involves a vast assortment of tools, some of which are material objects and some of which are not. The list of necessary tools may grow according to the tradition being followed, but some tools are common to most Wiccan traditions. These tools include the cauldron, athame, chalice, broom, bell, bolline, wand, symbols, Book of Shadows, censer, and atrology.

An Overview of Wiccan Tools

Wiccans use their tools during magic and formal rituals at esbats and sabbats, and these objects play a variety of roles. Some traditions have strict requirements regarding each tool's shape, size, and material. The particular tradition is the guide when tools are selected. A teacher, elder, or the vendor can help in selection of the appropriate tool.

Many students new to Wicca hastily acquire all of the tools they find listed in the book they are studying. This can be quite an expensive prospect. Most teachers recommend acquiring tools over time. It may take years to find just the right athame, wand, or Book of Shadows, and as a student progresses in the Craft, she may find herself amassing a collection of several athames, cauldrons, chalices, or other items.

Are the Tools Really Necessary?

In a word, no. Tools are useful in helping direct energy or signaling the mind that you are in sacred space. Certain objects can enhance energy or please the entities with which you are working. Tools also make things feel more magical, or make an altar look nicer, but they are not an absolute necessity.

Some witches gather a "traveling witch kit": a small box or pouch in which they carry a miniature incense burner, small candles, and tiny symbols of the elements.

Basically, you can use tools as a crutch, to help you work your magic, but you may wish to experiment with tool-free magic to get a feel for your own power and abilities. There may be times when you need to do magic and have no tools available to you, or it isn't convenient to wave a knife or burn incense. In these cases, your mind is the most powerful tool available to you. Don't be afraid to use it without material tools.

Should I Make Tools or Buy Them?

It depends on your tradition and your personal abilities. Some traditions ask students to make their own athames and provide instructions for how to do this, but urban Pagans may find this prospect difficult. And unless you happen to have access to large quantities of iron and a foundry, making your own cauldron will be quite a feat.

Be careful who touches your tools after consecration. It is considered impolite to touch someone else's tools without asking. If necessary, reconsecrate your items to remove impurities it might have picked up from other people.

Not so with other tools. There is probably an arts and crafts store near you that offers classes in which you could make and decorate your own pentacles, censers, and chalices. Several community colleges or arts and crafts stores offer jewelry making classes if you want to make a necklace or other wearable art from your sacred symbols. However, all of these items can also be purchased ready-made at New Age or occult stores, or even home-decorating stores that specialize in imported or unusual goods.

Regardless of whether or not you make or buy your tools, you don't need to spend a fortune right away. The most important aspects to consider are how likely you are to use it, and whether or not you feel comfortable with it. Take your time when selecting your tools. When the time is right, you will find the tool that is best for you. It may take years, but that's okay.

Consecrating Your Tools

Immediately upon making or buying a new tool, you should cleanse it and then consecrate it for ritual use. In addition to physical cleansing, you will want to remove any energy, positive or negative, the tool has attracted while outside your possession. Popular methods include exposing the tool to the light of the full moon overnight, setting it on sea salt, washing it in spring water (or in the ocean or a stream), or burying it in the earth. The appropriate method depends on the tool. If your tool is made of wood or a form of metal susceptible to rust, you will most likely want to avoid soaking it in water for an extended period. Once your tool is cleansed, perform a consecration to dedicate it for magical purposes. Once consecrated, don't use the tool for any other purposes.

Cauldrons of Many Sizes

A cauldron is exactly what you might think it is, a round iron pot with a curved handle that sits on three legs. Prior to stoves, they were placed in hearths for household cooking. Today they are predominantly used during ritual to burn incense or parchment paper as part of a spell. Some people light ritual fires within a cauldron.

Cauldrons today come in a variety of sizes, from one-inch round to hold incense charcoal, to 100-pound cauldrons suitable for very large gatherings or permanent backyard use. Always place your cauldron on a trivet or hot pad. Cauldrons are made of iron and heat up very quickly, including the legs and handles. Never pick up a cauldron immediately after use unless you use a hot pad.

Some cauldrons are treated with paint or other solvents and there have been concerns about lead exposure, so be careful when selecting a cauldron for use in the kitchen or to make food or potions to be consumed. It may be preferable to prepare potions in another container. Consult your herb manual for guidance or purchase an iron camping cauldron from a sporting goods or kitchen store.

The cauldron is associated with the direction of west and the element of water. It is a tool for transformation, signified by the many cauldrons mentioned in ancient Celtic legends and myths. The most famous mythological cauldron belonged to the goddess Cerridwen and is credited with giving Taliesin his knowledge. This significance can also be seen in the very act of simply transforming raw materials into another state, such as paper into ash, or raw food into a meaty stew.

Athame, a Ritual Knife

Athame (pronounced *ah-thaw-mee* or *ath-uh-may*) is the most commonly used Wiccan tool. Also called a black-handled knife, an athame is used for ritual purposes. It is usually double-edged and dull.

Wiccans use the athame to cast the circle or direct energy during ritual. It also represents the god during a ceremonial Great Rite. It is associated with fire and the southern direction, or the east and the element of air, depending on the tradition.

What is peace-bonding?
It is a method of declaring your intention of nonuse. You may choose to attach your athame to its sheath or holder with a plastic tie that must be cut with scissors for removal, or by sewing your athame into the sheath. If you choose to sew it, it should be so secure that the weapon cannot easily be removed, and it should be obvious to observers that this is the case.

Types of Athames

Athames come in a variety of forms, sizes, and shapes. The serpentine athame is commonly made of metal or crystal and has a curved body. The Gardnerian tradition uses a steel, sickle-shaped blade with a long, wooden handle. Other traditions prefer an athame with a wooden handle and a metal blade with serrated or smooth edges. If you plan to work with faerie energies, be aware that the wee folk are reputed to dislike iron, and therefore a crystal athame would be preferable.

Many elaborate athames are available on the market today, or you can use a letter opener as an athame. If you are a solitary, choose a blade that speaks to you. Take your time when selecting your first athame, as you will be using it frequently in ritual.

Athames in Today's Society

Some traditions require that initiates carry their athames on their persons at all times. Certainly you should have it with you at meetings or rituals, and most private Pagan gatherings welcome them. However, in this modern age there are restrictions on where you can carry your athame.

Regardless of the material it is made from, an athame may be considered a weapon. If you are visiting a place where weapons are prohibited, it is best to leave your athame at home. You can challenge the system; other religious groups, such as the Sikhs, have won the right to carry their peace-bonded weapons at schools. However it is likely that forcing the issue will result in your weapon being confiscated, or your being refused passage.

If you are planning to attend a Pagan gathering in a public place, check to see if athames are permitted. Athames may be prohibited by law, by their insurer, or to allay fear among laypeople who may be in attendance. If athames are permitted, you may be asked to peace-bond your weapon.

Witch's Wand

The wand is similar in use to the athame. This tool should be between twelve and eighteen inches, or roughly the distance from your extended middle finger to your elbow. The wand is used to direct or raise energy. It is commonly associated with the element of air or fire, depending on the tradition.

When searching for wand wood, it's best to look for a branch that has already fallen from the tree, but if you must cut a branch, ask permission from the tree and thank it afterward.

A wand can be made of wood, and popular materials are ash, oak, hazel, and willow, but any type of wood will do if it speaks to you. If a particular type of tree is prevalent in your area, or you feel a connection with it, a branch from it might be your best choice. Wooden wands can be decorated with feathers, beads, and symbols, and topped with a crystal, but a plain wand will work just as well.

Some wands are long, cylindrical crystals. Often you will see very ornate wands wrapped with wire and embedded with crystals, but this isn't necessary, and they aren't particularly useful if you find them uncomfortable to hold. You may wish to have two or three wands for various purposes.

Other Tools

Other tools commonly used in Wiccan rituals and ceremonies include the chalice, broom, bell, bolline, and censer. The descriptions of each tool follow.

Chalice or Goblet

The chalice can be made of metal, wood, glass, or clay and may be either plain or ornate. The chalice is used during the "cakes and ale" portion of the ritual (described in the next chapter) and is associated with female energy, fertility, water, and the west. It can also hold liquids that will be charged for use during healing rites.

The chalice symbolizes the goddess during a ceremonial Great Rite. To perform a symbolic Great Rite, the sexual union of the God and Goddess, the priestess holds the chalice while the priest lowers the athame into it. A symbolic Great Rite is typically performed at Beltane.

The Witch's Broom

Contrary to folk legend and Hollywood productions, witches do not fly on brooms. The broom is a phallic symbol, and it is often used to sweep negative energy out of an area where a ritual is to be performed. The sweeping is ceremonial, and the broom need not actually touch the surfaces it is sweeping.

Brooms are also used during Wiccan wedding ceremonies. A broom is placed before the feet of the couple after they have said their vows and before they walk back down the aisle. They step over it as a symbol of fertility and entering a new phase of life. Usually, the broom would be formed from twigs or wheat and a tree branch. The bride or her attendants then decorate the broom with colored ribbons and dried flowers and herbs that symbolize the bride and groom, as well as prosperity, fertility, happiness, abundance, or health.

Household brooms are not suitable for ritual purposes, so you'll need to purchase one or make it yourself. A ritual broom can be constructed from branches and twigs, branches and wheat, or other materials. Brooms are often decorated with dried flowers, crystals, and other items.

Ring the Bell

The bell is an optional tool, but it does have several purposes. On the practical side, some Wiccans use it to call people to circle. In ritual, it can be used to dismiss negative energies, to open or close the circle, or to invite the goddess to join you (the bell is associated with feminine energy and with the element of air).

The vibrational energy of a bell is quite strong, and it can also be used to solidify spells. If you use a bell, it can be of any size. Some people enjoy using ankle bells during ritual dances. They make a nice accompaniment to drumming while people dance around a blazing fire.

Another Type of Knife

The bolline (pronounced *bow-leen*) is also known as the white-handled knife. In most traditions, it is used for cutting herbs or carving symbols into candles. Most "white-handled knives" are not actually white-handled, but are sharp. Some people use sickles for harvesting magical herbs from the garden. A kitchen knife is suitable as a bolline as long as it is consecrated and limited to magical use thereafter.

Burning Incense

A censer is a container in which you burn incense. Censers come in many shapes and sizes and may be made of metal, ceramic, or glass. When using incense charcoal with a censer, it is best to put sand or kitty litter into the bottom of the censer to insulate it from the heat of the charcoal. Nonmetal censers can crack or explode if exposed to excess heat—be especially careful with glass ones. Metal containers should be placed on a ceramic trivet or a hot pad if you don't use sand or kitty litter. In addition, allow a censer to cool or use a hot pad to pick it up after you use it. If you are using incense sticks or cones, the kitty litter or sand isn't necessary.

Wiccan Symbols

There are several symbols of importance to Wiccans, and the specific role of each symbol varies by tradition and sometimes gender. Two symbols, the pentacle and the triple moon, are common to almost all traditions and to both sexes.

Pentacle, the Five-Pointed Star

The pentacle is universally associated with witchcraft in Western society, and it is the most misunderstood of all the Pagan symbols, with the possible exception of the Norse swastika, to be discussed in Chapter 9. A pentacle, quite simply, is a five-pointed star with a circle around it. Often, you will see pentacles with the arms interwoven at the cross-points.

◀ A simple pentacle is a popular pendant for necklaces. Pentacles can also be designed to look like Celtic knotwork.

It is most common for Wiccans to use pentacles with the point at the top as a symbol of protection. It also serves as a symbol of Wiccan faith, much like a Christian cross may represent Christian faith. An inverted pentacle is used by some darker paths, but it is also used by some Wiccan traditions, such as Gardnerian, to imply that an initiate has achieved the second degree (or level) in their training.

A pentagram is defined as a five-pointed star. Its geometric shape has no magical significance until you consecrate it as a piece of jewelry or for magical work.

Wiccans do not use the pentacle to symbolize Satan. The five points of the pentacle symbolize the five elements of earth, air, fire, water, and spirit. The circle symbolizes the cycle of life. In another interpretation, the five points symbolize the five stages of life: birth, childhood, adulthood, old age, death.

Pentacles are commonly worn as jewelry, or tattooed on the body. They are also drawn in the air or carved onto candles during rituals and spellwork. Flat disk versions of the pentacle suitable for setting on an altar are available. Some practitioners set their spell materials on top of the pentacle during magic. A pentacle can be made out of any material, but if it's intended to support a hot object like a cauldron, a ceramic one would work best.

Triple Moon

The triple moon is a circle with opposing crescent moons on either side. It is a goddess symbol, as well as a lunar symbol. When used to represent the goddess, it is a depiction of her three phases: mother, maiden, and crone. It is also a symbol of the phases of the moon: waxing, full, waning, and new (dark). Women more commonly use the triple moon, but men wishing to establish a deeper connection with the goddess find this symbol useful as well.

▲ The triple moon can also be shaded with a dark moon at the center.

The Book of Shadows

The Book of Shadows (BoS) is a magical journal, reference manual, and spell book all rolled into one. Covens often have a common Book of Shadows that their initiates copy by hand into a book of their own. The use of a BoS varies. Some Wiccans use them strictly to record correspondences, chants, spells, and rituals and design it to be a book that can be passed on to future generations. Others choose to record their meditations and journeys in the book, and it becomes a personal journal, a record of their magical lives.

If you print pages to attach to a bound BoS, use double-stick tape rather than glue to attach the pages. Glue-stick adhesive can evaporate, and household glue will thicken and warp the pages.

How you use your book is up to you. Traditionally, a BoS is handwritten, and the pages can be decorated with drawings and symbols. However, as technology has progressed and personal computers and graphics software have become readily available, the BoS has evolved as well. Many Wiccans now also possess a Disk of Shadows, a computerized record of all the spells and rituals they've collected over the years, or had e-mailed to them by witchy friends. People who are very accustomed to typing everything often choose to type the information to be included in their BoS and then print it out to be pasted into a bound book, or three-hole punched and placed in a binder.

There are no hard and fast rules governing the appearance of a Book of Shadows. It may be a binder, a bound book stamped with the words "Book of Shadows," an ornately carved wooden box, or a spiral-bound notebook. This last option is good when learning, but might be impractical if you plan to keep your BoS through the ages.

Astrology and Wicca

Many Wiccans closely follow astrology. In addition to knowing their sun signs (the position of the sun in the zodiac when they were born), they are aware of their moon signs (the position of the moon in the zodiac when they were born), and the positions of all the other planets in the signs as well. There are several computer programs that can provide you with a birth chart. You can also run transited charts, which tell you which signs your planets have migrated to.

Check Your Timing

Before doing magic, some Wiccans consult an astrological calendar to determine which phase the moon is in, if the moon is in a sign favorable to working, and whether or not the moon is void-of-course, an astrological term meaning it is not in any sign. Moon void-of-course periods, which can be a few minutes to an entire day in length, are considered bad times to perform magic or make legal agreements or new contacts.

It is also important to check if Mercury is in retrograde (when Mercury appears to be traveling backward in its orbit as viewed from the earth). Mercury goes retrograde approximately four times a year, for roughly three weeks at a time. During Mercury retrogrades, it is unwise to sign contracts or start new projects and you should use extra caution when driving. It is also wise to back up your computer files and avoid buying new electronic equipment.

If you find yourself having a lot of arguments or muddled communications, check the calendar. Mercury might just be in retrograde or the moon may be void-of-course.

Planetary Correspondences

Planet	Day	Element	Color	Sign	Metal	Stone	Herb	Properties
Sun	Sunday	fire	gold	Leo	gold	topaz	Saint John's wort, frankincense	creativity, fatherhood, success
Moon	Monday	water	silver	Cancer	silver	moonstone	willow, lotus	emotions, motherhood, intuition
Mercury	Wednesday	air, water	violet	Gemini, Virgo	mercury	opal	lavender, sandalwood	communication, travel
Venus	Friday	earth, water	green	Taurus, Libra	copper	rose quartz	daffodil, rose	partnerships, beauty, sex
Mars	Tuesday	fire	red	Aries	iron	carnelian	dragon's blood, pepper	aggression, lust, conflict
Jupiter	Thursday	air, fire	purple	Sagittarius	tin	amethyst	cedar, cinquefoil	business, education, law
Saturn	Saturday	water, earth	blue, black	Capricorn	lead	sapphire	hemlock, mandrake	thrift, obstacles, restriction
Uranus	none	air, fire, water	blue-green	Aquarius	uranium	quartz	clover	unexpected occurrences, invention
Neptune	none	water	light blue	Pisces	pewter	aquamarine	lotus, water lily	visions, art, healing
Pluto	none	water	black	Scorpio	chrome	obsidian	foxglove, dogwood	order, sudden change

Planetary Correspondences

Each planet is associated with specific signs, elements, colors, planets, herbs, stones, and properties. These are the items to consider when consulting an astrological calendar to determine which sign the moon should be in when you perform your spell. Choosing the sign ruled by the most beneficial planet is helpful. You can also consider stones and other items that will boost the energy of your spell.

Daily Correspondences

In addition to the planetary correspondences, each day of the week is also associated with a sign, color, stone, herb, and specific properties. You may wish to choose a day for your spell before considering the planetary aspects, because the two are closely aligned.

Daily Correspondences					
Day	**Sign**	**Color**	**Stone**	**Herb**	**Properties**
Sunday	Leo	yellow	citrine	sunflower	health, success, career
Monday	Cancer	silver	moonstone	willow	emotions, spirituality, psychic powers
Tuesday	Aries, Scorpio	red	ruby	nettle	passion, sex, aggression
Wednesday	Gemini, Virgo	purple	agate	lavender	memory, education, contracts
Thursday	Pisces, Sagittarius	blue	lapis lazuli	cinnamon, cedar	business, politics, law
Friday	Taurus, Libra	pink	rose quartz	rose	love, beauty, harmony
Saturday	Capricorn, Aquarius	black	jet	wolfsbane	protection, real estate, karma

Chapter 6

Wiccan Practices

Wiccans have a large number of different religious practices, most of which are related to rituals and the use of magic. These practices incorporate concepts from a wide variety of areas, including herb, stone, and color lore, astrology, meditation and visualization, and several forms of divination. Not all of these practices are used in every ritual, or even every day, but most Wiccans are familiar with all of them.

Wiccan Rituals

Ritual plays a large role in a typical Wiccan's life. Rituals take many forms, from short and simple divination or thanksgiving rites, to long and involved sabbat rituals. The rituals performed on sabbats honor a stage in the Wheel of the Year, and may include a magical working. Rituals are also performed on esbats and those almost always include magical working. Initiations are yet another form of ritual.

The length of the ritual depends on its purpose; spells are usually shorter than a full sabbat rite. Some Wiccans find that the deities who have chosen them require a brief daily ritual honoring them, or they may wish to start with a morning rite to greet the new day or draw cards on how the day will unfold. Some people also have a ritual of meditation or divination inside sacred space.

Ritual Format

Most Wiccan rituals follow a standard format, but there are variations and they can be customized to suit a particular purpose or tradition. The following is a good example of the steps taken during a typical ritual:

1. Grounding and centering
2. Casting the circle
3. Calling the quarters
4. Invoking the deity or deities
5. Sabbat or esbat observances (if appropriate)
6. Magical working
7. Cakes and ale
8. Releasing the deities
9. Releasing the quarters
10. Releasing the circle

Grounding is the act of releasing any excess energy from your body. Centering is the act of anchoring the energy you need in the center of your body. Some Wiccans visualize roots extending from their body into the earth and then draw energy back up through those roots. This helps prevent them from being overwhelmed by energy during ritual.

Casting the circle is a method of creating sacred space around you. In order to cast a circle, the practitioner points her athame, wand, or the finger of her dominant hand toward the earth and walks clockwise, or *deosil*, in a circle around her altar and ritual area. She then visualizes a sphere of energy forming around her. Some traditions use formal words when casting the circle, or have a specific set of instructions for doing so. It is traditional to start in the east or the north. When the circle is released at the end of the ritual, the practitioner returns to where she started and walks counterclockwise, or *widdershins*. As she walks, she pulls the energy back into her athame, wand, or finger.

The circle keeps negative, uninvited spirits or energy out and contains positive energy so that it can build up on itself. It also sends a signal to your brain that you are engaged in a sacred activity.

After casting the circle, invite the quarters (in this case the four directions represented by the elements, not the four Lesser Sabbats in the Wheel of the Year, which are also known as quarters):

· East is air.
· North is earth.
· West is water.
· South is fire.

Some traditions alter the element/direction correspondences to suit their beliefs, or to recognize the actual locations of those elements. For example, for practitioners who live on the East Coast, it might make more sense for water to be to the east. The quarters are there to protect the practitioner and lend additional energy to her working. It is traditional to start with the east or the north and go clockwise around the circle. When the quarters are released, the first one called is the last one released.

If the ritual is held on a sabbat, the special observances, like dancing the Maypole at Beltane, are conducted next. It would generally include a statement of the purpose of the sabbat, the mythology behind it, and some celebration of the current roles of the deities being called. Some traditions perform elaborate pageants as part of their ritual. Rituals performed on esbats include something to honor the full moon and the extra power it provides.

After the observances have been completed, the magical workings are conducted. Magic performed at sabbats is usually designed to benefit the world at large, such as a working for world peace or to heal from a catastrophe. Healing magic for individuals can also be done on sabbats. Other types of magic are performed in ritual, but not on the sabbat days, unless it is an emergency.

Cakes and ale is similar in some ways to the Christian Eucharist. The cakes represent the goddess and the bounty of the earth, while the ale represents the god and the bounty of the vines and trees. In addition to honoring the gifts of the gods, the cakes and ale help to ground practitioners after intense energy work.

The cakes are traditionally offered to the god and goddess first, then passed clockwise around the circle, with each person offering them to the person to her or his left (or the cakes may be presented by designated people who move around the inside of the circle). The high priest and high priestess may receive them first or last. The cakes are offered to each person with the phrase "May you never hunger," and the ale is offered with the phrase "May you never thirst." "Blessed be" is the appropriate response.

Deities in Ritual

Deities are invited to every ritual performed, and should be treated with utmost respect. When Wiccans invoke deities, they invite them rather than command them to appear. The gods don't like being ordered around. When they are released, they should be thanked for their presence. Once a deity has helped achieve the desired results, a rite of thanks or an offering is appropriate. Before inviting deities to join a ritual, Wiccans decide on the focus of the ritual and which deities would be the best guests.

Setting up an Altar

Altars serve as a focus for worship. Most Wiccans have at least one altar in their home. They may also use a separate, specially erected altar during rituals and spells. Group sabbats generally take place around an altar set up specifically for that ritual.

Keep your altar clean, neat and dust-free. Leaving your altar in a state of disarray will reflect back on your life, causing it to be in disarray. Updating it seasonally forces you to keep your altar current and tidy.

Permanent home altars take many forms. Some people have one household altar that holds a representation of the god and goddess and the elements, magical tools, and any items charged or created during a spell. Many Wiccans choose to update their main altar seasonally by adding or removing items pertaining to the current sabbat or changing the altar cloth. Some Wiccans have individual altars for each member of their family, or altars for different rooms, for example, an abundance altar in the kitchen or a love altar in the bedroom.

The first time you set up an altar, perform a ritual to consecrate it. Begin by ritually cleansing the area where it will be, then set it up. As you lay each object on the altar, consecrate those that haven't been consecrated yet, and state their purpose on the altar. Over time, you may add new quarter representations, tools, or new god and goddess depictions.

Spells and Chants

Spells and chants are the most common form of magical workings performed during ritual. Spells and chants can also be used outside of ritual space, should the need arise.

A chant can be used to invoke a deity, call a quarter, cast the circle, raise energy during ritual, or charge a magical item so it will continue the magic once the spell is done. Chants typically rhyme, and they are repeated several times to reinforce the power of the spell or ritual, so they should be short enough to be easily remembered. Chants can be spoken or sung, but singing is more common. You can find several CDs that contain elemental, circle, or invocation chants.

Chants can also be said outside of ritual. For example, if you are facing a challenge at work, you might say a quick chant to release the pressure and help you focus. Usually this would be a chant that you said in ritual, which you are now using to give the spell a boost or draw that energy back up.

A spell is more specifically associated with magic, and a spell may contain a chant. Spells are usually done inside a magical circle for the practitioner's protection, although some Wiccans choose to forgo the circle for simple spells. A spell usually involves several steps and may include candles, oil, incense, and visualization. All of the items are carefully selected to amplify the power and help achieve the desired results. The deity invoked should be related to the desired result.

Both chants and spells can involve lengthy preparation, especially if you prefer to write rhyming chants and invocations. When you first begin performing spells, you may wish to consult one of the many books on the topic and use spells written by others. Over time, you'll be able to write your own spells, and eventually you may choose not to write spells down ahead of time, and instead gather the necessary materials and then say the words that come to you once you are in ritual space.

Herbs and Essential Oils

Beyond the traditional use of herbs for cooking, Wiccans use herbs for healing, magic, and decoration. Most herbs have medicinal as well as magical properties that have been established through years of folk use, although some have also been medically tested.

It is best not to attempt to use herbs without consulting an expert guide unless you have a lot of knowledge about them. Many books have been published on the medicinal uses of herbs and the proper preparation of them. When used medicinally, herbs are often made into teas or mashed into compresses to be applied to the skin. They can also be sprinkled in baths.

Several herbs have come to be associated with concepts like remembrance, love, peace, etc., that can be applied to the practitioner's magical needs. Herbs can be placed in charm bags to carry on your person or burned to enhance the visualization of your desire. They are sometimes distributed at rituals as a symbol of the season or the working just completed.

Herbs come in two grades: cooking and decorative. If you plan to use dried herbs for consumption, ask the store if their herbs are cooking grade. Herbs at craft stores generally aren't, but your occult store may have them. Health and organic food stores that sell bulk herbs generally do have herbs suitable for consumption.

Herbs also make nice seasonal decorations for altars and the home. They can be woven into small brooms or decorative pentacles to hang over the altar for the upcoming sabbat, or they can be scattered on ritual altars or even the ground if you are in a place where it will not disrupt the natural environment. Fresh herbs make a nice addition to flower arrangements.

Essential Oils

Wiccans use essential oils derived from plants for many of the same purposes as herbs. Oils can be applied to the skin as part of a healing ritual, as a blessing, or for purification during a ritual. Essential oils can also be added to a preritual purification bath or dropped into an aromatherapy burner or disperser to set the appropriate mood during the ritual or any other time. Several oils have a relaxing or soothing effect and are popular among Wiccan office-workers who keep a small burner on their desks.

Essential oils are also frequently rubbed onto candles during spells. This is called "dressing a candle." In order to dress a candle, dab oil on your thumb and forefinger. Rub the oil from the ends to the middle of the candle if you are doing a ritual to attract something to you, and from the middle to the ends if you are doing a banishing ritual. Don't rub the oil in a back and forth motion. When you get to the middle, if you're doing an attraction spell, remove your fingers and return to the bottom of the candle for the next upward stroke.

Oils come in two grades: perfume and essential. Always look for essential oils, because perfume oils are often blended with chemicals or other oils that make them impure.

Candles and Incense

Candles represent deities or the element of fire and the southern direction, and so are frequently used in ritual and magic. Wiccans burn candles during spellwork to help transmit their desires to the gods and the universe. Candles can also serve as a focal point during visualizations.

When used to represent the god or goddess, there are a variety of options. Silver or green tapers or a candle in the shape of the female figure can be used for the goddess. Red or gold candles, or male-shaped candles, are used for the god. They are generally lit when the god or goddess is invoked and extinguished when they are released. Some people use three candles—white, red, and black—to represent the maiden, mother, and crone aspects of the goddess.

For spellwork, candles are often rubbed with oil and may have symbols carved into them. The size of the candle is not very important, but consider whether this is a candle that will be used multiple times, or just for one day. Never reuse a candle from an old spell for a new spell. In most cases, it is best to burn spell candles all the way down and then either bury the drippings or save them for Imbolc.

If you must leave home, go to bed, or have a curious pet or child and the candle has not yet burned down, put it and its holder in a fire-resistant area like the bathtub. That way if it tips over, it won't ignite anything else and the wax will be easy to clean up.

The most important aspect to consider when choosing a candle for spellwork is its color. Each color is associated with specific attributes or properties that correspond to the desired result. If the desired result is represented by several colors, you can burn several candles, or you can buy beeswax sheets in the appropriate colors and roll your own candle. If the desired result has several aspects, it would be appropriate to choose a color for one aspect and an oil or herb for another. The color of the altar cloth can also play a symbolic role. White can be used in place of any other color.

Color Symbolism	
Color	**Attributes**
Red	passion, fire, anger, action, sex
Orange	career, action, justice
Yellow	inspiration, confidence, memory
Green	prosperity, growth, the goddess, fertility
Blue	healing, communication, business, calm
Purple	influence, ambition, power
Pink	romantic love, peace
White	purity, innocent love, spirituality
Black	protection, banishing
Brown	neutrality, uncertainty, the earth
Gold	the sun, male power
Silver	the moon, psychic powers, female energy, intuition

Burning Incense

Incense comes in the forms of loose herbs, self-burning sticks, self-burning cones, and resin. All forms are suitable for magic and ritual, and some people burn incense for preritual purification, room purification, meditation, and divination. Loose herbs and resins such as frankincense and myrrh must be burned on incense charcoal, which are small black disks that can be found at occult stores and some natural food stores. The advantage to burning loose herbs and resins is the ability to control how long it burns. Sticks and cones have the advantage of not requiring charcoal, but they do leave messy ash behind.

Some people are allergic to smoke, including incense smoke, so ask before smudging (wafting smoke over) someone or igniting billowy incense in indoor group rituals.

Even though it is burned, incense represents the element of air, and also represents the direction of east. For sabbat rituals, some Wiccans like to use the same incense regularly, while others like to vary it according to the herbs associated with the season or the sabbat. Incenses are available from several different parts of the world, so it shouldn't be too difficult to locate one appropriate to the chosen pantheon or deities that will be called.

Stones and Crystals

Stones carry their own special power. Everything from river rocks to diamonds can have a place in magic because they all come from the divine and their energy can be harnessed and amplified. River rocks can be painted with symbols and transformed into rune stones. Wiccans also use stones to make altars, meditation wheels, and labyrinths. Holding a stone can help the practitioner ground after ritual.

Crystals are a subset of stones; they are special earth formations and many cultures have noted their special energetic or healing properties. In addition to diamonds and other gemstones, which cultural traditions have endowed with properties like chastity and faithfulness, other crystals have magical properties. For example, rose quartz amplifies love energy, and onyx is a wonderful healing stone.

There are hundreds of crystals, and it is possible to find one suited to almost every need. Crystals work by collecting and amplifying energy. Before using a crystal, it is necessary to cleanse it of any residual energy it absorbed while being handled in stores or during mining. To cleanse a crystal, run it under pure spring water, or set it on sea or rock salt for three days. After use, some translucent stones become cloudy. This is a sign that they need cleansing, but it is better to cleanse your crystals after each use than to wait for a sign. If a crystal collects too much energy, it may break.

When used in magic, crystals can be rubbed with oil and charged with your energy to help ensure the desired result. The stone can be left on the altar, or you can carry it with you until the desired result is achieved. Once a spell has come to fruition, be sure to cleanse the crystal before using it for another purpose.

The use of crystals has become controversial because they are mined, and the mining process may cause environmental damage. And even though crystals do grow and so are replaceable, the time frame for this is eons, not decades. You must decide where you stand on this issue before using crystals.

Practicing Meditation

Mediation is an important part of Wiccan practice. It is a way to check in with your subconscious and to commune with your matron or patron deity, the god and goddess, or spirit guides. During meditation you can meet and learn about forces stronger and more knowledgeable than yourself and receive guidance toward the right action. Meditation also allows you to check in with your body and make sure it's all right.

Meditation can be difficult to learn, especially for Type A personalities, because it involves quieting the mind, focusing on breathing, and learning not to pay attention to the millions of thoughts that are triggered as you try to quiet the mind. It may take you years to master the practice, but it is well worth the effort.

Forms of Meditation

There are many forms of meditation, some of which are easier to master than others: visualization, journeys, trance dancing, and self-guided meditation. You can write your own meditations, find them in books, or buy prerecorded meditation tapes or music. If you decide to undertake a meditation practice, it should be a fairly regular occurrence, whether it's weekly or daily.

Meditation has been proven to reduce stress, help victims of trauma mentally recover, assist with physical healing, reduce the effects of heart disease, and keep the mind sharp. Many doctors recommend meditation or meditation-based relaxation techniques to their patients.

Visualization

Visualization is mainly used for magic and manifestation. It is the art of picturing or imagining the desired outcome of your spell or magical working. Visualization, like all forms of meditation except trance dancing, is done with closed eyes. Try to broadcast your desired images, sounds, tastes, textures—as many senses as you can manage—onto your mind's eye, which is roughly located behind your forehead. Some people have difficulty with this and instead picture things just generally around them. Use whatever method works best for you.

Guided Journeys

Many prerecorded meditation tapes take the form of guided journeys. You can also find journeys in books, but it can be difficult to remember all the steps, so it is best to tape them and play them back during your meditation. A guided journey usually has a specific purpose. Typically backed by music or Native American drumming, a gentle voice tells you what to picture as you begin the journey and then gently guides you back to full consciousness. A guided meditation is probably the best way for beginners to learn this practice.

Trance Dancing

Dancing is another form of meditation, although it is a more active form. When trance dancing, you release your body to the beat of drums or other rhythmic music. If you reach a deeply ecstatic state, you may receive visions or messages. Bonfires lit during or after rituals are very popular places for trance dancing. For this reason, you may wish to keep your eyes open when trance dancing. Dancing into a fire is a sure way to cut the experience short.

The repetitive motion of drumming can also help you reach a trance state. It is best to use a *djembe* or *doumbek* for trance drumming unless you have already mastered another type of drum like a bodhran. This is because the beats of the *djembe* or *doumbek* are the most variable and require the least concentration. Instead of worrying about the music you are creating, beat the drum as you feel moved to and allow your body to carry your mind along with the rhythm.

A bodhran (pronounced *boar-on*) is a Celtic drum played with a shaped dowel called a tipper. It is round and flat with a skin top. A *djembe* (pronounced *gem-bay*) is a goblet-shaped, wooden drum with a skin top. It is from Africa and is played with the hands. The *doumbek* (pronounced *doom-beck*) is a similar-looking drum of Middle Eastern origin. It is made of metal with a skin or Mylar top and is played with the fingertips.

How to Get into Trance

Self-guided meditation is the most difficult form of meditation to master. The first step is to learn meditative breathing and to develop a method for walking yourself down into the trance state. There are several helpful books and tapes on possible methods. Once you learn how to enter the meditative state, your subconscious mind will lead you where you need to go. If it helps, light candles and incense and play special music as a mental cue that you are about to meditate. You may also wish to set a timer to call you out of meditation if you have a habit of falling asleep or meditating for hours on end.

To enter the trance state, relax your body, close your eyes, and focus on your breath. Count your breaths from one to ten, then start back at one. Don't allow any thoughts to distract you. If you do focus on a thought, acknowledge it and then return to counting at one. The counting will help quiet your mind. Once your mind is quiet, see if any messages come to you, or ask a question of the universe. When you are done, count down from ten to one. Stretch to awaken your limbs, then open your eyes.

Meditation Journal

Like dreams, memories of meditations and the messages received fade quickly. It is best to keep a journal nearby so you can record the details afterward. Make sure to date each entry. Every so often, you may wish to reread your journal and see if any places, animals, people, or lessons are repeated frequently. Those animals may be your guides, and the people could be deities or nature spirits who wish to have a deeper connection with you. Places visited repeatedly could be sacred sites for your magical dreamscape, or which you can mentally visit during times of stress.

Your magical journal can be anything from a bound book to a spiral-bound notebook or binder. If you have artistic skills, you might want unlined pages so you can draw visual images of what you saw. You can record your journeys with a standard pen or pencil, or consecrate a special one. The important thing is to record each one. You may want to start with the elements that stand out, or just record the entire experience from beginning to end.

Divining the Future

Divination is the practice of consulting some form of an oracle for messages, answers, or predictions of the future. Popular methods for divination include the tarot, I Ching, scrying, and runes (runes will be covered in Chapter 9). Most Wiccans use some form of divination before a spell to determine if it will have the desired outcome. Some also do a morning divination to see how the day will go, or if there is a particular message to focus on for the day.

Tarot Cards

Tarot is one of the most popular forms of divination. A tarot deck consists of seventy-eight cards: twenty-two Major Arcana and fifty-six Minor Arcana. The Major Arcana represent archetypes and reflect the life cycle. When they appear in a spread, they are considered to have a stronger influence than the Minor Arcana cards. The Minor Arcana has four suits, and roughly corresponds to a standard deck of playing cards. The four original suits were coins, staffs, wands, and swords, but many modern decks have updated the suits as pentacles, wands, cups, and swords. Each suit is related to specific attributes, and has the numbers one through ten, plus an ace, page, knight, queen, and king.

The first appearance of the tarot in its current form was in the fourteenth century, but its origin is unknown. Some believe it was invented in France in the fourteenth century, while others believe it originated with the god Thoth in ancient Egypt.

I Ching, the Book of Changes

The I Ching, also known as the Book of Changes, is a very complicated Chinese divination system. At over 4,000 years old, it is the first form of divination known to man. I Ching is comprised of a set of sixty-four hexagrams that translate the knowledge of the subconscious to the conscious mind. The six-line hexagrams are based on the binary yin/yang symbol. To create a hexagram, stocks or coins are tossed into the air and the order in which they land is compared against a book containing the meanings of the sixty-four symbols and the various interrelations of all the possible line combinations.

Gaze into a Crystal Ball

Scrying is a form of divination performed by gazing into a crystal ball, a bowl of water, a flame, or a scrying mirror. As you do so, you think of a question, quiet the mind, and stare into the device until an answer is received. The answer could be a picture you see, or it may appear in your mind. It could also be auditory.

Scrying is usually done in a darkened room. If you want to use a scrying mirror, you can make your own. All you need is a glass side-table topper that you can paint black on one side. Set a candle in the middle and then stare into the reflection of the flame with a question in mind.

Wiccan practices take a variety of forms. Together with celebrations, beliefs, and tools, the four elements form the basis of the Wiccan faith. Other Neo-Pagan faiths, such as Asatru, may seem to have similar elements, but they are applied in a different way.

If you're new to divination, you may find the tarot an easier form to work with at first. Scrying requires meditation skills, and the I Ching requires more study.

Chapter 7

Asatruar Beliefs

The religion of Asatru is based on the ancient practices and beliefs of the Vikings (especially those of Iceland) and of other Germanic groups from Scandinavia, Denmark, and Germany. Asatruar beliefs are reconstructionist, since they are drawn from surviving historical documents and archaeological evidence. The modern Asatruar do not consider their faith an exact replica of the ancient way of life because they recognize that some of the old practices are not appropriate or applicable to modern life.

The Eddas

Most of the beliefs and practices of Asatruar are based on the Eddas, which are a thirteenth-century collection of Norse poems that provide religious and magical guidance. Some of the Eddas are stories, while others are closer to proverbs in nature.

Contained within the Eddas are wisdom and advice for leading a good life and interpreting the runes, which are a Norse divination system. The legends of the gods and heroes help Asatruar understand their deities and provide a framework for appropriate methods of worship. Finally, the Eddas help Asatruar connect with the ancient faith they are rebuilding by detailing the Norse worldview from the creation of the world to the end of it at Ragnorak.

The word *Asatru* means "loyal to the Æsir." Practitioners of Asatru are known as Asatruar, which is both singular and plural, but most prefer to be called "Heathens" and call their practice "Heathenry." Asatruar may also refer to themselves as "the True." They rarely refer to themselves as Neo-Pagans.

Origins of the Eddas

The *Poetic Edda* recounts the mythological sagas of the Norse gods and heroes. There is also a *Prose Edda*, written by Snorri Sturluson, which records mythology but also provides instructions on writing Norse poetry. The *Prose Edda* dates to around 1220 C.E. It is not known precisely when the poems within the *Poetic Edda* were composed, but scholars believe that many were composed as early as the ninth century or as late as the twelfth century.

It is believed that most of the poems were composed in Iceland, but some may have come from other areas. It is unknown when or how the legends themselves were formed, because the Norse had an oral tradition long before they were written down.

The Norse Pantheon

The Norse pantheon is divided into two groups, the Æsir and the Vanir. The gods of the Æsir are related more strongly to battle and intellectual or spiritual pursuits, while the gods of the Vanir are more closely connected to nature, prosperity, and human emotions. According to the Eddas, the Æsir and the Vanir were once at war, but later made peace.

Asatruar worship the various deities in the pantheon, but they do not bow down to them. Instead, the gods are approached with love and respect so that Asatruar may learn to live and work with them. The relationship is rather like that of an elder to a child instead of a master to a servant.

The Æsir

The Æsir live in Asgard, one of the sky realms. The gods of this realm are the fierce sort, historically associated with the Vikings and their warring ways. You might like to think of them as holding more masculine or left-brain traits. The leader of the Æsir is Odin (Woden). He is the god of magic, poetry, and runemasters, or people who work with the runes (a system of divination). Odin is associated with the raven, the eagle, and the wolf, and his tool is the spear.

Tyr (Tiw) is the god of law, justice, and oaths and carries a spear. Thor (Thunar) is a warrior god and rules loyalty. He also has some ties to agriculture. He is associated with the hammer and the goat.

Among the goddesses of the Æsir is Frigga, the wife of Odin. She is the goddess of marriage and childbirth. She maintains domestic order and is connected with prophecy. Her tool is the distaff, which is used for spinning thread, so she may be related to the Norns (the three fates) and the web of *wyrd*, or fate.

The Vanir

During their war with the Æsir, the Vanir lived in Vanaheim. When peace was made, some of the gods of the Vanir moved to Asgard. The gods of the Vanir are gentler gods and connected to farming and living off the land. They would be more akin to feminine or right-brain attitudes. The goddess Freya is the most prominent among them. She is the goddess of magic, sex, love, and health. She is also a battle goddess and rules the Valkyries. Her tool is the Brisingamen, a magical necklace.

The god Loki is neither Æsir nor Vanir. He is a trickster god, similar to Native American trickster gods like Coyote, and is also associated with wildfires. He is difficult to work with because he cannot be controlled, even by the other gods. In legends, Loki seems to switch allegiance easily because he is attached to nothing in the human world or the otherworld.

Freya's twin, Frey, is one of the gods of the Vanir. He is associated with fertility in all its forms and erotic love. He carries a magic sword and is related to the natural processes of land and air. His animals are the stag, the horse, and the boar. Njord (Njorth) is the father of Frey and Freya. He rules the sea, but is also a peacemaker. It was he who ended the war with the Æsir, and his tool is the axe.

Other Norse Spirits

Asatruar also work with and honor other spirits, who are neither divine nor human. These figures are mentioned in the Eddas, and are also reflected in the myths of other cultures. They include the Norns, Valkyries, Disir, and Land Spirits.

The Norns

The Norns are similar to the Greek Fates. They weave the thread of *wyrd* (the web of fate). There are three Norns:

- Urd, the oldest, rules the past, or "that which has become."
- Verdandi, in the middle, rules the present, or "that which is becoming."
- Skuld, the youngest, rules the future, or "that which should be." Skuld has the power to rip up the web and end a person's life.

According to the Asatruar, the future is not set in stone, but it is guided by the *orlog*. The orlog is understood as the law of the universe, but it is also a record of a person's actions. An individual's past actions shape her personality, which shapes her future actions. The *wyrd* is set—it cannot be changed—but a person's reaction to it can be. For example, if it is a person's *wyrd* to contract cancer, that person can't change that fact, but he can choose his reaction to the diagnosis. The individual can choose to fight and keep up his spirits, or he can choose to mourn his fate and give in to the disease.

Asgard contains twelve palaces of the gods. Valhalla, made famous in *Beowulf*, is but one of these palaces. It is the home of the Einherjar, the dead battle heroes, and Odin resides there.

The Norns are also charged with tending the Yggdrasil, the World Tree, and guarding the magical Urd Well that lies below the tree. According to legend, they sprinkle the tree with water from the well once a day. The Norns may be ruled by Freya, who some believe spins the thread that they weave.

The Valkyries

The Valkyries are Odin's daughters. Among the legends, the number of Valkyries varies between nine and thirteen. Armed with spears and helmets, they roam the battlefields determining who will die and who will live, although sometimes the decision is in accordance with the will of Odin. They also conduct the dead heroes to Valhalla. In Valhalla, they are hostesses, but this isn't considered a servile role. Like the Norns, they have some connection to Freya, who is also associated with choosing the dead in battle.

The Disir

A third group led by Freya is the Disir, also known as the Vanadis. The Disir act as go-betweens for the people and the gods. A Disir is connected to a family, and may even be a female ancestor. They ride into battle to guard their wards and can choose whether or not to bind them in battle, or release those binds. When not in battle, they may help guarantee family abundance or protect lands. Images of the Disir are often placed on a family shrine to honor them and they are worshiped at the festivals of Winter Night, Yule, and Disting.

> The Disir are sometimes called the Mothers and may appear wearing black or white, depending on their purpose. They sometimes appear in groups, but they should not be feared. They are there to help their wards.

In addition to warding a family, they assist in childbirth and claim the newly dead. Because the Disir are prophetic, they can attempt to interfere in the actions of their wards to prevent harm from coming to them. For example, if a person is going to get into a car accident on her way to work, her family's Disir might create a distraction that will keep her from leaving on time, which will also prevent the accident.

The Wights

The wights are spirits Asatruar both honor and interact with. The wights take many forms. One is the house-ghost, a male spirit tied to a house, a burial mound, or a family. A house-ghost guards the property and home of the family, and may assist with chores. It brings luck to the family to which it is bound, but may take the luck away if displeased. House-ghosts are also fond of playing tricks. It is customary to offer them porridge and beer or whole milk on Thursdays to keep them happy. They are also given a special offering at Yule.

Light Elves, Dark Elves, and Dwarves also play a role in Asatru. The Light Elves are connected to Frey, and may have some influence on the weather. They are considered messengers of the gods. Dark Elves are dead people and reside in mounds. Gifts for them are left on these mounds at Yule. The Dark Elves may serve a purpose similar to the Disir. Dwarves are also dead people, and they are connected with dreams. They are magical and wise, but they are also deceitful and carry grudges. It is believed that the dwarves crafted the tools of the gods because they are great craftsmen.

Land-wights are natural beings connected with streams, stones, and other natural landmarks. They protect the land from attack and are often given gifts of food and drink to secure protection and ensure their happiness. Unhappy land-wights can bring misfortune or interfere with a person's work.

Fylgia are attached to specific people. They take the guise of animals or female spirits. Each person has a fylgia, but her presence is hidden. Fylgia may be connected to the shamanic form of magic called *seidhr*. In other faiths, they are known as fetches or spirit guides.

> The Jotnar are a race of giants that lived before the world. According to the Eddas, the world and all its inhabitants were created from the decaying body of the giant Ymir. The giants are elemental in nature, and are not worshipped. They will play a role in the destruction of the world at Ragnorak.

Asatruar Cosmology

Asatruar believe that the world is composed of nine realms, all of which are a part of the Yggdrasil, the World Tree. Some divide the World Tree into three interconnected levels, while others see the nine realms as nine roots of the World Tree, or eight realms around the human realm. Beings from each of the realms interact with beings from all the other realms.

According to the three-level theory, the three lower realms lie beneath the tree. The first realm is Hel, the land of the dead. Next is Swartelf-home (Svartalfheim). It is the home of the dwarves and the forces that bring structure into being. The third lower realm is Etin-home (Jotunheim). The Jotnar as well as the forces of chaos and order reside there.

Above the lower realms are the three middle realms. The first is Midgard, or Middle-Earth. This is the earth, the realm of humans. It is connected to Muspell-home (Muspelheim) or the land of fire, and Nifelhome (Nifelheim), the land of ice. The interaction of these two realms brought the world into being.

At the top are the three celestial realms of the gods. The first is Asgard, the kingdom of the Æsir. The second is Vanaheim or Wane-home, the kingdom of the Vanir, where some of them still reside. And finally, there is Lightelf-home (Lightalfheim), the realm of the Light Elves and the seat of the intellect as well as fertility.

Asatruar Values

The Asatruar values are reflected in the Nine Noble Virtues, which offer a moral compass. They also make considerations for their reputations and the honor their families will retain after they die.

Asatruar are very principled people, but that doesn't mean the faith is without joy. If a life is well lived, there should be plenty of time to gather with kin and celebrate, but there are also times to work hard, and perhaps even to battle.

Nine Noble Virtues

The Nine Noble Virtues are a guide for living a good, just life. These values are not recorded in ancient lore, but were developed by modern Asatru organizations based on wording in the *Hávamál*, a collection of poems in the *Poetic Edda*. Most Asatru consider them ample moral guidance. The Virtues are not rules like the Ten Commandments, but are single words that embody important personality traits. These Nine Noble Virtues are:

1. **Courage:** This is not merely the lack of fear in the face of danger. It is also the courage to stand up for the rights of others and yourself. It is the courage to live according to moral values even when it seems all around you are violating them.
2. **Truth:** Honesty, which is a key part of maintaining personal honor.

It is also allegiance to the gods and your religious truth.

3. **Honor:** What drives you to act according to the Virtues and what is right. Without honor, you are nothing. It precedes your arrival in new places, and follows you after death.

4. **Fidelity:** Being faithful to your commitments, both to your friends and family as well as the larger world.

5. **Discipline:** This is really self-discipline, working hard to keep yourself on the correct path. It is also getting yourself back to work if you've relaxed a little too long.

6. **Hospitality:** Welcoming people warmly into your home and treating others with respect. It is also treating your house spirits with the dignity owed them.

7. **Industriousness:** Not just working hard at your chosen career, but working hard at your faith. It is forming a kindred if you can't find one to join.

8. **Self-Reliance:** Instead of or in addition to seeking help from other people or the gods, you do what is necessary to fulfill your own needs and desires.

9. **Perseverance:** Continuing in the face of difficulty, whether it's in your personal life or a challenge to your faith from the outside.

Oaths and Oath-Breaking

Oaths made by and between Asatruar are taken very seriously. An oath is much more than a casual promise—it's a pact and a solemn promise to perform some action. A popular type of oath is the oath of Frith, in which Asatruar promise to uphold the honor of a person or the group as a whole. Oaths can be sworn during rituals called *blots* or *sumbels*. They can also be made outside of rituals. It isn't usually necessary to write them down, but witnesses may be present.

An oath should be broken only in dire circumstances. For example, let's say your oath-brother has developed a drug habit. He is stealing from friends and family members to support the habit and refuses to get help. In this case, you would tell him that you are breaking the oath and explain your reasons for doing so. You would also need to inform anyone who witnessed the oath that it is now broken. Of course, having broken the oath, you could make a new oath to be there for him when he's finally ready to get help, and breaking an oath doesn't necessarily mean that you have to sever all ties to him.

 Because oaths are taken so seriously among Asatruar, it is wise to consider your oaths carefully and to avoid making oaths until you know the other person very well. You might wish to view it as signing a contract. If you wouldn't sign a contract to a similar effect with that person, then don't make the oath.

After Death

Most Asatruar believe that life continues in another form after death. This could mean residing in one of the halls of the dead in Hel or Valhalla. Neither place is like the Christian Hell. Hel is calm and peaceful, and Valhalla features great feasts. The dead might also remain in the burial mound and watch over their relatives, or travel between the realms to keep an eye on their families.

Because there is so much emphasis on living a good life according to the Nine Noble Virtues, there is little fear of death for Asatruar. Death is merely a transition, and the result of it depends on how the person lived. It is believed that one part of an individual could be reborn in a new person within the family line, especially if that new person is given the same name, or a person's entire soul could reincarnate in a new body within the family.

Myth of Asatruar Neo-Nazism

A common point of confusion among non-Asatru Neo-Pagans, and the wider community, is the perceived racism of the faith. This perception is related to another branch of Norse Paganism, Odinism. Odinists are usually loyal only to Odin, and may or may not be Asatruar. Unfortunately, some white supremacists and Neo-Nazis have adopted Odinism. Because followers of Norse traditions highly value their ethnic heritage, some use this belief as an excuse for racist beliefs and activities. The rise of the Neo-Nazi movement has also led to renewed corruption of some Asatru symbols.

True Asatru welcome all races, genders, and sexual orientations. They are not homophobic or anti-Semitic. While those who are actually of Norse descent honor their genetic heritage, they don't look down on those with other heritages. For example, an Asatruar of German descent might celebrate German culture at a festival or make a trip to Germany to visit the land of his heritage, but that doesn't mean he doesn't appreciate the contributions of other cultures to his local area or will never visit any country other than Germany.

Hierarchy and Organization

Like Wicca, Asatru does not have a strict structure or hierarchy. It is acceptable to practice the faith alone, and there are small groups that may be a part of a larger group. These small groups may or may not have a formally trained priesthood.

Asatru Priesthood

The Asatru priesthood is comprised of the gothar. Priestesses are called *gythia,* and priests are called *gothi.* In old Iceland, the gothar were the lawmakers. They met at the AlThing once a year to make laws and conduct what would now be called courts.

Modern members of the gothar lead rituals for the other members. They also maintain *hofs,* or gathering places, and keep the tools used in ritual. It is common for the gothar to maintain libraries for the use of other members, or for use in training new students. They may also seek new members, but Asatruar don't proselytize; instead, they might post a notice about an upcoming meeting at a local Pagan store and invite interested people to attend.

Kindreds and Hearths

Asatruar who choose to work with a group join or form a kindred (also called a hearth). A kindred has at least one male and one female member; five seems to be the optimal number for a new kindred. The kindred may or may not have a leader. The members may be related by blood, or they can simply be a group of friends interested in worshipping together. Many kindreds meet regularly (for instance, weekly) to study lore or Asatruar practices. They also gather to celebrate Asatru festivals.

Once a kindred has become well established, it might advertise for new members, conduct training, and hold larger rituals and gatherings. The first kindreds in the United States were formed in the 1970s. Two of those original kindreds survive today.

Larger Groups

In addition to the many small kindreds, there are also larger groups with which the smaller kindreds might choose to register. One is the Asatru Folk Assembly, which maintains a list of kindreds. A second is the Asatru Alliance, a loose coalition of kindreds that publishes a magazine listing the various member kindreds. A third group, the Troth, calls their smaller groups hearths. They have a second type of group called a garth. A garth is a group led by one of the trained elders—a godwoman, a godman, or an elder still in training. Garths are often more public than hearths.

Asatru is a legally recognized religion in today's Iceland. They have a single church where all Asatruar go to worship. With over 400 members, it is the fastest-growing religious group in the country.

Prevalence of Asatru

It is not known how many Asatruar there are. Like Wicca, Asatru is rapidly growing. The religion is especially popular in Iceland and Scandinavia, and some parts of Germany. Asatruar are scattered throughout the United States, and due to the independent nature of the faith, many practice alone. Guessing from the number of smaller groups that have registered with larger organizations, it is safe to say that there are at least a few thousand Asatru in the United States.

Chapter 8

Asatruar Holidays

Asatruar hold a variety of celebrations. In addition to honoring the seasonal cycle of the year, some of the holidays focus on certain gods or spirits and their historical importance and role in human life. They may also focus on the personal transformations Asatruar undergo as individuals or as part of a kindred. Among Asatruar, most of the holydays are also seen as times to celebrate kinship.

Asatruar Holiday Calendar

The Germanic peoples celebrated three major feast days to mark important turning points in the agricultural cycle. Modern Asatruar continue to celebrate these festivals, and have added other holidays, many of which are based on smaller, local festivals mentioned in old calendars. Each festival has a personal meaning in addition to its agricultural association.

The Asatru Alliance and the Troth have both put out festival calendars for their member kindreds, and other smaller groups offer calendars too. Observations of the various holidays vary from kindred to kindred. Most of them honor Yule-Tide, Summer Finding, Walburga, Midsummer, Winter Finding, Winter Nights, and Einherjar.

When choosing which holidays to celebrate, follow the guidance of the leader of your kindred or select those that are most appropriate to your region. If you work alone, then honor the major holidays and whichever minor ones call to you.

In addition to the major holidays, there are smaller feast days sprinkled throughout the year. These might be days of remembrance for Viking or Germanic heroes, or festivals and rituals to honor specific gods. Observances of these holidays vary among various Asatru groups.

Yule-Tide

Yule-Tide runs twelve days, from Mother Night on December 20 to Yule, or Twelfth Night, on December 31. The most important of all the Asatruar festivals, Yule-Tide begins the night before the winter solstice, the shortest day of the year. In northern Scandinavia, the sun does not rise at all on the winter solstice, and in old times it was very important to conduct rituals to ensure that the sun would return.

During Yule-Tide, it is easier to connect with the recent dead, ancestors, and the gods because the veil between the worlds is thin. Apart from honoring those who have passed, Yule-Tide is also a celebration of kinship and the return of the light. The days will begin to get longer after Yule. In northern regions, the change is rapid.

Yule Customs

The first night of Yule-Tide honors Freya and the Disir. Frey is honored on other days of the twelve-day festival because he is the god of fertility and he can help bring back summer. Thor may receive offerings, because he is also associated with the return of spring. Some kindreds also honor Sunna, a sun goddess.

Yule-Tide is a time for great feasting and swearing oaths. A Yule oath was originally sworn on a hollowed boar, but in modern times it is appropriate to swear on a cake or loaf of bread shaped like a boar. Oaths can also be sworn on a drinking horn, a cup, or the Yule wreath. These oaths might take the form of "New Year's Resolutions."

Yule is one of the three original Germanic feast days. The "Twelve Days of Christmas" descend from Germanic Yule traditions. In some areas, it was celebrated later in the year. In England, "Old Twelfth Night" falls on January 13. Twelfth Night should be honored with a raucous party.

Yule Associations

Many of the traditions and customs associated with Christmas come from the old practices of the Germanic peoples. The spirits were said to roam the land at this time, and elves, trolls, and other spirits had to be invited into the home or chased away. A Yule tree could be brought inside and decorated with gifts for them if they were to be welcomed. Many Asatruar still do this in modern times, in addition to using their traditional holiday tree decorations.

The holiday wreath may symbolize the sun-wheel or an oath-ring, both of which were important to the old people. If you have one, your wishes for the coming year can be woven into the wreath. The Yule log is another Germanic symbol of the returning sun. Fir and pine would be good choices for the log because it symbolizes the might of the soul. Asatruar who don't have a fireplace can leave a candle burning all night instead.

Summer Finding

Other names for Summer Finding are Ostara and Easter. Summer Finding falls on the vernal equinox, or the first full or new moon that falls after it, and marks the return of spring. It also honors the spirits of the land and the gods associated with fertility and spring. The word Easter is drawn from the name of Eostre, the goddess of spring.

At Summer Finding, it is traditional to color eggs and plant them in the earth. This custom may stem from the idea of planting a symbol of fertility in the earth, or they may originally have been gifts for the land spirits. The eggshells are kept all year to protect one's family. Some people paint blown eggs or buy or make wooden egg ornaments to hang on an Easter tree, as is still traditional in Scandinavia. Rabbits are often associated with this season, and are a symbol of the goddess Eostre.

Rituals should be held in honor of the goddess of spring, usually Eostre. Freya and Frigga may also be honored with offerings to help stimulate the fertility of the earth and celebrate the renewal that comes with spring. The gods do not play a major role at Summer Finding.

Eostre was not universally celebrated as the goddess of spring in the Germanic regions. She was mainly a German and Anglo-Saxon deity. Much of her lore has been lost through the ages. In some areas, the day was honored as Sigrblot (Blessing for Victory).

Walburga (May Day)

Walburga is also known as Waluburg's Night, Walpurgis Night, Walpurgisnacht, May Day, May Eve, or May Moon. It is actually two holidays, one falling on April 30, the other on May 1. The day and evening together honor both the dark and light halves of the year. It is a very magical holiday for those who practice magic.

In more southern areas of Germanic dominance, Ostara was the second festival of the year and hailed the start of summer. In some northern regions, the festival was delayed until Walburga due to the late start of the planting season. The northern areas had a very short, but very abundant, growing season.

May Eve

On May Eve, Asatruar celebrate the night of the witches and the dark side of the year. It is a time to honor Freya's and Frigga's darker aspects as goddesses of the dead. It is also a time to honor the heroes that have fallen. Magic is very powerful on May Eve, especially when aided by Odin and Freya or Frigga.

May Eve is also a ribald night dealing with Freya's passionate side as the goddess of love and sex. Young men and women look forward to and prepare for the festivities of May Day. Some Asatruar couples re-enact the marriage of Odin and Frigga. Those who are single might choose this magical night to cast a love spell.

May Day

May Day, on May 1, honors the light half of the year and the bounty of spring. It is also dedicated to Freya, in her role as a goddess of love. In some regions, May Day was considered the start of summer. It honored the fruitfulness and abundance of the coming season.

On May Day, it is traditional to carry the Maypole in procession to the ritual gathering. It should then be set upright so people can dance around it. Some gatherings also feature a fire for jumping, which is believed to bring good luck. Decorations of greenery, flowered wreaths, and bunches of wildflowers are all appropriate.

Midsummer: The Summer Solstice

Midsummer falls on the summer solstice. At Midsummer, nature is at fullness. Offerings are made to all the gods to thank them for their gifts. All activities are faced outward, toward action, because Midsummer was historically the beginning of the Viking conquest season.

Midsummer is the longest day of the year, and in more northern regions, the sun will not set at all. This is the day to honor the sun goddess Sunna. Some Asatruar also honor Balder, the sun god. For some, Midsummer marks the start of the light half of the year.

It is traditional to start the day with a Greeting to Sunna. Asatruar also dance the Maypole again, make wreaths, and jump over fires. It is again appropriate to decorate with flowers, greenery, and all the other bounty of summer. Members of the Troth might also burn a corn dolly or a small model Viking ship filled with offerings.

Winter Finding

Winter Finding is also referred to as Harvest. It falls on the fall equinox and begins the winding down of the cycle of the year. Because it nears the end of the harvest season in northern regions, it is a festival held in order to give thanks for the abundance you have received. This abundance can be agricultural in nature, perhaps for the vegetables you grew in your garden, but it can also be for your satisfying work or financial well-being.

At Winter Finding, it is appropriate to honor Odin, Freya, and/or Frey and offer them thanks for the fruitfulness of the past season. The meat harvest will come later, so this is a time to celebrate the grains, fruits, and vegetables that were reaped during the summer months. It is also a time to be aware that the cold will soon be returning and to prepare for shorter days.

In keeping with the harvest theme, Asatruar may hold a large, public harvest gathering to share the abundance, or a kindred might gather together for a hearty feast. Decorations should center on grains such as wheat and late summer fruits or vegetables.

Winter Night

Winter Night is known by many other names, including Vetrablot, Winterfyllith (Winter Full-Moon), Alfablot (Elf-Blessing), Disablot (Dis-Blessing), and Frey-Blessing. It is the last of the three major festivals celebrated by the original Germanic peoples.

Rather than celebrate Winter Finding, some Asatruar hold Freyfaxi on the fall equinox. Freyfaxi is dedicated solely to Frey, the fertility god, and is a time to thank him for his gifts. Some place Freyfaxi in late August rather than late September, and honor both days.

Winter Night takes place around mid-October, either between October 12 and 15 or the nearest Saturday, or on the first full moon after the autumn equinox. It is honored as the Norse New Year, the end of the harvest, and marks the beginning of a period of introspection and indoor activities such as making crafts and reading the runes. It is also a celebration of kinship with the living and the dead.

Winter Night Customs

In old times, it was common to bless the "Last Sheaf" in the field as a gift to Odin. An offering of milk, ale, or mead poured onto the earth is an acceptable alternative and is more common in modern times. Winter Night was also the animal harvest, when animals that would not survive the winter were slaughtered. Given that most modern-day Asatruar aren't butchers, they instead follow the modern practice of simply taking the time on Winter Night to remember where their food comes from and give thanks for those who provide it, deities and humans alike.

Winter Night is also a time to honor the dead and the ancestors. A ritual can be held to honor the Disir and Freya in the guise of Vanadis. Frey and Freya should be thanked for the fruitful harvest. It is also common to ask for an abundant harvest next year. Any feasts should be quiet and respectful of the dead. An offering to the family Disir is also appropriate at the meal.

Winter Night Associations

In addition to the Disir and Freya, Odin and other gods of the dead are associated with Winter Night. Ghosts, trolls, and other nonhuman beings ride on the Wild Hunt during the dark period that follows it. They are said to roam the roads at night, and it is a time to use caution when traveling late. Decorations for ritual and feasting would follow the harvest theme, but Halloween-oriented items aren't appropriate.

In keeping with the New Year theme, it is a good to consider personal accomplishments over the past year and to consider goals for the next year. A *sumbel,* or toasting ritual, is appropriate for making oaths and promises for the coming year.

Einherjar: In Honor of Veterans

On Einherjar, Asatruar honor those who have fallen in battle and given their lives to protect others. In the United States, this holiday is most commonly held on Veteran's Day (November 11). The Troth hold Einherjar on Memorial Day (last Monday in May). November 11 is also the chosen day for most European Asatru. Those in the Southern Hemisphere usually choose a day associated with one of their own days of remembrance, such as April 25, ANZAC Day, in Australia. Einherjar is not related to the cycle of the seasons, but is an important day for Asatruar, some of whom are veterans or have military family members.

On Einherjar, it is appropriate to visit the graves of military heroes, or to make an offering to them at home. Memories of the deceased are quietly shared in ritual. Unlike the other Asatruar holidays, it is not a joyous occasion.

It is believed that those slain in battle now reside with Odin and his other warriors in Valhalla. Odin has chosen them, and it is an honor to be there. Although Einherjar is quiet, it is not mournful, but merely respectful to those who willingly gave their lives in service of their country or their kin.

Other Holidays

In addition to the holidays shared by most kindreds, there are certain holidays that are celebrated by some, but not all, Asatruar. These include Thorrablot, Disting, Loaf-Feast, Thing-Tide, and feasts to great heroes. Vikings like Erik the Red and Leif Ericson both have days in their honor. Also remembered are Raud the Strong, Eykind Kinnifri, Gudrod of Gudbrandsal, King Radbod of Frisia, and Queen Sigrid of Sweden, all of whom fought against forced conversion to Christianity. Some of them suffered and died for it, while others held the new faith at bay a little longer. Individual kindreds may also celebrate separate feast days to certain gods, or honor days mentioned in the old Icelandic calendar.

Thorrablot, the Feast of Thor

Thorrablot takes place in mid- to late January and is named for Thorri. Although Thorri is not the same as Thor, modern Asatruar use this day to celebrate a feast to Thor. Thorri is a winter spirit, and it's also appropriate to honor him. The feast is designed to strengthen your spirit and keep the winter doldrums from getting you down.

The feast is Icelandic in origin, and is still celebrated there today. In Iceland, it is a cultural celebration, as well as a time to honor the coming spring. Icelanders use this day to hold a winter feast or party. Asatruar also celebrate their Viking nature with feats of strength or share their craft skills with their kindred.

February 14 is also honored by some as the Feast of Vali. Vali is the god of vengeance and rebirth. Vali bears no resemblance to St. Valentine or the traditions of Valentine's Day, but the tradition has stuck due to the similarity of names. Some Asatruar celebrate love and family on this day.

Disting and Charming of the Plow

Those who honor Disting do so on February 14. Charming of the Plow is held on February 1, at the time when the earth is just beginning to thaw. The feast marks the nearing end of the period of introspection. Gatherings focus on preparing for spring and the planting time. Offerings of bread can be made to the earth as thanks for its renewed fertility. Frey and the Disir are especially honored at this time. Rather than including Frey, some Asatruar use the day to honor all the goddesses.

Loaf-Feast

Loaf-Feast celebrates the first grain harvest. It is mainly honored by members of the Troth. It is also referred to by the Celtic name Lughnasadh or Lammas. At Loaf-Feast, the "First Sheaf" to be harvested from the fields is offered as a gift to Thor in his role as a harvest god. Today, common practice is to bake a loaf of fresh bread and offer that instead.

Loaf-Feast marks the nearing end of summer and the coming period of hard labor necessary to ensure the harvest of all the crops before winter comes. In old times, this period also marked the end of the Viking conquest season. The men would return to harvest the crops and prepare for winter. Modern Asatruar aren't out pillaging new lands, so instead they take this time to consider their accomplishments for the year and all that they hope to achieve during the remaining months before Yule.

Thing-Tide

Taking place on approximately August 23, Thing-Tide is held at roughly the same time as the old Icelandic AlThing. Thing-Tide is a time of large gatherings. Kindreds come together to deal with administrative matters and renew their kinship.

Thing-Tide might be a good time to get married. In the old times, it was also the time when the courts meted justice and disagreements were solved. Thing-Tide is also a good time to resolve major disagreements within the kindred.

Chapter 9

Asatruar Tools and Practices

Several tools and practices have been developed to assist Asatruar in observing their faith. As with the beliefs and holidays, these are drawn from the traditions of the ancient Germanic people of Iceland, Germany, and Scandinavia. But again, the modern tools and practices aren't at all exact replicas of those used in the original faith. Some of them are new creations unique to modern life. Whether old or new, all of these tools and practices play an important role in the Asatru faith.

Adoption of Faith

The Adoption of Faith ritual, sometimes called the Profession of Faith ritual, is an important ritual undergone by many Asatru. It's not one of the original Norse rites because back then it wasn't necessary. Most Asatruar today are not born into the faith, and therefore often want a ritual in which they formally accept their new faith. It's similar in intent to the Catholic confirmation ceremony, but not at all similar in how it's actually performed.

The Adoption of Faith has three parts. First, it is a declaration of an individual's belief in the gods. Second, it is a declaration of a person's intention to worship them through the Asatru faith and a vow to give up the faith in which the initiate was raised, or other faiths he or she may have dabbled in. Third, if an Asatruar is joining a kindred, she is swearing her loyalty to that group and its members.

The ritual itself is quite simple, and is usually performed outside of a blot. Initiates declare their intent before a gothi or gythia and then make an oath on the kindred oath-ring. A Profession of Faith can be performed at a holiday rite, or at a regular meeting.

If you are not a member of a kindred, you can become an Asatruar by stating before the gods, "I am Asatru," and then living your life according to the Nine Noble Virtues, honoring the Asatru holidays, and following the Asatru ways.

Blot: An Asatru Blessing

The blot, literally "blessing," is the most common form of ritual in Asatru. The blot is used for holiday rituals, magic, and rituals held on special occasions such as births or marriages as a way to honor the gods and reaffirm a person's connection to them. Blots (and all other Asatru rituals) are best performed outside, but indoor rituals are acceptable when the environment is not amenable to outdoor worship.

The tools required for a blot include a hammer, a drinking horn or cup, a bowl, and an evergreen sprig. Other tools vary depending on the purpose of the ritual. Generally speaking, a blot consists of nine parts. Some Asatru kindreds refer to the steps by different names, but the purpose is the same.

1. **Hallowing** is the creation of ritual space. It is traditional to draw the symbol of the hammer (an upside-down T) in the air in the four cardinal quarters of north, east, south, and west. If the practitioner has a permanent ritual space, this step can be skipped.
2. The **Reading** is simply a reading from one of the Eddas that states the mythic basis for the ritual.
3. The **Rede** is a second statement of the rite, this time of its modern nature with a link to the mythic purpose.
4. The **Call** is the invocation of whichever deities are being invited to ritual. The words can be from an Edda, newly crafted in the old poetic language or method, or from the heart. It is common to use kennings, or descriptive names such as All-Father for Odin, to call the deities. As the deities are called, the Asatruar praises them and specifies their roles in the ritual. If magic is being performed during the blot, the Asatruar can also specify how they will help her achieve her desired result.
5. **Loading** is the process of charging and blessing the sacred drink, which can be mead, ale, or juice. The beverage is then poured into the drinking horn or cup.
6. **Drinking** from the cup is the next step. The cup is passed around the circle and each participant takes some, being careful to leave a little at the end so it can be poured into the blessing bowl. As each person sips, he or she makes a toast to the god being honored.
7. The **Blessing** is done by sprinkling some of the sacred drink from the bowl onto the altar with a sprig of evergreen.
8. The **Giving** is a sacrificial offering of the sacred drink to the deities, invoked by pouring the contents of the bowl onto the earth. The blot is now complete.
9. The **Leaving** releases the sacred space and formally ends the rite.

The Rite of Sumbel

A *sumbel,* sometimes spelled *symbel,* is a drinking, boasting, and toasting rite. It is a way to praise one's ancestors, toast the gods, strengthen kinship, tell stories, publicly state personal goals, and make oaths. A sumbel can follow a blot, or it can be held separately. A feast almost always accompanies a sumbel, which is good if the drinking horn is filled with alcohol. Getting drunk is not the goal, but it quite often happens at a lengthy sumbel.

Asatruar don't have a dress code when it comes to ritual. Some choose to wear Germanic attire modeled on the old styles, while others wear jeans and a T-shirt. Asatruar do not usually work naked or in the robes associated with Wicca. The vendors who cater to members of the Society for Creative Anachronism are a good source *(www.sca.org)* for Germanic attire.

To begin a sumbel, the host states the purpose of the gathering and fills the ale horn. The horn is then passed around the table and each person says or sings something as an offering. A sumbel should consist of at least three rounds, but it doesn't have to stop there. The first round is dedicated to the gods and goddesses, the second round to the ancestors and heroes, and the third and subsequent rounds to whatever the participants choose to say.

While a sumbel involves a great deal of drinking, it is still a holy rite. The drink has been dedicated to the gods, and that lends an air of sanctity to the rite. Asatruar join with their kin and bonding with their gods in a sumbel.

Other Rituals

In addition to the Adoption of the Faith, the blot, and the sumbel, Asatruar have several minor rites. Some of these are performed daily; others are performed as needed. One such rite is a blessing to the gods, addressed to the Asatruar's matron or patron deity. The frequency of the rite depends on the requirements of the deity. Some people also bless their food and drinks, a ritual similar to saying grace before a meal. Other rites include Greeting the Sun Rite and the Hammer Rite.

Greeting the Sun

Even though Greeting the Sun does not derive from ancient lore and is optional for Asatruar, many practice this rite. The blessing is performed up to four times a day, at sunrise, midday, sunset, and midnight. The rite is designed to help practitioners connect with the sun and the flow of energy throughout the day.

Evidence of ancient sumbels derives from the Norse epic *Beowulf* and other ancient tales of warriors being introduced to new clans via sumbels. These were chances to prove identity and confirm honor. Some time was also spent praising the host, in Beowulf's case, his new king.

Greeting the Sun can be an elaborate rite, or it may be said quickly and quietly. It's more important to acknowledge the moment than to perform an involved rite. Asatruar recognize that in our modern world, religion and other life concerns have to blend well together, and sometimes allowances have to be made for things like a midmorning business meeting.

Hammer Rite

The Hammer Rite is used to create sacred space around the working area at the beginning of blots, other rites, and before doing magic. The basic method involves drawing the hammer sign at the four quarters (north, east, south, and west) and toward the sky above and the earth below. Some people also draw the sign at northeast, southeast, southwest, and northwest. Whether four or eight signs are drawn, together they create a sacred area similar to the Wiccan magical circle.

The Hammer Rite can be performed with a ritual hammer, a pendant, a wand, or the hands. Regardless of the tool used to draw the sign, it should be drawn large and with great vigor. A swastika can also be substituted for the hammer sign (its meaning is explained later in this chapter).

The hammer sign is made by drawing a line through the air from the top to the bottom, then by drawing a horizontal line from left to right below the vertical line, as if drawing an upside-down T. At each step, appropriate words are said, and these chants, calls, and blessings vary among different kindred. Several books listed in the recommended reading (Appendix B) offer excellent, detailed descriptions of the Hammer Rite.

Ritual Space

A stead is a permanent ritual space where kindreds can hold meetings and rituals. Ideally, it is a separate space preserved just for this purpose. A small ante-building on a property or a room within a home can be used as a stead. Some well-funded kindreds have purchased buildings just for this purpose.

The Asatru stead is decorated with the important symbols and holds a permanent altar, or harrow. Symbols are also hung over all the entrances to protect them. Small statues of the gods and goddesses are kept within the stead and it might also be the home of the kindred's ritual tools and library. The stead is blessed as holy space, and therefore it isn't always necessary to perform hallowing when rituals are held there.

In an ideal world, every kindred would have a stead, but this isn't always possible. Some kindreds are formed in large cities where apartment-living leaves little room for a permanent structure. In this case, a stead can be created whenever it's necessary by hanging up ritual decorations such as god images or the symbols, and placing the altar in the appropriate area.

An Appropriate Altar

Some Asatruar have a permanent altar, while others have a temporary one, depending on their needs and space allowances. Indoor altars are usually made out of wood. Outdoor altars are usually made of stone. Some Asatruar kindreds call their indoor altars "stalls" and their outdoor altars "harrows." They can be as simple as two boulders with a flat stone laid across the top or a pair of two-by-fours with a wooden plank nailed to the top. The ritual tools are placed on top of the altar.

There are no hard and fast rules about how an Asatru altar should be set up. As long as it's large enough to hold your tools, and the bottle of mead and drinking horn won't tip over, whatever you use is fine.

Asatru Shrines

In addition to the ritual altar, some Asatruar maintain shrines to their matron or patron deities, or to their house-spirits. Outdoor altars can also be built for the land-spirits. In both cases, the shrines are used to leave offerings. For outdoor offerings, some Asatruar build a small pile of rocks and place offerings inside or in front of it.

Ritual Tools

Asatru rituals are simple, and so are the tools used in performing them. Asatruar tools consist of a drinking horn, an offering bowl, a hammer, an oath-ring, a knife, a rune wand, and a sword. Most rituals also include an evergreen sprig for sprinkling the ritual drink.

Given the limited quantity of tools, most of them should be fairly easy to acquire. Renaissance fairs and Society for Creative Anachronism vendors are good sources. And many Asatruar choose to make their tools themselves.

Drinking Horn

Every Asatruar has a drinking horn, and it gets used a lot. The drinking horn is usually fashioned from a hollowed-out animal horn. The end is then cased in an ornately decorated metal holder. Most holders have feet to allow the horn to stand at an upward tilt to prevent spills. Some horns also have a strap so the horn can be carried over the shoulder.

The horn is used in sumbels and blots. While ale and mead are the typical beverages consumed from a horn, juice is also acceptable. The horn isn't usually used for beverages consumed outside of sumbels or blots.

Hlautbowl (Offering Bowl)

The *hlautbowl* is the offering bowl used in blots. It might also be used during a sumbel to make occasional offerings to the deities. Most hlautbowls are made of wood from a fruit- or nut-bearing tree. In addition to the common bowl used by the kindred, Asatruar usually have their own bowl for blots performed at home.

The bowl is placed at the center of the altar. During the blot, an offering is poured into a drinking horn, and then the beverage is blessed. After the drinking horn has been passed, some of the remaining drink is sprinkled onto the altar and hallowed area with an evergreen sprig. Finally, the remaining drink is poured into the bowl, the bowl is raised as an offering to the gods, and the contents are poured onto the earth as another offering.

Thor's Hammer

The hammer, usually a Thor's Hammer, is used for hallowing ritual space in blots. It is a symbol of Thor's great power and of the Asatruar's kinship with the gods. Many Asatruar have their own hammer in addition to the one used at group rites.

Asatruar hammers vary in size. A mallet and sledgehammer are both good options, but a ball-peen hammer probably isn't appropriate because of its shape. A hammer pendant can also be used in ritual.

Oath-Ring

A kindred usually only has one oath-ring. It is a round ring, probably closer in size to a bracelet than to a ring that can be worn on a finger. The ring should be unbroken and is usually made from metal. Copper, gold, and silver are good choices.

The kindred use the oath-ring for the formal swearing of oaths by its members. The Adoption of the Faith and the accompanying oaths are also sworn on the ring. Because the ring is unbroken, it symbolizes the unbreakable nature of the oaths, except in dire situations, as noted earlier.

Sax and Rister

The sax (knife) is another personal tool that is not used in blots or sumbels. The sax is used for rune magic and to cut the wood used for runes. It can be any size or shape, but should fit comfortably in your hand. It should also be sharp enough to cut wood cleanly and easily. The sax used for rune magic shouldn't be used for other purposes.

Some Asatruar have a separate tool called a *rister* that they use to carve the runes into wood. This tool has a sharper point than a knife, and might have a cylindrical rather than a traditional blade. Again, it should fit comfortably in your hand and should be kept sharp enough to allow you to cut rune shapes into wood with little fraying.

Gandr (Wand)

The wand, also called a *gandr*, is another personal tool mainly used in rune magic. During magic, it can be used to perform the Hammer Rite to bless a sacred space. The wand is always made of wood, and Asatruar sometimes carve runes into it. If you do so, you should try to fit all twenty-four on the wand. The wand can be as small as the palm of your hand, or run from the tip of your index finger to your elbow, similar to the Wiccan wand.

The Ancient Alphabet of the Runes

The runes are an old Norse alphabet and are used as a divination system. Each rune is also associated with a god or holiday, and has magical properties as well. The runes are seldom used for writing these days, unless they are written during magic.

Who made the first runes?
The exact origin of the runes is not known, but according to legend, Odin hung himself upside down from the Yggdrasil for nine nights in order to receive them. He then gave them to the people as a gift.

The word *rune* means "secret" or "mystery." It also means "to whisper," "to roar," and "to inquire." The runes signify what is hidden from you, both mentally and spiritually, and invite you to question deeper. Each rune consists of a sound, a stave (or glyph), and the lore associated with it. All three blend together to create powerful magic. The lore is useful for divination. For example, the rune *tiwaz* is pronounced *tay-wahz* and it is shaped like an arrow pointing upward. It represents justice, conflict, order, and the god Tyr.

It is believed that the runes were formed before 200 B.C.E. The oldest runic alphabet is called Elder Futhark. Elder Futhark consists of twenty-four runes, which are broken down into three sets called *aettir*. Younger Futhark evolved in Scandinavia. It reduced the set to sixteen glyphs. When Asatruar refer to the runes, they are usually speaking of the Elder Futhark.

Learning the Runes

Before you can work magic with runes, or use them for divination, you have to understand them. It might help to do practice readings with the runes, but don't put great store in what you discover until you've truly mastered them. It is best to start by reading the lore associated with each rune. The lore can be found in the Eddas as well as several newer books.

As you learn the runes, you might want to sound out or sing their names. You can also draw them to familiarize yourself with the glyphs. Try rewording the lore in your own language, and then check it against the original to be sure the meaning is the same.

Making Your Own Runes

Once you have learned the runes, you can make your own set for regular use. Runes are also available ready-made, but they have greater power when they come from your own hand. You may wish to buy a set so you can learn them, then make your own once you are familiar with them.

Runes are usually made from wood, with the glyphs carved into them and colored with red paint or ink. You could also find a set of stones you like and paint the symbols onto them. Once the stones are complete, keep them in a drawstring bag or a lined wooden box.

Craft your runes one at a time. It may help to enter a meditative state and focus on the lore as you create each individual glyph. This isn't to say that you can't cut all your pieces of wood or polish all your stones at once. It does mean that rather than carve them all, then go back and paint them all, you should complete each one before moving on to the next rune.

Rune Divination

Rune divination is the main form of divination in Asatru. Usually the runes are drawn from the bag and cast in some sort of pattern. Patterns and recommendations for interpretation can be found in several books. For now, it's enough to know that the main factors to consider are each rune's place within the whole set, its place within its subset, the name of the rune, and the lore that accompanies it.

One popular method for casting the runes is past, present, future. One rune is drawn to represent each category. You can also draw one rune each morning and use it as your guide for the day, or to be aware of some related lesson you will learn that day or a challenge you will face.

Special Symbols

Asatruar have several symbols useful for magic and ritual or to represent their community or the gods. When used in magic, the symbols help create and draw power. Some symbols are used as protection talismans. They can also be worn as symbols of faith and of being a member of the Asatru, or of dedication to a specific deity. Some of the symbols have also taken on modern, unintended meanings that corrupted their original intent.

Irminsul

The Irminsul is the symbol of the pole connecting the worlds that was destroyed by Charlemagne during one of his many quests to eradicate Paganism in Norse regions. The Irminsul symbolizes the unity of the nine realms, as well as the creation of humanity from a pair of trees. Runesters sometimes use it as a reminder of how Odin suffered in order to receive them.

◀ Irminsul is a symbol representing the pole that connects the realms.

Thor's Hammer

Thor's Hammer is usually pictured upside down. It is a symbol of Thor and his power. It is also a symbol of fertility, protection, creativity, and sanctity. In the old times, a Thor's Hammer was given to a bride to guarantee her fertility. Today the Thor's Hammer symbol represents Asatruar faith. Some wear it as a pendant while others have it tattooed on their body. The hammer pendant or tattoo can take a variety of shapes and is often elaborately decorated.

◀ Thor's Hammer is a symbol of Asatruar faith.

Valknut (Triple Triangle)

The *valknut* is a symbol of sacrifice to Odin. Those who wear a valknut are usually dedicated to Odin. To some, the valknut symbolizes the triple nature of Odin. Odin is also sometimes said to be part of a triad with Vali and Ve, and the valknut would symbolize this as well. Finally, the valknut is a symbol of the nine realms and their interconnection.

▲ Valknut   ▲ Asatru swastika   ▲ Solar cross

Swastika and the Solar Cross

The swastika and the solar cross are both symbols of Thor. The swastika is one of the most misunderstood Neo-Pagan symbols due to its adoption by Hitler during his regime. Prior to then, the swastika was a peaceful symbol of luck and the power of the sun.

Because of the Nazi connection, some Asatruar choose to use the solar cross, or solar wheel, instead. It has the same magical and religious connotations as the swastika. The solar cross is also used by Neo-Pagans outside of Asatru.

Asatru and Magic

The practice of magic is not as prevalent in Asatru as it is in Wicca. Nevertheless, there are two methods of magic available to Asatruar, and it is believed that both are based on the actual practices of the old people. The first type is *siedhr*, which is shamanic in nature. The second type is *rune-galdr*, or just *galdr*. Magical practitioners are referred to by the general term *vitki* (magical practitioner), but also have specific names within each type.

These forms of magic require a lot of practice and experience. Neither is easy to master and both require magical and mental control and focus. If you want to learn either form, it might be best to seek out an experienced teacher who can guide you and help you avoid pitfalls.

Siedhr, Shamanic Magic

Siedhr (pronounced *seith*) is ruled by Freya and Odin. Odin is the only male god known to practice seidhr, having been taught by Freya. Seidhr is the dominion of the goddesses of the Vanir. The word itself means "seething" or "boiling," indicating that great emotion was required to perform seidhr in the old times. The most detailed description of a seidhr ritual can be found in Erik the Red's Saga.

A *haegtessa* is a priestess of the Norns. She uses divination to understand your web of *wyrd*, and may use magic to alter it, if necessary. Haegtessa are dedicated to Freya or Frigga.

A female seidhr practitioner is called a *seidhkona* (seeress) and a male seidhr practitioner is called a *seidmadhr* (seer). Rather than relying on tools, seers use trance to roam the other realms. Experienced seers may be able to enter trance at will, while others use rhythmic beats, such as drumming or chanting, to help them achieve a trance state. Drumming isn't traditional, but because it is part of the heritage of the American land, it is acceptable to many seers. Hallucinogenic drugs are rarely used, or required, by modern seers, but some might take a legal herbal substance to help them reach the trance state. Other seers might use sexual energy to help them reach the trance state.

Once in the trance state, a seer may shapeshift into other animals to communicate with other spirits. Sometimes seers receive messages they transmit back to the real world. In this way, seidhr becomes a divination method, similar to the soothsaying. Magical change performed in seidhr is achieved through mental force rather than manipulation of the physical elements, as in Wiccan magic.

If you are interested in practicing seidhr, it is important to first become experienced with meditation and trance. You should also spend some time learning about the other realms before attempting to use them for magical change. Your first order of business when learning seidhr is to locate your fetches—your animal and spirit guides in other realms.

Rune-Galdr

Rune-galdr (pronounced *gall-door*) is a form of magic practiced with the runes. The runes are used to create talismans that will draw your desire to you, or change your *hamingja*, roughly translated to mean "luck." Runesters may also work with galdor-staves, which are magical symbols that predate runes. If you haven't yet made your own runes, you must do so before practicing rune-galdr or the magic will have no effect.

The ability to shapeshift in other realms comes to the most powerful seidhr after a lot of practice. Only movie superheroes can shapeshift in the earth realm, but with practice, you might be able to make would-be attackers think you've suddenly turned into a tiger.

In rune-galdr, you first choose the runes you intend to use based on their lore and your intent. Once you've created ritual space, you might sing the runes in a chant designed to increase their power. You could also carve a bind-rune or write the chant out in runes. Bind-runes are created from a set of runes combined to create one symbol. For example, if you or your partner were pregnant and you wanted to protect the baby, you might combine the rune for fertility with the rune for protection by either drawing both symbols and connecting them, or by creating a new symbol by combining elements of the two.

Chapter 10

Druidic Beliefs

Druidry, like Asatru, is a modern reconstruction of an older faith. The original Druids were a professional class with great political power among the Celts. This group was crushed following the Roman invasion, but their legends survived. The practices of modern Druids are based on what is known of the beliefs and practices of the ancients, but updated for modern times. As with Asatru, it would be impossible to practice the faith as it was originally conceived because the world has evolved far beyond anything the Druids could have imagined.

Organization and Hierarchy

Over the course of the last few decades, several prominent Druid organizations have emerged in the United Kingdom, Ireland, and the United States. Each organization is unique in some ways, but many similarities do exist. For instance, most Druidic working groups are called groves, regardless of which larger organization, if any, they belong to.

Do Druids have sacred texts?

There are no sacred Druid texts similar in nature to the Christian Bible. The ancient Druids followed an oral tradition. Guidance for practicing modern Druidry can be found in Celtic myths and legends that were written down in the Middle Ages.

The Order of Bards, Ovates, and Druids

OBOD traces its lineage back to the Ancient Order of Druids, founded in 1717. After numerous fractures and splits, Ross Nichols refounded the order in the 1960s. OBOD offers an extensive three-year training course for its three-degree system. Studies begin with the bardic level, then move up to ovate, and then to Druid. As each level is completed, the student undergoes an initiation ceremony.

A chief leads the order. The chief's term of office is not limited to a specific time frame. Other officers include the pendragon, the scribe, and the modron. All four have spiritual roles in the organization and specific duties in ritual.

Groves belonging to the OBOD are led by Druids and hold regular meetings, rituals, and may offer initiations and training. In addition to groves, OBOD has seedgroups. Some Seedgroups are more casual groups that work together when they choose. Seedgroups do not require a leader who has achieved the Druid grade. Groves and Seedgroups belonging to OBOD are found in the United States, United Kingdom, Ireland, continental Europe, and Australia.

British Druid Order/Druid Network

The Druid Network grew out of the British Druid Order. Neither group offers organized training similar to that of OBOD, although they do recognize the three Druidic degrees. In both groups, members can remain at any grade for as long as they wish, and training is through personal study and experience. Both groups offer affiliations for groves around the world, and host larger events and gatherings, generally in the United Kingdom.

Ár nDraíocht Féin

Issac Bonewits founded Ár nDraíocht Féin (ADF) in 1983 as a North American Druidic group. The name means "Our Own Druidism" in Gaelic. ADF emphasizes scholarship, inspiration, and Pagan spirituality.

ADF members come from all over the United States and Canada. ADF is led by a Mothergrove, but the groves also have some degree of local control. Membership is open to members of groves and solitary Druids. ADF groves, which are led by three voting members over the age of eighteen, hold regular meetings and public rituals.

ADF does not offer degrees—instead, all members are considered equal. But it does provide two training programs. Dedicant training lasts one year and covers the basics of Druidry. The Study Program provides training specific to individual specialties, such as healing or becoming a member of the clergy.

The Henge of Keltria

The Henge of Keltria was established as an offshoot of ADF in 1987. The focus of the Henge is on Celtic Druidry, whereas other groups might incorporate practices from other cultures. Their training program is divided into three Rings, with the highest Ring divided into three specialties: bard, seer, and priest. Each segment of training may last a year or more and concludes with an initiation.

Local groups belonging to the Henge are organized into groves and study groups. Groves are required to have at least three Henge members and to adhere to Henge bylaws, but are otherwise autonomous. The Henge currently has groves and solitary members in the United States.

Druidic Grades

The Druid organizations that offer degrees usually offer some version of the old Druidic classes: bard, ovate, and Druid. Each specialty has an important role within Druidry. Each role also offers a unique insight into or experience of the Druidic path.

A bard is a teller and keeper of lore. Bards relate the stories of the land and inspire others to connect to the land. The skills a bard must acquire involve learning to listen to the land and attuning to the elements. Bards also learn how to creatively express all that they learn.

An ovate's skills relate to prophecy and divination. Ovates learn to communicate with the spirit realm to discover how and why something is happening. Ovates may also learn greater spiritual healing skills, and use a variety of oracles in addition to spirit communication.

The age of a Druidic organization has no impact on its validity as a group. It's also not necessary to belong to any group. There are solitary Druids, although many find that their experience of the faith is enhanced by interaction with other Druids.

A Druid combines the skills of the bard and ovate and adds to them with additional training. Druids learn to travel between the two realms and make visits to the otherworld. They serve the role of priest and teacher, and preside over rituals for holidays and rites of passage. The main goal of each Druid is to reunite the earth and its people and to create peace between all the realms.

Are All Druids Pagan?

Druidry is a religion *and* a philosophy, but it may be either one or the other. It all depends on the individual's personal understanding of Druidry and its role in that person's life.

For those who consider Druidry a religion, a Druid is a Neo-Pagan because the ancient Celts were Pagans and the priesthood was a part of that religion. Generally speaking, members of ADF and the Henge of Keltria are Neo-Pagan Druids. Members of OBOD, the British Druid Order

(BDO), and the Druid Network may or may not see themselves as Neo-Pagans, but the majority do consider themselves Neo-Pagan.

In addition to Christian Druids, there are also Jewish Druids, Buddhist Druids, even Wiccan Druids, although generally Wiccan Druids will eventually become Druids by religion as well. Druids are found in all faiths and walks of life.

For those who consider Druidry a philosophy, a Druid is not necessarily a Neo-Pagan. Druidry's essential components are reverence for and connection to the land and learning to access divine inspiration. For non-Pagan Druids, such as Christian Druids, the land is a representation of the divine God. Christian Druids view Druidry as a mystical school, a method for accessing the divine nature and creation of God.

Debate about Modern Druidry

There's also some debate about whether or not modern Druids are really Druids. Some claim that only the ancient Druids were "real" Druids. Others claim that modern Druidry is a revival that can rightfully take the name Druid.

Those who doubt the modern Druids' authenticity are mainly concerned with vocabulary. To them, the Druids were a specific people from a specific time. They don't agree with the new application of the old term.

Those who claim that modern Druids are "real" tend to view modern Druidry as a reconstruction or re-creation of the old ways. Like Asatruar, they don't claim an unbroken lineage and don't believe they're following the old ways exactly. Instead they feel a connection to the same spiritual inspiration as the old Druids, which they believe has modern applications and validity.

Druidic Cosmology

Druids seek to learn more about themselves, nature, and the natural spirits. Their worldview is largely based on the triplicity of the universe and everything in it. This view affects their idea of the afterlife. The image of the *awen* (illustrated on page 133) is a perfect example of this belief system.

Triplicity

In the ancient Celtic World, everything came in threes. For example, the world was seen as made up of three realms: land, sea, and sky. Modern Druids see the world the same way. The land is the realm of humans, nature, and nature spirits. The sea is the underworld and the land of the ancestors. The sky is the realm of the gods. The world can also be divided into three circles:

1. **The Circle of Abred** is the realm of the living and the dead.
2. **The Circle of Gwynvyd** is the realm of immortal beings.
3. **The Circle of Ceugant** is the realm of the one source, or God.

In addition to the triplicity of the world, there is also a triplicity of the beings in the world. Gods, humans, and ancestors all share the world and may work together. The divine creative force of the world is sometimes described as the Mother, the Father, and the divine Child, the cycles of which are reflected in Druidic seasonal celebrations.

Nine is another important number to Druids. It features prominently in Celtic myths and legends. Heroes were sometimes advised to travel beyond the ninth wave. The Cauldron of Vocation was said to bring nine gifts. Brighid is a triple goddess with nine aspects.

View of the Afterlife

The afterlife is a part of the triple nature of the world. Death is merely a part of the cycle of life—birth, death, and rebirth—and Druids see death as a transition. The dead reside in Annwn, the underworld, the place of death and transformation. All souls transition through life by traveling through the spirals of Abred, which is the living, elemental realm. As souls move up this realm through several incarnations, they eventually escape it and join the land of Gwynvyd, where the wise ones and the gods reside.

The Awen Symbol

Awen, also known as *imbas* (pronounced *eem-vas*), is the source of all inspiration and one of the most important facets of Druidic belief. It is flowing energy, the flow of divine inspiration, and can be found in all things. Druids seek to learn how to access the power of nature and establish a cooperative relationship with the spirits of nature so they can call on them for assistance.

◀ **Awen:** The three dots of the awen symbol signify the positions of the sun throughout the year: the spring equinox, the summer solstice, the fall equinox, and the winter solstice. The three rays symbolize the paths of wisdom, knowledge, and inspiration. They are also related to the three drops of knowledge from Cerridwen's cauldron.

To access awen, Druids chant its name: *ahh-ooo-ennn*. It can also be drawn, traced, or otherwise re-enacted to fully connect with it. Learning to access awen is the key to Druidic magic and worship.

Druidic Deities

Some Druids honor no deities at all, and see Druidry as an internal path to healing and self-knowledge, and Druid gods as archetypes. Most Druids, however, see the gods as elemental forces or unique beings. Those who work with gods draw from a variety of pantheons.

The majority of Druids work with Celtic deities. The Celtic gods most frequently found are Irish, Welsh, British, and sometimes Gallic. The gods from all these regions have similar traits, but they have different names.

British Deities

The British gods are divided into the Children of Don and the Children of Llyr. Of the Children of Don, the three major gods are:

· **Arianrhod,** often called the Lady of the Silver Wheel, is the goddess of the stars. She has roles in time, birth, and initiation.
· **Gwydion,** her brother, is the god of the sky, magic, and poetry. He is also considered a father god.
· **Lleu Llaw Gyffes,** their son, is a hero god of many skills.

The children of Llyr are:

· **Manawyddan** is god of the sea.
· **Bran** is a war god and guardian of the land.
· **Branwen** is a goddess of love and death.

In addition, the British had a few deities not associated with either of the two main families.

· **Rhiannon** is a beautiful horse goddess.
· **Arawn** is god of the underworld.
· **Cerridwen** is the corn goddess and a prophetess; she keeps the cauldron of inspiration and rebirth and is often considered a dark mother.

Irish Deities

The Irish gods are collectively known as the Tuatha Dé Danaan, the children of Danu, the mother of all and goddess of rivers.

· The **Dagda** is the Good God, the lord of knowledge, and the father god.
· **Morrigan** is one of the triple goddesses of war and death. Her aspects are called Nemhain, Badb, and Macha. She is also connected to the fertility of the land.
· **Angus Og** is the god of love, but not always joyous love.
· **Lug** is the shining god of many skills and the lord of light. He is also

sometimes a guide of the dead.

- **Brighid,** another triple goddess, is the goddess of healing, poetry, and smithcraft.
- **Manannan Mac Lir** is the sea god.
- **Crom Dubh** is the harvest god and guardian of the sacred bull.

Some Druids choose to honor gods from other pantheons. ADF encourages the veneration of all the Indo-European gods, but not all in the same ritual. The Norse or Saxon gods may also be the focus of Druid groves, although followers of the Norse gods are more likely to become Asatruar.

Gallic Deities

The Gallic gods don't have divisions, and only a few have retained prominence:

- **Esus** is a god of trees and cranes.
- **Taranis** is the god of thunder, the wheel, and the oak tree.
- **Teutates** is a warrior god.
- **Cernunnos** is often depicted as a horned fertility god and the lord of the animals.
- **Epona** is a horse goddess.

Together, Taranis, Teutates, and Esus form a triad of powerful gods.

Myths and Misunderstandings

Druids have been the subject of many fanciful depictions over the years. Some of the depictions are based partially on fact or conjecture, but some are not. The myths that persist revolve around ritual blood sacrifice, Stonehenge, and Druidesses.

Blood Sacrifice

Modern Druids practice neither human nor animal sacrifice. While it is true that the original Druids made blood offerings during some of their rituals, as did priests from most other ancient religions, the extent of the blood sacrifices is up for debate. There is some evidence that bulls were sacrificed at Beltane and Samhain and that other animals were sacrificed on other occasions.

Most of the records of their human sacrifices come from their invaders, whose accounts are not unbiased. The Greek philosopher Posidonius was the first to mention that Druids practiced human sacrifice, and Julius Caesar and others adopted his conjectures. According to them, prisoners were placed inside a giant cage shaped like a wicker man and burned as an offering to the gods. They also claimed that a Druid would stab a man in the back with a sword and then use his death throes as a form of divination. Actual Celtic records and archaeological evidence don't bear out these claims, which are now believed to be propaganda tools used by the enemies of the Celts.

Stonehenge

In the early days of the study of Stonehenge, the theory was put forth that the Druids erected Stonehenge. Later archaeological science proved that Stonehenge was built over a period of 1,400 years, ending around 1600 B.C.E. It is not known precisely who built it or why, but it was completed well before the Celts arrived in Britain.

Newgrange is another sacred site of interest. It is a stone barrow with a small slit cut into it. On the morning of the winter solstice, the light of the rising sun passes through the slit and illuminates the interior chamber for seventeen minutes.

It is known that the Druids recognized the sacred nature of the site and of other stone circles, and used them for Druid rituals. Stonehenge is astronomically aligned so that the summer solstice sun rises exactly over the heel stone and the light falls on the center of the monument. Modern Druids have adopted Stonehenge as one of their own sacred sites and have worked with English Heritage to gain access to the site on holy days like the summer solstice.

Witches and Sorceresses

Celtic women were on fairly equal footing with Celtic men, and had most of the same rights as men. These rights carried over into the priesthood, where evidence of female Druids is clearly found. After the arrival of the Christian church, the female Druids were recast as evil witches and sorceresses. This myth continued through to the early Druid revival of the 1800s and the first Druidic organizations were only open to men. Modern Druids, however, are both male and female and both genders are considered fully equal. Some female Druids refer to themselves as Druidesses.

Druidic Values

Druids see their faith as a path toward personal healing, a strong connection to the land, reverence for the ancestors, and balance. Because Druidry is both a religion and a philosophy, its rituals and holidays offer a deep look into the personal psyche. The bardic path allows for the exploration and exercise of individual creativity, which may have been squelched by too many years of society's emphasis on logic. The ovate path helps practitioners learn to look deeper within themselves for answers and mentally communicate with the otherworld about their life and choices. The Druid path offers yet another way to delve into the otherworld to undergo deep healing and learn how to use the gifts of the land to assist with that healing.

Modern Druids are animists who believe all living things have spirit. In addition, the land contains spirit, and everything in the world is part of a web of connection. The rock is connected to the tree, which is connected to each person, who is connected to the rock. Tolerance and equality for all living things and all systems of belief are stressed in Druidry because of the interconnection of everything.

Druids greatly revere their ancestors from several sources. First, they honor their genetic ancestors, the people whose blood flows in their veins. Second, they honor the ancestors of their heritage, the original Druids and keepers of the land. They honor the work the early Druids did and their modern spiritual connection to them. Finally, they honor the ancestors of the land where they live, the spirits that reside within the land, the trees, and the plants that inhabit every living space.

By nurturing a deep connection to the land and the ancestors, Druids seek to achieve balance, which is often the final step in healing. Balance means that you return to the earth what you take from it. You live always in awareness of your impact on the earth, and seek to lighten not only your impact, but the impacts of others as well. Druids are environmentalists who work toward balancing the earth's needs with human needs.

Prevalence of Druidry

Druidry is a large and growing movement. It is predominantly practiced in the United States, United Kingdom, Ireland, Europe, and Australia. The City University of New York American Religious Identification Survey determined that there are 33,000 Druids in the United States.

Given the lower populations of other nations, the numbers there are also lower. OBOD claims 3,000 members and other groups have significantly fewer members. Membership in any organization is not required of Druids, so there are probably many who practice as solitaries or belong to unaffiliated groves.

Most Druids live in English-speaking countries, but groves are also developing in other nations like France, Germany, and Slovakia. It would probably be safe to assume that there are at least 50,000 practicing Druids worldwide.

Chapter 11

Druidic Holidays

Although the ancient Celts honored only three or four holidays that were universal to all of them, modern Druids have adopted an expanded holiday system similar to the Wiccan Wheel of the Year. The eight holidays can be divided into two sets: a solar cycle and an earth cycle. Together, the eight holidays follow the natural cycle of the year, the natural cycle of human life, and the cycle of the seasons.

Twin Holiday Cycles

Of the eight major Druidic holidays, four comprise the solar cycle and another four the earth cycle. The holidays overlap, so there is one holiday approximately every six weeks.

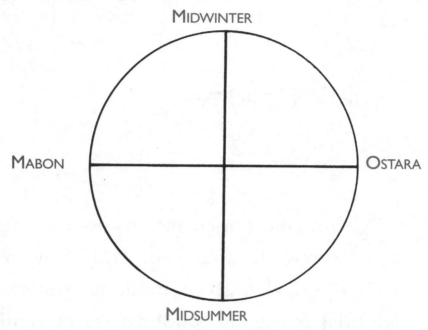

▲ The solar cycle is related to the fixed position of the sun.

Solar Cycle

The solar cycle consists of the two equinoxes and the two solstices. During fall and spring equinox, the day is exactly as long as the night. During the summer solstice, the day is at its longest. During the winter solstice, the day is at its shortest.

Solar cycle dates vary by a few days every year, but they were well known to the original Druids and the people that preceded them, as evidenced by the ancient megaliths like Stonehenge. The solstices and equinoxes mimic the human life cycle of infancy, childhood, adulthood, and old age.

The solstices are less noticeable in places like Southern California where even the longest day of the year is only fourteen and a half hours and the shortest day is ten hours, but they are very noticeable in a place like Dublin, Ireland, where the longest day is nearly seventeen hours and the shortest day is only seven and a half hours long. For British Druids, the experience of the solstices is very powerful indeed. For American Druids, the experience is less striking, but still important.

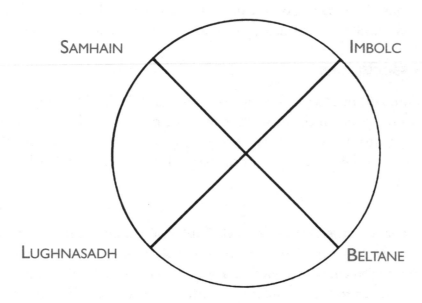

▲ The earth cycle is related to the experience of the seasons on earth.

Earth Cycle

The earth cycle follows the cycle of the seasons as experienced on Earth. Earth cycle holidays were honored as fire festivals by the ancient Celts. The sun plays a role in the seasons, but the actual experience of the seasons lags behind the sun's changes by several weeks. The earth cycle holidays are Imbolc, Beltane, Lughnasadh, and Samhain.

Imbolc falls in the middle of winter, when the earth is starting to awaken, and some blooms are emerging. By Beltane, spring is in full bloom. At Lughnasadh, summer is at its peak. And at Samhain, the harvest is complete as nature prepares for winter.

Samhain: Druidic New Year

Samhain, also known as Calen Gaeaf, Samhuinn, Ancestor Night, Hallowmas, and the Feast of the Dead, is celebrated from October 31 to November 2. Some Druids celebrate Samhain at the first frost or similar first sign of the coming winter; another option is to honor it on the full moon that falls in the sign of Scorpio, which runs from October 21 to November 21. Drawing on the past, Druids have developed several customs and associations to accompany this holiday and extend its meaning.

Samhain Associations

Samhain marks the first sign of winter and the beginning of the dark half of the year, which is also the beginning of the Druid year. It is a time to prepare for the coming darkness and to honor the earth's dark gifts. Darkness and death are part of the natural cycle and should be honored as such.

If at all possible, Druids hold their rituals outdoors, come rain or snow. However, if it's absolutely impossible to hold a ritual outside without freezing to death, an indoor ritual is acceptable. Although the rituals are connected to the sun and the earth, they are not always held during the day. Many also have a lunar association.

The three days of Samhain were not counted on the Celtic calendar. They were a time out of time to honor the forces of chaos, which will rule until the light returns at Midwinter. It was a time to reclaim the value of the darkness, to see the good in decay, to know that which dies and decays becomes fertilizer for next year's crops.

Gods associated with Samhain include Lug and Cerridwen. Its animals are nocturnal beasts or beasts that scavenge on death: the owl, the crow, the bat, and the mole. Food and drink should be dark in color or ethnically related to the practitioner's ancestors. Many Druids honor their ancestors by preparing dishes from favorite family recipes. Incenses should be heavy and pungent.

Samhain Customs

The central activity of Samhain, besides celebrating chaos and darkness, is mourning the ancestors. Ancient ancestors are honored, as well as those who have passed within the last year. The veil between the worlds is thin. Druids communicate with them and give them offerings as tokens of their affection or create an ancestor altar to honor them.

Alban Arthuan means "the Light of Arthur." The other three solar cycle festivals are known as Alban Heruin (the Light of the Shore), Alban Elfed (the Light of the Water), and Alban Eiler (the Light of the Earth).

Because Samhain is the beginning of the year, it is a good time to reflect on individual successes and failures during the last twelve months. It is a time to release anything unwanted and to make declarations about goals for the coming year. In her book, *Ritual,* Emma Restall Orr, a prominent British Druid, recommends that people face their fears of the darkness and release them. It is the time to sacrifice anything that is no longer needed.

Some Druid groves add a bit of pageantry to their rituals. Some Druids burn the Spirit of the Old Year. Some look to Celtic mythology for a story about the darkness overcoming the light and re-enact it in a little play. Another practice is to hold an Ancestor's Feast. Each person brings a favorite dish of the ancestor he or she wants to honor.

Midwinter: The Winter Solstice

The Midwinter festival is also known as Yule and Alban Arthuan, and it takes place on the winter solstice. Midwinter can actually be celebrated as two separate holidays: the Winter Solstice and Midwinter. The first celebration takes place on the actual solstice, while the second celebration may take place a few days later when the sun has begun to rise a few degrees to the east. Midwinter has several customs and associations connected with it.

Midwinter Associations

Midwinter honors the dark womb of the mother, who is preparing to give birth to the new child of light. The old sun has died, and the new sun is about to be reborn. The new sun is a male child, and the energies of male and female are combined at Midwinter.

Gods associated with Midwinter include Mabon, the child of light, and Modron, his mother. Incenses burned at Midwinter should be spicy in honor of the renewed warmth of the sun. Mistletoe is associated with Yule because it displays life, in the form of its berries and evergreen foliage, even in the winter. Holly is also a symbol of growth, warmth, and healing. The wren is connected with Midwinter and its call is said to tell the future.

Midwinter Customs

Midwinter is connected with many of the traditional activities of Christmas. The Yule log, said to protect the home from fires, should be burned for twelve days, until Twelfth Night. The date of Twelfth Night varies from country to country; some Druids follow their own local calendar, while others choose an ancient calendar to follow. The exchange of gifts between friends and family members is also practiced because Midwinter is a time for strengthening bonds with others and the community. It is a time to give back to the community if possible.

Druids decorate trees at Midwinter, but many try to find a potted evergreen that can be replanted rather than buying a cut tree, because cutting down live, healthy trees is considered a sign of disrespect for the earth.

In the Midwinter ritual, Druids celebrate the birth of the child of light by lighting a fire. A bonfire is too intense a flame, but a candle or a fire in a small cauldron is appropriate for this. To celebrate Midwinter, Druids often hold a pageant, re-enacting the birth of Mabon or the myths of other sun gods like Bel and Belenos. Aine or Aña can be honored as a mother. As Emma Orr points out in *Ritual,* Midwinter is also a good time to celebrate personal rebirth, emergence from the darkness of fear or limitation, and the internal shift from chaos to calm.

Imbolc: Feast of the Goddess

Imbolc, also known as Oimelc, Laán Arragh, Bridget's Day, Candlemas, Gwyl Forwyn, Gwyl Fair, Feast of the Maiden, and Feast of Mary, is celebrated on February 2. Some groves celebrate on the night before. Orr says Imbolc rituals can be held when the first lambs are born or upon first sight of snowdrops or hyacinths, the first flowers to bloom. A final alternative date is the full moon of the sign of Aquarius, which lasts from January 21 to February 21.

Imbolc Associations

At Imbolc, the crone is resting and her child is growing. She is a mother, but also a crone because the earth is not yet fully awake. The fire at this festival symbolizes the awakening child and new growth that comes from the warming sun. Candles are also symbols of inspiration, and the fire at this ritual might be smaller than other fires.

On the earth, the snow may begin to melt, lambs are being born, and the earth is shaking off the debris of winter, but it is a gentle shaking. Gentle incenses like sandalwood are best for Imbolc rituals.
A bowl is used to symbolize the womb of the earth and the mother.

It is customary to honor only the goddess at Imbolc. Brighid is the most commonly worshipped goddess. Here she is recognized as a fire goddess, and the goddess of inspiration. It is also acceptable to honor mother goddesses at an Imbolc ritual.

Imbolc Customs

Imbolc is a time for planting seeds, whether they are actual or mental. It is a time to recognize one's duty to nurture inner seeds of growth and the physical seeds of the earth. It is the time to consider personal goals and dreams, and to embrace inspiration. It is common to bless and burn candles of inspiration at Imbolc rituals.

Imbolc rituals are usually small and private. They are typically held indoors because the earth is still very cold. Thanks are often given to the winter spirits, who provide many lessons during this dark, inward period. By spring, new spirits will have taken over.

Pageants or plays held during Imbolc rituals are often based on myths of inspiration, something involving Brighid. Some Druids weave Brigit's Crosses while they tell her stories or share poems, songs, and other artistic expressions as tributes to her as the Patroness of the Arts. Storytelling by the hearth is yet another way to honor her.

Ostara: The Spring Equinox

Ostara, also known as Alban Eiler, takes place on the spring equinox and marks an important turning point, because winter will now fade quickly and flowers and new life will rapidly burst forth.

At Ostara, Druids bless the seeds they will plant if they live in colder regions where the earth is just now ready. In other areas, seeds are blessed at Imbolc. The seeds of new life, eggs and baby animals, are also honored. Some Druids bless an egg and take it home to plant in the earth. Many Druids include children in their Ostara festivities by hosting egg hunts and picnics. Most children's Easter traditions are appropriate for Ostara. Incenses should be light and airy, such as a spring scent.

The spring equinox, like the fall equinox, is also a festival of balance. It is a time to honor opposites: innocence but flirtation, frolic and the hard work of growth. Be aware that the spring passes quickly and its balance, the fall, will arrive soon.

The god at Ostara is growing, but he is still innocent. The goddess is a maiden, not yet sexually ripe. She and the god flirt innocently. In Ostara rituals, a young woman acts as the maiden. All those gathered make offerings to her and she offers blessings in return. The sun lord can also make an offering to her and the two can enact a delicate dance of love. Angus Og is an appropriate god to honor. Brighid is a maiden goddess.

Beltane: A May Day

Beltane is also known as Lá Bealtaine, Calen Mai, Belteinne, Bealteine, Bealtuinn, Roodmas, Summer Day, and May Day. It is celebrated on May 1 or at the first flowering of the hawthorn tree. Rituals can also be held at the full moon in the sign Taurus, which runs from April 21 to May 21. Several of the customs and associations of Beltane are drawn from its history as an ancient fire festival, but it also has no connotations.

It is also said that the ancient Celts extinguished their home hearth fires on Beltane and then relit them with coal from the Beltane bonfire. While you most likely don't have a permanently burning hearth fire at home, you could reignite your inspiration at Beltane.

Beltane Associations

Beltane is the beginning of the light half of the year. It is celebrated as the start of summer. Beltane is a very potent, sexual holiday because it is the occasion of the union of the maiden and the sun lord. Together they ensure the continued fertility of the land. The Lord of the Wildwood, Cernunnos, and the Green Man are appropriate gods for Beltane. Branwen and Blodeuwedd, a maiden made of flowers, are both goddesses connected with Beltane. Blodeuwedd is also Lleu Llaw Gyffes's wife.

At Beltane rituals, aphrodisiac incense such as damiana and jasmine are burned to stir sexual fervor. This is the day when the maiden becomes a mother who will once again give birth to the new sun lord at Midwinter. Life and death are both a part of sex; it creates life, but everything that lives must ultimately die.

Beltane Customs

Most Beltane rituals feature a fire or a pair of fires. The ancient Celts built hilltop bonfires on Beltane and drove their livestock between them to ensure their health and fertility. Modern rituals include activities such as jumping a fire, or running or dancing between a pair of fires to ensure physical and creative fertility, as well as fertility in every other area of life.

Beltane is a popular time for handfastings. The May queen and king may join in a symbolic or actual marriage, and then receive gifts from those present. Often the May queen and king preside over the dancing of the Maypole. Red and white ribbons are traditional, but myriad colors can be hung on the pole. Altars and ritual spaces should be overflowing with flowers, the symbol of this holiday.

Midsummer: The Summer Solstice

Midsummer, also called Alban Hefin or St. John's Day, takes place around the time of the summer solstice. Like Midwinter, it can be divided into two separate holidays: the Summer Solstice and Midsummer Day, held a few days later, on June 24. Some Druids celebrate the summer solstice with three separate rituals. The first ritual is held at dusk the day before the solstice. The next is at dawn on the solstice, and the final ritual is held at noon on the solstice day at the very peak of the sun's power.

Divination is a common activity on Midsummer. A good option is reading the *ogham* or the Druid Animal Oracle. Dream interpretation can be tricky, but it is an important skill for a Druid to possess.

Midsummer is the most male-centric of all the holidays. While the goddess had her day at Imbolc, the god reigns supreme on Midsummer. His influence on the intellect, courage, and wisdom are honored with offerings and thanks. It is also a time to thank the god for his role in personal creative expression.

Plays that explore the rays of the awen or re-enact the epic battle between the winter sun god and the summer sun god are appropriate at this time. Beli and Og are both gods of the sun disk who can be called on this occasion. It is common to light a bonfire as a symbol of the strength and power of the sun.

Lughnasadh: A Harvest Holiday

Lughnasadh is sometimes spelled Lughnasa and is also known as Hlaef-mass, Lammas, Gwyl Awst, the Feast of August, and Harvest Home. It is celebrated on August 1 or at the first sighting of ripe fruit or grain ready for harvest. It can also be honored on the full moon in the sign of Leo, which runs from July 21 to August 21.

Lughnasadh Associations

Lugnasadh celebrates the first fruits of the harvest. This harvest is first and foremost a holiday celebrating nature. In ancient times, this was the first fresh fruit or grain the people had tasted in many months. On a personal level, Lughnasadh is a time to give thanks for all the blessings that have been received so far and to consider what has been reaped and what is yet to be harvested.

If the ritual includes a play or pageant, practitioners might chase the Corn King and bring him back to the circle as a symbol of the gifts he gives at Lughnasadh so the people may eat. John Barleycorn may also make an appearance at a Lughnasadh rite. Lug is the most commonly honored god in his guise as an older father god. Altars should be decorated in the golds, oranges, and yellows of harvest and incense should be fruity. Goddesses for this holiday are fewer in number, but it is appropriate to call Aine, Eire, or Danu as the mother of the land, who allowed the harvest to grow from her womb.

Lughnasadh Customs

Like Beltane, many handfastings take place on Lughnasadh. In ancient times, the marriage might be permanent or just until the following Lughnasadh, and the same is true today. The marriages of Lughnasadh are symbolic of the marriage of Lug and the land of Ireland.

At rituals the earth and the gods are presented with physical representations of personal harvests. Some Druids make a wheat wheel to decorate the altar, or create other symbols out of shaped wheat. Games and feasting are very popular at Lughnasadh celebrations because the ancient peoples celebrated this festival with contests and games of skill. Bread, mead, and fruit are shared among grove members and friends.

Lughnasadh is also associated with apples, which are an otherworld fruit. They grow on the Tree of Life that grows in the otherworld. They are among the first fruits to ripen and hard cider is a popular Lughnasadh beverage.

Mabon: The Fall Equinox

Mabon, also known as Alban Elfed and Harvest Home, takes place around the time of the fall equinox. This holiday rounds out the solar cycle, as a balance of Ostara and the second harvest festival. It is another turning point in the year, coming at the beginning of the dying season as the earth prepares for winter.

At Mabon, thanks are again given for the harvest of the past year. It is a time to consider how personal gifts will be used and shared with others. For example, if an individual's gift is one of poetry, he or she could read a poem to the gods and to fellow grove members.

The Druidic holidays enhance personal connections to the earth and the experience of the seasonal and solar cycles on an individual's own life. The holidays follow two related cycles to create a unified whole. The rituals carried out on the holidays are enhanced by Druidic practices and tools, which also have uses outside of holiday rituals.

Chapter 12

Druidic Practices and Tools

Druid rituals tend to follow a standard format and feature an altar within sacred space, and a small set of tools is generally used. In addition to holiday celebrations, Druids also practice divination and study tree and animal lore to deepen their connections to the earth and help in their healing work. The ogham alphabet is used for divination, but also has other applications as well.

The Druidic Ritual

Druidic rituals are used to celebrate the holidays, honor rites of passage, or carry out special magical acts. They are designed to help practitioners connect with the land and the spirits, honor the gods and spirits, and seek blessings for the land and its people. The rituals have several important steps. The exact order of the parts varies by grove, as does the specific manner in which each step is performed, so this is an example of the basics performed by most groups.

Oak forests are the most popular ritual spots for British Druids. Ancient stone circles have also been adopted for certain rituals. These sites are not found in the United States, but meadows, fields, forests, and other open spaces are good places to hold rituals. If you have a big backyard, you could construct your own stone circle or plant a circular grove of trees.

Ritual Steps

The Druidic ritual is generally made up of twelve steps:

1. Call for peace
2. Create the circle or temple
3. Invoke the awen
4. Consecrate the elements and call the directions
5. Invoke the realms
6. Invoke the spirits
7. Offerings
8. Central purpose of the ritual
9. Blessings and grounding
10. Eistedfodd
11. Feast
12. Release the circle

Call for Peace

Each ritual begins with a call for peace. In the call for peace, Druids ask for permission to perform the rite from the guardians of the area that have been chosen for the rite. They are asked to remain peaceful during the rite.

Drawing the Circle

Next, the circle or temple is created. In Druidry, everything in the world is connected, so in order to create the ritual space, Druids temporarily sever those connections, creating a magic bubble around the proceedings. How strongly and completely those ties are severed depends on the purpose of the ritual and the practitioner's personal preference.

Do Druids use magic?

Yes, but not always in the same way as Wiccans or Asatruar. Druids generally use Transformational Magic. They attempt to transform themselves in order to be in harmony with the spirits of nature.

Invocation of the Awen

The awen is the divine inspiration that is an important facet of each ritual. The awen is invited to guide the rite and the words that are spoken.

Consecration of the Elements

Next, the elements are consecrated by blending burning incense, which symbolizes earth, air, and fire, and by sprinkling water around the sacred space and on the participants. Then the spirits of the directions are invited to join the rite.

Invocation of the Realms

Next, several spirits or energies must be invoked. First, the practitioner invokes the three realms of land, sea, and sky by honoring the well, the fire, and the Sacred Tree. The well is tied to the sea and its underworld powers. The fire is connected to the sky and its smoke travels to meet the gods. The Sacred Tree grows on earth and connects humans to the other realms.

Invocation of the Spirits

Next the spirits are invoked, who are comprised of ancestors and animal guides, the spirits of place, and the gods. These invocations can be performed directly, with words spoken to the gods, or their archetypal energies can be invoked through the telling of a story or a myth.

Try to be aware of the natural spirits of the land, and speak to them rather than speaking to British land spirits. Some British land spirits might have migrated with human immigrants, but in general in America, the spirits honored by Native Americans are more prevalent.

Making Offerings

Once the spirits and energies have been invoked, the practitioner makes offerings to them to thank them for their presence and the gifts they have given her or him. The offerings can be burned or spoken. Individuals are also welcome to make offerings. The final offering should be from the grove as a whole, and should be related to the main purpose of the rite.

Special Rites

For a holiday rite, the practitioner would now relate the myth of the holiday or perform some action related to the holiday, like burning his or her fears. If the rite is for purposes of divination, this is the time to request an omen. If the rite honors a rite of passage like a marriage, the practitioner would now perform the wedding ceremony. If the practitioner is performing personal magic, the spell, request, or thanksgiving rite would now be performed.

Blessings and Grounding

The blessings will often take the form of a cup of ale, mead, or juice, and bread passed around the circle. The blessings are also a way of grounding the energy that has been raised during the ritual.

Eisteddfod and Feast

The grounding can continue with an *eisteddfod,* which is the sharing of inspiration through songs, stories, or other expressions of creativity. A feast can also take place within the circle, or both the eisteddfod and feast can wait until after the ritual is over.

Opening of the Space

The final step of the ritual is the opening of the space. The spirits are released in the reverse order from which they were called. Next, the realms are released, again in reverse order. Finally, the directions are released in reverse order and the circle is reconnected to the web of the world; the practitioner does this by walking in the opposite direction from which the circle was cut.

Ritual Roles

Depending on the size of the grove and the specific Druidic tradition, there might be several required roles that people will need to fill. First, there is the chief or another presiding Druid who leads the ritual. He or she announces the steps that are about to be carried out. The pendragon, scribe, or other Druids will carry out the ritual steps. A bard and an ovate might be present to read invocations and determine omens. A separate person might be present to make the offerings.

Some Druids choose to perform this ritual alone; in that case, he or she performs all the steps. The ritual can be as simple or as complicated as the practitioner chooses to make it.

Prior to taking a role in a public ritual, grove members should practice through private rituals and small gatherings. Rehearsals are also helpful to work out the minor kinks. For rituals performed in public, it is also important to have speakers who can speak loudly and clearly and who won't get stage fright at an inopportune moment.

The Altar and Other Tools

In Druidry, no tools are absolutely required, but there are several tools that enhance or assist in ritual and the experience of the faith. The most common tools are the altar, bowl, wand, and knife. During rituals, Druids generally wear special robes.

Ritual Altars

There are no specific requirements for a Druidic altar. It can be inside or outside, depending on whichever works best, but outside is preferable. It can be a large stone, a tree stump, or a small table. The altar can be in honor of an ancestor, an element, a god, or several gods. An altar can also be to the awen, or it can be to something the individual wants to achieve.

An altar should be maintained regularly (daily, if possible). Doing so will strengthen the practitioner's connection to the focus of the altar. It can be decorated with power objects and symbols of personal beliefs. If power objects are used, they should be found rather than bought, because you can't always guarantee that a purchased object was collected with the correct intention. A feather found on the ground was freely given by the bird, but a bird feather purchased in a store may be the result of a slaughtered bird.

Ritual altars are usually decorated with the tools to be used in the ritual. It is typically in the center of ritual space and is sometimes called the Stone of Speech. It contains the incense and bowl of water. If candles are used during the ritual, or the practitioner has offerings, they can be placed there until it is time to make the offerings to the fire. The ritual fire, if small enough, can be on the altar or in front of it.

Ritual Bowls

The ritual bowl symbolizes feminine energy and the womb. The bowl and its contents represent rebirth, the unknown potential of birth, and the awen. It is a tool for transformation and a container for the elements.

A bowl can contain water, incense, fire, or a ritual beverage. A standard Druid ritual may use several bowls. Bowls can be made of any material, but they should be fire and heat resistant if they are to be used for burning items.

Sand or earth can be placed under the incense to absorb the heat.

The water in a bowl is often pure water or drawn from a sacred source. It can be well water, rainwater, spring water, seawater, or tap water, depending on the purpose and accessibility.

A ritual fire can be contained within a bowl or cauldron, which has the same associations as a bowl. The wood used for the fire should be connected to the purpose of the ritual. Many druids consult tree lore and their own personal connection to a tree when choosing the wood. A ritual fire can also be lit in a hearth or a fire pit rather than in a cauldron or bowl.

The bowl that holds the ritual beverage could also be a chalice. A bowl can be used to receive offerings from the chalice or other containers if pouring them on the fire would douse it. A more popular alternative is to pour the offering directly on the earth, but if the ground is frozen solid, this might not be possible. The goal of Druidic ritual is to leave no trace of the practitioner's presence behind.

Wand and Staff

The ritual wand is used to close and open the ritual circle. It also serves to strengthen the practitioner's connection to the tree it came from and her or his connection to trees and nature in general. A ritual wand should be the length of the user's arm from the elbow to the tip of the middle finger. Many Druidic wands are carved.

When choosing a wand and staff, consider your personal connection to various trees. Before cutting a branch to make your tool, request permission from the tree and then make an offering in return. You can also look for an already felled branch, but request permission from the spirits of the place before taking it. The day after a storm would be a good day to go in search of a staff or wand.

The staff is rather like a walking stick. It is a great deal larger than a wand, usually at least shoulder height. It can be carved or plain. The staff is a symbol of the practitioner's connection to the earth and his or her stability. Some Druids carry their staff when walking or hiking to help strengthen that connection.

Dagger and Sword

The dagger or sword is a symbol of masculine energy. It represents dignity, honor, clarity, strength, and desire, all of which are associated with male energies. Either can be used to sever the ties to the web of connection when casting the circle. The dagger can also be used to cut branches from trees or harvest herbs.

There are no rules governing the size or design of the Druidic dagger. The handle can be metal, wood, or stone, depending on personal preference. It can be carved or plain. The main concern is that it's comfortable to grasp and use.

Special Robes

Most Druids work in robes. Traditionally, the robes are white, but they can also be other colors. Depending on the grove, the color of members' robes might symbolize their rank within the grove or their path: bard, ovate, or druid. It might also symbolize a particular element with which the practitioner is connected or trying to gain a deeper connection to. In pageants, the robes might symbolize the performers' roles, such as yellow for the Corn King or a white or pale blue robe adorned with flowers for the maiden.

Ogham Alphabet

The ogham (pronounced *oh-um*) alphabet is an ancient Celtic alphabet that was most likely never used for actual writing. The symbols were once used to leave secret messages for others and were often carved into stones. The ogham consists of four sets of five letters plus five diphthongs (two-part vowel sounds, spelled as two vowels in English). The original twenty letters of the alphabet are believed to have developed sometime around 200 C.E., but may be older. The diphthongs were added later.

The oghams are lines drawn perpendicular or on a slant across a central line. The ogham was originally written vertically from bottom to top, but is now more commonly written horizontally. The system also had symbols to indicate spaces.

There are two versions of the ogham alphabet. The first, the Beth-Luis-Nuin, is mentioned by Robert Graves in *The White Goddess*. The second, the Beth-Luis-Fearn, is more commonly accepted among Druids.

Each ogham is named for a tree and deals with the lore of a tree. The oghams have also been connected to birds, colors, and other objects, concepts, or creatures. The trees that relate to the ogham vary, but there are a few standards. For example, B relates to the birch and L to the rowan. The letters are actually taken from the first letter of the ancient name for the tree; for example, birch is *beith*, rowan is *luis*. The alphabet serves as a mnemonic device for the original Druids. Their teachers connected the trees to lore and history to make it easier to remember.

The oghams can be used in magic. The symbols can be drawn and carried with you to bring the energy of the ogham into your life. For example, you could use the beith if you need to purify yourself of something.

Tree Lore

Trees, herbs, and plants are very important to Druids. They represent their sacred alphabet, they are used for healing, and many Druids name themselves after trees. Trees are the connection between the realms. Ireland was said to be divided into four lands, each occupied by a sacred tree with a fifth tree at the center.

The five most important trees are the oak, rowan, birch, apple, and yew:

- The **oak** is connected with strength, protection, and stability. Some say that the very word Druid derives from *duir*, the old word for oak.
- The **rowan** is useful for protection, youth, and prophecy.

- The **birch** is symbolic of beginnings, renewal, regeneration, and cleansing. It is also associated with the bard.
- The **apple tree** is the tree of life and is said to reside at the center of the otherworld.
- The **yew** is associated with death and decay because it is very poisonous, but this unique evergreen tree also lives for thousands of years. It is related to the ovate and is frequently found near sacred wells.

Other trees, such as the ash, willow, and hawthorn also frequently appear in mythology and legend.

Foremost among the herbs and plants most revered by Druids is mistletoe. Mistletoe is a parasite frequently found growing on oaks. It is said that mistletoe, which grows off trees rather than from roots in the earth, must never be allowed to touch the earth. It is sometimes called all-heal, but it is poisonous, so use it with caution. Verbena, or vervain, is gathered at Midsummer, whereas mistletoe is gathered at Midwinter. It is used as an offering to the gods. It is also considered a cure-all and is said to ward against evil spirits.

Herbs, trees, and plants may have useful properties, but they can also be dangerous. Before using any plants for healing, consult a reliable herbal dictionary or other knowledgeable source in addition to consulting your intuition and guides. For example, Saint John's wort is known to interfere with the birth control pill.

Debate about the Tree Calendar

In *The White Goddess* Robert Graves announced the existence of the Celtic Tree Calendar. It has since been proven that the Celtic Tree Calendar is his invention. There are no references to it in Celtic history, and the only Celtic calendar known to exist, the Coligny Calendar, doesn't correlate to the Tree Calendar.

According to Graves, each lunar month was named for one of the thirteen trees in the ogham. It begins at Yule with the birch and ends just before Yule with the elder. A second system starts the calendar with the

Reed Moon at Samhain and ends with the Ivy Moon. The trees in both systems are the same.

The Celtic Tree Calendar is based on the lines of the Song of Amergin, which is an actual historic poem, so some people have adopted the calendar for their own use. Most Druids ignore the calendar because it is a purely modern invention. Although some Druids honor the moon cycle, they do so without naming the months.

Animal Lore

Animal lore is also useful in Druid ritual, life, and divination. In addition to trees, the ogham alphabet has also been connected to birds, cows, and other animals. Animals have symbolic associations based on their habitats, behaviors, and historical roles:

- **Horses** are associated with Epona, their goddess, and with other gods.
- **Swans** are said to be faerie women.
- The **raven** is sacred to the Morrigan and banshees.
- The **boar** is related to war and death.
- The **stag** is a symbol of great spiritual power.
- The **salmon** is connected to wisdom and knowledge, according to legend.
- The **eagle** is able to fly up to the gods and can convey messages from them.

Selkies are mythological women who wear sealskins. They often remove their skins when on land. They are said to be more beautiful than human women. According to one legend, a man stole a selkie's skin and made her his wife, and their children had webbed toes. People with webbed toes are said to be descendants of selkies.

In order to determine the animals they are most connected to, and most need to learn from, Druids study scientific and historic information about them. Many Druids also choose to keep their power animals as pets, if it's possible and legal. If your power animal is an eagle, you are out of luck, but a cat is a good power animal pet.

Modern Druidic Divination Methods

Divination is a common component of a Druid's life. Divination is used as a guide for correct living, as well as for signs of what is to come and why. Ovates are trained in divination, but all Druids are free to use the various forms available. In addition to tarot, I Ching, or other methods popular among Neo-Pagans, there are a few systems popular among Druids.

Ogham Sticks

Ogham sticks are the most popular form of divination for Druids. The ogham letters are carved onto a series of sticks that can then be cast or drawn. Each of the trees associated with the letters has certain properties connected with it. Birch, for example, is related to protection and purity.

When reading the ogham sticks, Druids draw on their knowledge of tree lore and their intuition. They may consider the order of the sticks and how the concepts relate in that order. They may also consider the sounds of the letters. Some Druids cast the sticks onto a cloth marked with concentric circles and observe which circles the sticks land on and how they appear in physical relation to one another. For example, sticks crossed over each other would convey a different meaning than sticks lying parallel to each other.

Card Decks

Several people have developed card decks based on the ogham, tree lore, and animal lore. Many Druids use these decks in place of the tarot because they are more specifically suited to Druidic beliefs. The most popular decks are the Druid Animal Oracle and the Celtic Tree Oracle. There are also manufactured ogham sets, but you'd be better off carving your own.

Stephanie and Philip Carr-Gomm developed the Druid Animal Oracle. Philip Carr-Gomm is currently the chief of OBOD, and he created the deck in accordance with traditional Druid animal lore. The deck consists of twenty-nine animal cards and four dragon cards representing the elements.

Liz and Colin Murray developed the Celtic Tree Oracle. Each card depicts one of the twenty-five ogham letters and the tree connected with it. The lore of each tree is also included. The cards are an excellent way to learn the ogham so you can work with them without the deck.

Meditation

For those who have learned to communicate with the otherworld, meditation is the simplest and most straightforward method of divination. During meditation, you travel to the otherworld, or speak to spirits in the otherworld and ask questions. You might also be taken on a journey to a new area of the otherworld, or a familiar area, and the answer will be found along the journey or once you arrive at your destination.

Some Druids travel to an inner grove that exists only within their minds and spirits. They use meditation to access the grove and discover the answers lurking in their subconscious minds. The landscape can be as vast as that of the external otherworld, but all the answers lie within the individual.

Interpreting Natural Phenomena

The ancient Druids were skilled in the art of interpreting natural phenomena, such as cloud formation, bird flight, animal movement, and water movement. Modern Druids sometimes draw on these methods as well. Unlike the other systems, interpreting natural phenomena relies solely on the intuition. For example, if you were to divine from cloud formations, you would look for images in the clouds and then determine what that image meant to you. Seeing a snake might mean one thing to you, but something else entirely to another person.

Scrying—gazing into a stream, lake, river, a bowl of water, a candle flame, or a fire—is a popular method related to natural phenomena.

In this method, Druids try to determine the images and meanings in ripples in the water or the flickers of the flame; practitioners look for shapes in a large fire or in the foam of crashing waves.

Some Druids divine by gazing into a Druid Egg, which is a crystal sphere. Images don't appear on the sphere, but rather appear in the practitioner's mind. Staring into the egg gives the Druid's mind something to focus on so his or her intuition can explore.

Important Symbols

Druids have several symbols important to their faith and practices. Some of these symbols are found on ancient Celtic petroglyphs, while others are modern creations. In addition to the awen, other commonly used symbols are the triskele, triple spiral, world tree, and Druid sigil.

Triskele and Triple Spiral

Triskeles and triple spirals, also called triskelions, come in many forms. Versions of each have been found carved onto the entrance stone at Newgrange and petroglyphs of the symbols have been found all over the British Isles.

◀ Triskele symbol in its simplest form.

◀ Triskele symbol with three legs, also known as the symbol of the Isle of Man.

◀ The triple spiral, as it is most often depicted.

These symbols represent the triplicity central to Druidic and Celtic beliefs, and the interconnection of all things. The triskele symbol with three legs is the symbol of the Isle of Man and has been used on coats of arms. Triskelions have also been found in France and Italy, and were briefly used by the Nazis.

Druid Sigil

Some Druids wear the Druid sigil as a symbol of their faith, similar to the way Wiccans wear pentacles. The origin of the symbol is not known, but it is modern and not found in Celtic history. It was first used by David Fisher of the Reformed Druids of North America.

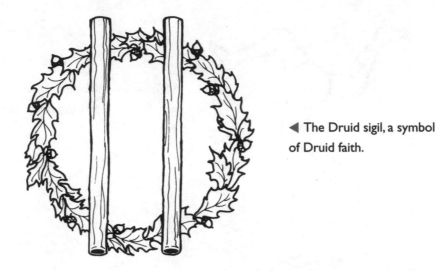

◄ The Druid sigil, a symbol of Druid faith.

The sigil is usually depicted as a wreath of leaves and two vertical staves, but can also be drawn as a plain circle with two lines. Some Druids replace the staves with a tree inside a circle. It is mostly used by members of ADF and is less commonly found in British Druidry. Other Druids wear the awen symbol as a sign of faith.

Chapter 13

Vodoun and Santería

African Paganism emerged over 1,000 years ago, and the original faiths are still followed in some parts of Africa, while in others the local populations have accepted the Muslim or Christian faiths. Santería and Vodoun are similar religions that grew from the practices of the slaves in the New World and their response to forced conversion to Christianity. Neither faith is Neo-Pagan, because both are continuations of the old Pagan ways of Africa, which have been modified to suit their New World setting.

Roots of Vodoun and Santería

The faiths that would become Vodoun and Santería formed among the West African tribes that spoke variations of the Akan and Fon languages and lived in the Yoruban and Dahomey regions, which are now Nigeria, Benin, Togo, Senegal, and the Guinea Coast. Because of the closeness of their languages and geographical regions, many of the gods share the same characteristics but have different names; other gods have the same names, but serve slightly different functions.

In addition to trading with one another, the Yorubans, Dahomeans, and Ashantis warred against one another and took slaves from one another's tribes, increasing the exchange of religious ideas. It was common for a conquered tribe to adopt the gods of the conquerors, because survival is a concept that is central to African religion. If someone else's gods seemed more beneficial, the tribe would switch allegiance.

In general, all the tribes worshipped a supreme creator god who was uninvolved with humans and unreachable to them. Instead, the creator established lower deities to interact with the people. These deities were believed to reside in nature and to rule over it. People also venerated ancestors, who were believed to have some sway over the well-being of the living. Although fate was understood as predetermined, the Africans believed in a trickster god who carried the messages of fate from the gods. If he could be convinced to change the message, then fate could be altered.

The Ashanti beliefs were slightly different in that their god was a triple god similar to the Catholic image of the Father, Son, and Holy Spirit. They were the only tribe to erect temples, and their ancestors were deified.

Each tribe had an elaborate set of priests, who were the only people able to communicate directly with the gods. These priests performed rituals and sacrifices necessary for survival and to maintain balance. In their world, everything had an opposite, a balance, sometimes expressed as the *Da*, which is akin to the Chinese yin/yang concept. The goal of religion was to keep people in balance with the gods, and with themselves. In addition to priests, the tribes had medicine men and sorcerers. The sorcerers were considered evil, but still had a role in survival and were turned to in times of extreme suffering. Both medicine men and sorcerers received extensive training in the use of herbs and plants.

In the New World

For over 300 years, slaves were kidnapped from the coast of West Africa and taken across the Atlantic to the New World. The bulk of the Dahomeans and Yorubans arrived in lands controlled by the French and Spanish (Caribbean and South America), while the Ashantis were taken to the English islands and later to the United States. Upon arrival in the Spanish islands, the slaves were forcibly converted to Catholicism, because they were seen as human beings and therefore their souls were worth saving. The slaves taken to the English islands were not considered equal to humans and their owners spent less time trying to force religion on them.

Emergence of Vodoun

Vodoun derives from the Dahomean word for spirit. Today it is also called Vodun, Voudou, Voodoo, and Sevi Lwa. It emerged in Haiti and the other West Indian isles as a response to enforced Catholicism and as an attempt to maintain the old ways.

The African slaves, with the help of their priests, assimilated their gods, called *loa*, to the Catholic saints. Through these saints they were able to continue to worship their original gods in secret. Due to a lack of training and the increased prominence of sorcerers, the priesthood died out. Instead, the people turned to medicine men and sorcerers for help. The sorcerers fomented uprisings and cast spells to improve the lot of the slaves. The medicine men, meanwhile, found new plants to work with and their practice continued unabated.

An 1804 uprising in Saint Domingue resulted in the establishment of Haiti as a free republic. Most of the Haitian slave-owners and other nonblacks fled to Cuba and other islands. It was around this time that

Vodoun traveled to New Orleans. In New Orleans, Vodoun was practiced openly, with public dances held in Congo Square. Both whites and blacks practiced the faith.

The government of New Orleans became concerned about Vodoun and sought to quell it with raids and new laws prohibiting it. Vodoun went underground again in the 1850s, and many of its practices were again hidden within Catholicism. A free black, Marie Laveau, declared herself the Voodoo Queen and attempted to reinvigorate it by giving the saints new, Vodoun-related roles, and manufacturing new saints when necessary. She also established the practice of charging for services and the annual ritual on St. John's Eve. Her daughter started the Monday night feast of spirits.

Hoodoo is associated with Vodoun, but is usually considered to be magic practiced by slaves from the Protestant English islands, and is separate from the Vodoun religion of New Orleans. It is more magical than religious in nature.

Emergence of Santería

Santería is derived from the Spanish term *santos,* or saints, and was initially a derogatory term. The religion was also called Lucumi, the Way of the Saints, and Regla de Ocha. In Brazil it is called Candomble and Nagos. Santería grew on the Spanish Islands, especially Cuba, Puerto Rico, and the South American Spanish colonies, and later made its appearance in the United States.

Like the followers of Vodoun, the African slaves in Latin American colonies, some of whom were priests, recognized the similarities between their deities and the Roman Catholic saints and assimilated the two groups. On the Spanish islands, slaves were also allowed to continue with their drumming and singing, which the owners saw as entertainment. In reality, it was an important facet of their faith and helped maintain its strength.

The British infusion of new slaves in the 1700s helped keep the old ways strong. It eventually transferred to the Hispanic peoples of Cuba, and also began to attract whites. It spread to the United States following the Civil War.

While being less diluted than Vodoun, Santería is not exactly like the faith practiced in Africa. Santería absorbed spiritism in the 1800s, which reawakened ancestor veneration, and adopted some of the ways of the Plains Indians. In addition, the religion of modern Nigerians has evolved while Santeríans attempted to preserve the older traditions.

Vodoun Beliefs

Vodounsis believe in a supreme god from which lower deities, called *loa*, emerged. They also honor their ancestors, but not necessarily as deities. For Vodounsis, their spirituality is part of their daily life, and their altars must regularly be maintained with offerings.

Vodoun Deities

The supreme God is called Nana Buluku, Olodumare, or Olorun. This god is unreachable and is removed from human affairs. Nana Buluku created the twins called *ibeji*, Mawu and Lisa, his female and male offspring, to interact with the people. They represent night and day and affect everyday life. The loa are also associated with tree spirits and are pantheistic in nature. Several important gods form a group called the Seven African Powers:

- **Legba:** god of the crossroads, trickster.
- **Orunmila:** god of wisdom.
- **Obatalá:** god of the sky and intelligence.
- **Ogún:** god of steel and iron.
- **Chango:** god of lightning and thunder.
- **Oshún:** goddess of love, art, and sensuality.
- **Yemonja:** the ocean, the Great Mother Creator.

In addition to the Seven African Powers, there are also a few other loa that are honored:
- **Ochossi:** god of the plants.

- **Shoponno-Omulu-Babaluaiye:** god of skin diseases, especially leprosy and smallpox.
- **Oyá** or **Damballah:** the goddess of the elements, also associated with the mind, wind, and transformation.

Numerous minor loa can be called on as the need arises.

Two Groups of Ancestors

Vodoun ancestors are divided into two groups. The first group includes those who did not die an honorable death and therefore are not honored. The second group is the *egun,* who did have an honorable death and who receive offerings. The egun have the power to influence the well-being of their family and can interact with the loa. Vodounsis have altars to their ancestors and often have additional altars to the loa as well. The Vodounsis consult their ancestors through prayer, seeking advice and help in resolving their problems. In addition to contact through prayer, Vodounsis consult their ancestors through an oracle that relies on four pieces of fresh coconut shell.

Vodoun and Santería are not Neo-Pagan faiths. Modern Vodounsis and Santeríans prefer to be called "spiritualists" in order to escape the stigma of evil that has been wrongly attached to their religions.

In Vodoun, the *da* is the energy field of the earth. When a person dies, her soul merges with the *da,* which then flows into nature. A part of a person's soul may also merge with her guardian spirit and reincarnate as a new person with some of the same characteristics as the old. In this way, the ancestors can return to the earth.

Vodoun Practices

In addition to venerating the loa and the ancestors, Vodounsis have several practices to help them adhere to the requirements of their religion. They hold rituals to honor the loa and the ancestors. They also practice divination and magic to correct imbalances in the *ache* (spirit, soul), often under the advisement of the Vodoun priesthood, the loa, or the ancestors.

> Horror movies often focus on Vodoun zombies, which are said to be the moving body of a dead person. In actuality, a zombie is a live person under the influence of herbs that create the appearance of death. The practice is rare in Vodoun today.

Priests and Other Practitioners

Vodoun priests and priestesses have several duties within the faith. In general, they run *iles*, which are groups of Vodounsis who practice together. Iles are considered families, although the members need not be related. The priests might be called *houngans*, and priestesses *mambos* (priestesses are also considered the mothers of the spirit). Priests and priestesses are charged with training new members, leading rituals, and performing initiations when desired. Students are called *omos*.

In addition to the priests and priestesses, Vodounsis receive help from several other magical practitioners. Root-workers are herbalists trained in the proper use of plants and herbs. A ju-ju woman or man is a magician who might use magical means to attain the desired result. A two-headed woman or man is a medium who can contact the ancestors or loa for advice.

Vodoun Divination

Vodoun offers several options for divining a person's fate, the magical actions required to correct an imbalance, the offerings a loa requires, or to get an idea of what is happening in an individual's life. In addition to using coconut shells, Vodounsis gaze into a bowl of water, interpret the arrangement of cowrie shells, or interpret their dreams as forms of divination. Any other method of divination that speaks to the practitioner, such as the tarot or I Ching, is acceptable.

Ritual possession is another form of divination, but it is also a religious experience and something that laypeople can't control. You've probably seen images of possessed Vodoun dancers in movies or on TV, and the images are correct, but at the same time, it's much more than it appears to be. In Vodoun, possession is welcomed, and usually only comes to trained priests or priestesses who invite the spirits of their loa into their bodies. The loa then convey messages to those gathered.

Magic and Ritual

In general, magic and ritual are used to correct some imbalance in the flow of energy, or to make amends for an abuse of power. All that is taken must be returned to the loa, and this is done through offerings and rituals. Before a loa is invited, his or her *vever*, or insignia, is drawn on the ground with cornmeal or grain. After a loa is called, offerings can be made. In some cases, an animal sacrifice may be necessary, but only in cases of life or death. The sacrifice is always done in a humane manner.

The dolls associated with Vodoun are more commonly depictions of loa, saints, ancestors, or the self, rather than victims of negative magic. For magic aimed at others, a photograph of that person usually gets better results than a doll.

Magic in Vodoun is both negative and positive. Blessings are preferred, but sometimes the difference is in the eye of the beholder. For example, a Vodoun practitioner might do a spell to help heal someone suffering from a grave illness. From that person's perspective, this is beneficial to the sick person. But suppose the magic prolongs the life of the person who is being healed, and she has already decided it is time to die and bring a permanent end to her suffering. In her eyes, the magic isn't helping her.

Some Vodounsis intentionally use negative magic. Hexes may be necessary to stop a greater evil or threats to life, such as a serial killer stalking the neighborhood. Vodounsis have several terms for hexing: A person can be *crossed* or *fixed,* which usually means it's something that person brought on himself through his own action. A person can also be *hexed* or *hoodooed,* which means someone else has cursed her. When a person is cursed by someone else, she can "turn the trick," which means she can figure out through which method she was cursed and turn the magic back on the person who cursed her. Magic can be transferred by eating cursed food, touching a cursed item, or cursed items can be buried under the front stoop, in the yard, or placed under the bed.

With Vodoun magic, it is usually best to use it in a way that is clearly for the benefit of all. For example, if you hate your coworker and she constantly harasses you, you could do a spell to make her get a new, better job somewhere else. That would help both of you, but it also might have been simpler just to do a spell to get a new, better job for yourself.

Santerían Beliefs

The religious structure of Santería has been maintained better than Vodoun's. In addition, Santerían beliefs are more elaborate, and their gods and ancestors require more attention. In the United States, some Vodounsis have added these beliefs to their own ways.

Santerían Deities

The Santerían gods are called *orishas*. As with Vodoun, they honor a supreme god, Olodumare or Olorun, who created the orishas and then ended his involvement with the world. The orishas also have several *caminos*, or manifestations, which represent the various roles they play. In Santerían mythology, the orishas are all members of the same family and interact with each other. They also interact with humans. Each person has a mother and father orisha, and the dominant orisha is called the *eledá*.

The seven highest orishas are called the *Siete Potencias*. The *ashés*, or central forces, of the orishas reside within their dedicated *santeros* (priests) and afford the santeros certain powers and abilities. These orishas are:

- **Obatalá:** the lead god who rules purity and patience.
- **Eleggua:** the god of the crossroads and the future.
- **Shangó:** the god of thunder, lightning, dancing, and drumming.
- **Yemayá:** the mother goddess and ruler of the oceans.

- **Oshún:** goddess of beauty, sensuality, pregnancy, and rivers.
- **Ogún:** god of iron and war.
- **Oyá:** goddess of storms who resides at cemetery gates.

Numerous other minor orishas are also recognized, but they do not merge with santeros as the Siete Potencias do. A few of the more prominent include the following:

- **Osian:** the god of all plants.
- **Aña:** the spirit of the sacred bata drums.
- **Iroko:** a tree spirit who resides within kapok trees.
- **Babalú Ayé:** a god associated with diseases.

The power of the orishas also resides in the *otanes*, or sacred stones. Although the orishas are depicted as saints, the saint images can be discarded and replaced, whereas the stones cannot. The saints are used to help non-Santeríans understand the nature of the orishas, but santeros know that the two are different spirits. A figure of Eleggua is also often kept in a small cabinet behind the front door and the otanes are kept in special covered containers.

In both Santería and Vodoun, magic is only effective if both the magician and the recipient believe in its power. Just the idea that you have been cursed may be enough to bring you harm if you believe in its power. You don't have to know you've been cursed for it to work if you are a believer in the faith.

The Role of Ancestors

Santeríans also revere their ancestors. When a person dies, his relatives hold a proper Catholic mass nine days afterward, but they also confer upon the dead a *misa espiritual*, which is similar to a séance. *Espiritismo*, or possession by ancestors, often takes places at a *misa espiritual*.

Ancestors have *bóvedas*, altars, erected in their honor, and may receive rituals for years to come. The ancestors are sources of advice and guidance. In some cases, ancestors are elevated to orisha status, but this is usually only the case with great leaders.

Santerían Practices

Santerían practices are much more ordered than Vodoun practices. The priesthood is elaborate and hierarchal; several initiations are required to reach the highest level of the priesthood. In addition, several methods of divination and magic are available.

Priesthood Hierarchy

The first level of the priesthood is the *madrina* or *padrino*, the godmother or godfather. They teach new initiates and advise those who have been practicing for some time. The next level of the priesthood is the *santero* and *santera*, priests and priestesses. Priestesses are also sometimes called *iyalorishas*. They lead rituals of all forms and can offer herbal cures and do magic. They are also skilled at divination. A *babalao* has achieved the highest level of priesthood possible. Babalaos are exclusively male in Cuba, Puerto Rico, and the United States, but Brazil has female babalaos. In addition to the priesthood are *brujas,* witches, and *curanderos,* healers.

Whether or not a person becomes a santero or santera is determined by his or her fate. Babies born with a caul, or birth remnant, on their faces are said to be born with special abilities. The seventh daughter of a seventh sister is also especially gifted.

Initiation Ceremonies

Santeras and santeros receive at least two initiations, and possibly more. The first initiation is the Catholic baptism, usually given at birth. All Santeríans receive this initiation, whether or not they will become santeras or santeros. If the Santerían's fate dictates it, he or she undergoes a *kariocha* at some later point, possibly in childhood, but there is no set time. To receive the kariocha, a Santerían must complete training that lasts up to three years, although in the United States it is often condensed down to three months. At the kariocha, the *ashé* of one of the initiate's *eledá* is embedded into his or her head. After the kariocha, the person is officially a santero or santera. Later, a santero or santera can have kariochas to the other orishas of the Siete Potencias, if it is fated to be so.

Santeros and santeras are considered novitiates for the first year after their initation. During this time, they wear white, perform numerous rituals, and obey taboos as required by their orisha. Santeros also receive additional training in magic, ritual, and divination. Following initiation, santeros wear the *collares*, or beaded necklaces. The colors of each necklace represent certain orishas, and santeros wear one for each orisha to whom they are a santero or santera; for example, a santero to Shangó would wear a red and white beaded necklace.

Magical supplies for Vodoun and Santería can be found at botanicas. Most major urban centers have at least one botanica. They stock candles, oils, herbs, figurines, and other ritual tools. It used to be traditional for Santeríans to grow their own herbs, but as more people began to live in cities, this became difficult. Purchased herbs are perfectly acceptable.

Methods of Divination

Santeríans use several methods to divine fate, the needs of the orishas, or the cause of personal imbalance. Practitioners interpret the arrangement of *ikins* (palm nuts), *obi* (four pieces of coconut), or *diloggún* (sixteen cowrie shells). In addition, Santeríans examine an *oguelo*, a divining chain, for guidance. *Charada* is a system for determining lucky numbers, but it is very complicated.

Divination is often used to determine when initiation is appropriate and who a practitioner's first orisha will be. Santeríans divine their *itá* at their first initiation. The itá comprises the rules, taboos, and predictions for the rest of the person's life. For example, a practitioner might be told to stop eating meat and that he cannot earn a lot of money from his services as a santero. Divination is also used to determine the sacrifices and offerings required to appease an orisha.

If an individual is suffering some ill, she, her santero, or a healer can divine the reason and the cure.

Magic and Ritual

As with Vodoun, balance is key to Santería, and imbalances must be corrected through rituals and magic. Ritual is more common to Santería than magic, but both have their places. Santeríans hold several types of rituals in addition to kariochas. *Pembés* are feasts held in honor of an orisha. These feasts often feature *oru*, sacred music that is drummed and sung. Each orisha is associated with a specific beat. When played properly, the oru will entice the orisha into possessing a santero and conveying beneficial messages. Santeros also hold funeral rites and rituals to honor ancestors.

Rituals sometimes feature sacrifices. Sacrifices may be required to give thanks to or appease an orisha, to prevent an orisha from getting angry or some action from taking place. Sacrifices are also a part of every initiation. The sacrifices made in thanks or at initiations are cooked and eaten by the guests. Regardless of the purpose of the sacrifice, the animal is killed humanely. The sacrifices signify that everything a person receives must also be returned and helps keep balance. Only babalaos may sacrifice four-footed animals, and this is rare. Chickens are the most common choice. The number associated with the orisha determines the number of animals sacrificed, or other offerings made. Orishas are also associated with colors. Santeríans often decorate their altars and choose the color of the candles they offer based on the colors associated with their orishas.

Magic rarely takes a negative form. It is more common for it to be used to correct an ill or an imbalance, and is often based in herbs. Santeros prepare *omieros*, magical herbal infusions that heal people or prepare them to be healed by a medical doctor. The selection of the herbs is guided by the orishas, and permission must be received from the orisha that rules the herb before it can be cut. A *despojo* ritual is a ritual herbal cleansing.

Prevalence of Vodoun and Santería

The precise number of Santería and Vodoun adherents around the world is not known, largely owing to the secrecy maintained by many members. This secrecy stems from years of oppression and persecution, and even in places where it's no longer necessary, secrecy is still practiced by many of the older practitioners. Both religions became more public in the 1980s and 1990s.

Vodoun seems to be more widely practiced than Santería, but this may be because Santeríans sometimes say they are Catholic when asked what their religion is. Estimates of Santeríans range from 22,000, as determined by the ARIS study done by the City University of New York, to over 5 million. Santería is growing quickly, especially in the Hispanic immigrant and black populations of the United States. It is practiced in Europe, South America, North America, and the Caribbean islands.

The number of Vodoun adherents is not known, but it's high, probably in the millions. It is practiced in the Caribbean (especially Haiti), the United States, and South America. Some estimates measure those who worship the orishas without dividing them into religious groups, and these estimates range up to 75 million. These estimates may include people following their native religions on the African continent.

Chapter 14

Shamanism

Shamanism is not a religion, but rather a practice and a philosophy that can be used within any religious framework. Shamanism has its roots in the earliest human cultures, and continues to be practiced in numerous native cultures today. Today, it is a growing practice among Pagans and non-Pagans alike, who find it to be a valuable addition to their lives.

Roots of Shamanism

In its earliest form, shamanism was a religion, in the sense that shamans had religious roles in the tribe. Their primary function was to maintain harmony between the human realm and the spirit realm. Not every member of a tribe was, or could be, a shaman. Becoming a shaman required a calling and extensive training.

Shamanism did not develop uniquely in one place, but rather emerged at various places around the globe as a part of the evolution of humans. Despite the seeming differences between shamanic cultures, Michael Harner, a noted anthropologist, discovered that certain practices and beliefs are common to nearly all shamanic cultures. He calls these commonalities "core shamanism."

For the ancient shamans, and the people they served, a shaman was the central healer of the tribe. According to them, illness or suffering was caused by disharmony with spirit. If a shaman could remove or repair the disharmony, the person would recover. Divination was also within the realm of the shaman, who used it to help individuals and the tribe.

Shamanism is not the only religious practice that seemed to appear at the same time in far-flung locales. The construction of pyramids also took place in roughly the same period in Egypt, China, Mexico, and other locations, and none of these cultures had contact with each other at the time. Some of the pyramids were strikingly similar in design, but had very different uses.

Although shamanism is still practiced in its original form among some native cultures, the practice has also been opened to Westerners. For Westerners, shamans have become one of many types of healers available. In Western cultures today, the duties of the shaman are fulfilled by several people, like the herbalist, energy healer, priest, or therapist, whereas the native shaman used all of these skills together.

Over Time

Shamanism is thousands of years old, and the practice remained roughly the same during that period. Even today, you can look to native cultures and discover that many of their current methods and tools have not changed for millennia. For these tribes, the shaman is still an important religious figure.

> Some shamans are psychopomps, meaning they help the dead travel to their spirit destination and may deliver any last messages to the human realm. Westerners serving as psychopomps rarely receive the proper training to carry out their missions.

Although shamanism has continued unbroken in some places, in others it has been persecuted to near extinction. The native people of Siberia practiced shamanism well into the 1930s, when Stalin crushed the practice. In North Korea, shamanism was suppressed first by the Japanese, then by Korean Christians, and finally by the communist government, but pockets of practitioners can still be found. In the United States, many of the practices of Native Americans have been restored, and for many tribes, were never completely destroyed.

In the 1950s, Michael Harner began his research into shamanism in South America. He continued this exploration for years, and in the 1970s he began teaching it to Americans. In the 1980s, Harner established the Center for Shamanic Studies. It is now called the Foundation for Shamanic Studies and continues to welcome new students. Members of the foundation have also visited other nations to help them recover their original shamanic practices.

A Point of Contention

While most people agree that shamanism is an acceptable practice for Western and native people, there is some debate about whether or not the term *shamanism* can be accurately applied to these practices, and which cultures actually practiced it.

The term *shaman* is not a native term. It was first used by Europeans to explain the practices of native Siberians. The word does appear to have roots in the Turko-Mongolian languages, and variations of it appear in many cultures on the Asian continent.

In addition to the term *shaman,* some tribes use the terms *medicine people, elder,* and *priest,* among others. When speaking about religious leaders of current native tribes, it's best to use the term they use as a sign of respect.

Some people say that because anthropologists used the word to describe a specific people, it should not be used to describe the practices of any other culture. They also claim that the shamanic practices of people like the Celts, Norse, and other cultures cannot be established, and therefore consider the combination of Celtic or Norse beliefs and shamanic practices invalid.

It is important to note that anthropologists have applied the word *shaman* to many cultures for decades. It has evolved to mean the practices that include trance and ecstasy as a means of accessing the spirit realm for the purposes of healing. People who use the term *shaman* to describe the practices of Native Americans, for example, are applying the modern definition rather than its original meaning. People who combine shamanism with other cultural frameworks point to lore that suggests that while other cultures didn't use the word shaman, or any words similar to it, they still engaged in shamanic practices.

Whether or not you use the term shamanism to describe your practices is up to you. If you feel that the word applies to what you do, then use it. If you feel it would be improper to use it, then find a new word for what you do. *Journeying* is a possible alternative term.

Modern Practices

The modern practice of shamanism falls into two categories. The first category consists of native shamans adhering to the practices of their tribes and having received all the training and fulfilling all the duties of a traditional shaman. The second category consists of Western shamanic practitioners who have adopted shamanic practices and use them to some degree, but do not perform all the functions. That is, a person can use shamanic practices without being a shaman.

Native Shamans

Traditionally, a native shaman receives a call to shamanism. The shaman would then be trained to enter the shamanic trance state and journey to the spirit realm by elder shamans in the tribe. Traditional native shamans are also trained in shamanic healing methods such as sucking out a spiritual implant and soul retrieval.

Traditional native training is open to members of a tribe. It is not unheard of for a Westerner to receive native shamanic training, but it is rare. As a nonmember, a person must earn the trust of the tribe before an elder would be willing to teach her or him to become a shaman. The shaman must also see some sign that the nonmember has the calling. Michael Harner was trained by a Jívaro shaman only after spending a great deal of time studying the tribe as an anthropologist, and after repeated requests for a deeper understanding of their ways.

Western Shamanic Practitioners

Western shamanic practice takes a variety of forms. Some people incorporate it into other religious practices, but their shamanic practices are based on cultural knowledge. Examples are Druids who visit the otherworld in spirit and Asatruar who practice seidhr. Some people combine shamanism with other belief systems to produce a new kind of shamanic practice. Celtic shamanism uses traditional shamanic practices such as power animals and spirit journeys, but also draws on Celtic mythology and otherworld lore as a guide for the topography of the spirit realm.

Shamanic practices can be used for personal healing and to establish a deeper connection to the earth. These uses are just as valid as the outward healing performed by true shamans. Westerners who practice Reiki and other energy healing modalities might use shamanic techniques to enhance healing, but they wouldn't necessarily be called shamans, because they aren't using pure shamanism.

Shamanic Tools and Methods

The tools and practices used by Western shamanic practitioners are based on those of traditional native shamans. The exact specifics vary, but the most frequently used tools are the call to shamanism, trance and journeys, physical challenges, rhythm instruments, and power animals.

The Calling

Before becoming a shaman, a person must receive the call. In traditional societies, the call can either come in the form of an ancestral heritage or a grave illness or injury. A person can also choose to be a shaman, but it is more traditional to receive a call.

If you are not a member of a native tribe, you might not recognize the call right away, or you might not be aware of your ancestral heritage. If you feel drawn to shamanism, think back on your childhood. Were you ever so seriously injured that others feared for your life? Did you have a long, intense illness that endangered your life? Have you had a near-death experience? Are there stories of relatives who spoke to spirits and used spirit-healing techniques?

When the Celts referred to someone as being "taken by the faeries," it meant the person was gravely ill and usually unconscious. The Celts believed the person's soul had been taken to the otherworld by the faeries. Legends tell of people who were deathly ill for months or years who then suddenly regained health. After they awoke, they possessed new gifts for healing.

If you've received the call, go on a spirit journey to contact the spirits who called you and advise them that you are ready to begin your training.

You can also attend shamanic workshops and read books on the topic, but experience is the best teacher. You may want to seek out a trained shaman to help you.

If you haven't received the call, that doesn't mean you can't use the methods. You can be trained just as a called shaman, but you may find it more difficult in the beginning. With time, you will be able to master the techniques necessary for your own life.

Trance and Journeys

Most shamans and shamanic practitioners do the bulk of their work through trance. Trance is not the same as becoming unconscious, although it may appear that way to observers. Mircea Eliade, another noted anthropologist, called the form of trance unique to shamans "ecstatic," meaning they achieve a state of mental and emotional overload, but the experience is controlled in some way.

When shamans are in the trance state, they journey to the spirit realm where they interact with their power animals, ancestors, gods, and other spirits. They make conscious choices and decisions while there, but they are also detached from themselves. Shamans follow the spirits and go where they want them to travel. They may find themselves taking fanciful flights, but they can end the experience when they choose to.

Usually the spirits that appear to a shaman in the spirit realm are familiar figures in that person's culture. If the individual has no concept of a rare African beast, he or she is unlikely to see one in the spirit realm. A person's entrance to the spirit realm, whether it's a cave, a spring, or some other portal, will also be from his or her own culture or frame of reference.

Physical Challenges

Traditional shamans have a variety of methods of achieving the trance state, especially for the first time. In many native tribes, an initiate is sent on a vision quest that might involve sleep deprivation or fasting. The vision quest lasts several days and the initiate usually goes alone and brings very little with him or her. He or she spends days chanting, drumming, or just watching and listening. Eventually the shaman slips into the trance state and receives the first journey.

Some Western shamanic practitioners also go on vision quests or engage in fasting and sleep deprivation, but most learn other methods for entering the trance state, such as meditating to drumming tapes or live drumming. The most important aspect of the initial trance journey is a sense of humility or pitifulness. Fostering pity for the beings in the spirit realm will make them want to help you. At the very least, you should go to them from a position of being less than they are, of requiring their assistance.

Rhythm Instruments

Drums and rattles are useful for reaching the trance state. The drums and rattles used for journeys are not the same as a rock band's drum kit or a silver baby rattle. Drums appropriate for shamanic trancework are found among native peoples, such as African, Native American, and Asian tribes. The rattles are made of natural materials like dried gourds or dried plants with bulbous heads containing seeds.

For shamanic journeys, avoid guided meditation tapes. They will not produce a shamanic experience, because you don't control the journey at any level. Some shamanic drumming tapes have a guided meditation and drumming on one side so you can learn how to enter the portal, but once you've mastered that, use the other side, which contains pure drumming with no speaking.

When drumming or rattling to reach the trance state, you should produce a monotonous rhythm. The point is not to create an interesting beat, but to hypnotize yourself. If someone else is drumming, you might dance to the rhythm, but it's a dance of the body, not the mind. If you don't have someone to drum for you and haven't yet mastered shamanic drumming for your own journeys, several native drumming tapes are available.

Power Animals

Power animals are not pets or familiars. Power animals reside in the spirit realm. They are archetypal spirits such as a bear or cat. The animals aren't limited to those we find on earth, but can also be dragons, unicorns, and other legendary creatures. Power animals are typically mammals or birds, but can also be reptiles or fish, so long as neither is showing fangs or teeth.

On your first shamanic journeys, go in search of your power animal before you do anything else. It is your guide in the spirit realm and keeps you from losing your way. With practice, you will be able to shapeshift into your power animal in the spirit realm. Your power animal also keeps you healthy in the human realm. If you fall ill, check in with your power animal to see what's wrong.

You're not limited to one power animal. You can have several, and they may change over time. You might first work with a bear, but then later shift to a wolf or crow. If a power animal has decided to move on, let it go and seek another one.

Incorporating Shamanism into Any Path

Shamanic practices can be a beneficial addition to your current spiritual practices. They can help you achieve healing on a deeper level, and enhance your treatment of others if you are a healer by profession. Proper training, adoption of a regular practice, and keeping journals will help you adapt shamanic practices to your own beliefs.

Adequate Training

Before adopting shamanic practices into your regular practices, you should receive proper training. The best way to master shamanism is to be trained by an experienced shaman. You can seek out a shaman from a native tribe, but you might have better luck with a workshop aimed at Westerners. There are also several books that provide exercises useful in mastering the practice.

Don't expect to complete your training in one weekend. It takes months or years to master shamanic practices. With each journey, you get a little better, and may spontaneously develop new skills you haven't learned yet. Give yourself time to grow within your practice, because that's what it's really about.

Regular Practice

When you decide to adopt a shamanic practice, it's important to do it regularly. You should plan to journey or drum at least weekly. Power animals and other spirit guides require regular visits and interaction, or they might decide to go see someone else. Regularly using your shamanic practices also keeps your skills in top form. The more you do it, the easier entering the trance state will be.

Part of your regular practice may involve healing others. If you keep your shamanic pipes oiled, so to speak, the correct shamanic cure will be more readily apparent to you and you'll have an easier time applying it. Attempting a soul retrieval if you haven't journeyed in several months will be difficult, if not dangerous.

Is a drug-induced journey the same as a trance journey?
Some native tribes used, and continue to use, powerful hallucinogens to reach the trance state. Most Western shamanic practitioners frown on the practice. The substances used by native shamans are pure and shamans have been trained in their safe and proper use. Western drugs do not have the same effect and may endanger your physical and mental health.

Keeping a Journal

Most shamanic practitioners keep a written record of their journeys. The journal will help you keep track of where you've been, what you saw, who you spoke to, and what was said. You may notice a certain message being repeated or find that a certain destination was particularly helpful. You'll also discover which methods for achieving trance work are best for you.

Record your journey as soon as it's over so it's still fresh in your mind. It's best to mark your journeys with a date and time. You could also add details like the moon phase if you are closely attuned to the lunar cycle.

You may choose to record the images that most stand out and then reread them and see what else comes up. If you can't remember everything, don't worry about it. As you become more accustomed to recording your journeys, your records will be more complete.

Practices That Suit Your Beliefs

Because shamanism is a philosophy and a practice rather than a religion, you can easily modify it to suit your beliefs. The location of your journeys and the figures you see all depend on your personal framework. You can also choose a specific type of drum, rattle, or chant that relates to your belief system. Research the lore of your personal path to see if any of the practices of that ancient culture were shamanic in nature. Alter the shamanic techniques you've learned so they align with the practices of your preferred culture.

For example, if you follow an Egyptian pantheon, your journeys can center around the pyramids or the Nile. Rather than entering the otherworld through a cave, you could crawl through an entrance to one of the pyramids. Rather than speaking to the bear, you could speak to the phoenix. Instead of visiting a tribal spirit, you would work with Isis and Osiris.

The popularity of shamanism waned for many years, but it has experienced a resurgence as more people recognize the value of the ancient ways in modern life. As a modern practitioner, you have several tools and practices to draw on when making the practice your own. Not everyone is called to shamanism, but if you feel called to it, you will find the practice very rewarding.

Chapter 15

Other Neo-Pagan Traditions

In addition to the three main branches of Neo-Paganism—Wicca, Asatru, and Druidry—as well as Pagan faiths like Vodoun, Santería, and shamanism, there are other Pagan faiths that have fewer followers. Some of them are based on the traditions and practices of an ancient culture. And there are Pagans who do not adhere to any specific tradition and instead follow a do-it-yourself model. For those who live in the United States and Canada, there are also Native American practices to consider.

Hellenism: Greek Reconstructionist Paganism

Hellenism, also called Hellenismos and Hellenic Reconstructionist Paganism, is a form of Greek Paganism. As the term *reconstructionist* suggests, Hellenism is an attempt to re-create the religion of ancient Greece. Their beliefs and practices are based on ancient Greek texts, such as the works of Homer and archaeological evidence and theory. Two prominent Hellene organizations are Hellenion and the Omphalos.

The ancient Greeks had no written holy book. Their religion was based on their society and their region, but the ancient writers recorded some holy practices in their works. Other practices, like the Eleusinian Mysteries, were strictly guarded and only fragments of the old rites survive today.

Hellenic Beliefs

Hellenes worship the twelve Olympian gods and goddesses as well as non-Olympian Greek deities and heroes. Some Hellenes refer to the Greek gods by their Roman names. Hellenes also honor nature spirits and their ancestors.

Hellenes attempt to adhere to the classical values of the Greek city-states, but don't believe it would be beneficial to completely re-create those societies. It's not necessary for Hellenes to receive training as priests in order to interact with their gods, but the Hellenion does have a training program.

Hellenic Practices

Hellenism is a devotional religion, which means that their central acts are worship, prayer, and making offerings to the gods, ancestors, and nature spirits. Their ritual calendar is based on festivals found in the calendars of the Greek city-states. The rituals are held in honor of the gods and goddesses, heroes, and the agricultural cycle. They follow a lunar year of twelve months, with an occasional thirteenth-month year to reconcile the difference between the lunar cycle and the solar cycle.

In addition to public rituals, Hellenes may make offerings to the gods at home. The home and family are very important to Hellene life, as they were in ancient Greece. Any family observances, such as weddings and funerals, are also performed according to the ancient model. Some Hellenes practice magic and some do not. It's a personal choice, and those who practice magic do so in private.

Kemeticism: Egyptian Reconstructionist Paganism

Kemet is the ancient name for Egypt; Kemeticism, also called Egyptian Reconstructionist Paganism and Kemetic Orthodoxy, is a re-creation of the religion of ancient Egypt. Kemeticism is based on archaeological evidence and theory about the practices of its people. Detailed records of the ancient beliefs and practices survived through the ages, and Kemetics apply them to modern needs. Major Kemetic organizations include the International Network of Kemetics, the Isiac Religious Society, Akhet Hwt-Hrw, and the House of Netjer.

Kemetic Beliefs

Kemetics believe that the Egyptian gods and goddesses are distinct beings, but all are derived from the same source and are interconnected. These gods together are called the Neter, which is the whole. Kemetics also honor their ancestors, who are believed to influence the lives of their families.

Kemeticism is more than a religion—it is a way of life. Kemetics honor their gods and adhere to the ancient Egyptian values in order to maintain *ma'at,* the balance of all things. Justice, truth, and right action are all important to Kemetics.

Kemetic Practices

Specially trained priests and priestesses aren't necessary for Kemetic worship, but the House of Netjer does offer ordination. Kemetic priests, as well as unordained Kemetics, may hold large re-creations of the ancient temple rites of Egypt on days listed in the ancient Egyptian calendar. They try to stick as closely to the original script as possible. Kemetics also make prayers and offerings to the gods and their ancestors at their home shrines.

Ancient Egyptian artifacts are owned by many major museums around the world. Modern Egypt encourages scholarly study of its heritage and mounts traveling exhibitions. If you want to see an actual Egyptian temple, but can't afford to travel to Egypt, the Metropolitan Museum in New York has one on permanent exhibit.

Kemetics do practice magic, usually through trance. Trance can also be used to receive messages from the gods or the ancestors. Other oracles are consulted outside of trance, and dreams are believed to hold special significance.

Senistrognata: Celtic Reconstructionist Paganism

Some people who are drawn to the ancient Celtic culture practice Senistrognata, which is a new name for Celtic Reconstructionist Paganism. Senistrognata is also called Aurrad (pronounced *ow-rath*) or Gaelic Traditionalism, among other names. Celtic Reconstructionists attempt to re-create the ancient Celtic religion as it was originally practiced. It is based on what is known today about the Celtic tribes of the Iron Age. Imbas is the most prominent Celtic Reconstructionist organization.

Senistrognata Beliefs

Celtic Reconstructionists worship the ancient Celtic gods, but because each Celtic region had specific deities not shared by other regions, they usually try to limit their worship to gods from one area. They also honor their ancestors and the nature spirits of their current local region. The earth is especially revered, and it is believed that it is divided into three realms: land, sea, and sky.

Because little archaeological evidence of the ancient Celtic tribes survived intact, most Celtic Reconstructionist beliefs are based on information contained within Celtic mythology and folklore. They also honor a set of nine values found in mythology. The values are similar to those of Asatruar.

Senistrognata Practices

The main festivals of Celtic Reconstructionists are limited to the four found on the original Celtic calendar: Samhain, Imbolc, Beltane, and Lughnasadh. Those who honor the gods of a specific Celtic region might also re-create local festivals from those regions.

Family and tribe are central to Celtic Reconstructionists. The head of the household, rather than a priest or priestess, leads rituals. They may gather with other groups or a larger clan for the major festivals, but also hold monthly or daily rituals at home.

When magic is used in Celtic Reconstructionism, it is mostly done in a trance state. Prayer and offerings are also used in magic. Divination is performed with the ogham and through dream interpretation rather than more modern systems like the tarot. Some Celtic Reconstructionists also use folk magic methods still practiced in Ireland today.

Religio Romano:
Roman Reconstructionist Paganism

Religio Romano is also called Roman Reconstructionist Paganism. It is an attempt to revive the religion of the ancient Romans. The beliefs and practices of Roman Pagans are based on the works of writers like Ovid and archaeological evidence and theory. Organizations promoting Religio Romano are Nova Roma, the Societas Via Romana, and the Julian Society, which practices the form of paganism prevalent under Julian, the last Pagan emperor of Rome.

Religio Romano Beliefs

Roman Pagans worship the major Roman gods, such as Jupiter, Juno, and Diana, as well as nature spirits and Roman heroes. Some also honor older gods of Italy, such as the Etruscan gods. Like Hellenism, Roman Paganism is a devotional religion. Peace with the gods was of primary importance to the ancient Romans and they achieved it through sacrifices and offerings. Modern Roman Pagans say prayers and make offerings to their gods to ensure their favor.

Some people practice Greco-Roman Paganism, but according to most Roman Pagans, the two are quite different. While the gods have been assimilated to some degree, Roman Pagans worship them according to their preassimilation associations and myths.

Roman Pagans adhere to the values that were important to the ancient Roman state: dignity, dutifulness, and respectability. Piety toward the gods is especially important. Roman Pagans don't require initiation, but believe that simply worshipping in accordance with the old ways is enough to make you a Roman Pagan.

Religion Romano Practices

Because Roman Pagans no longer have access to the extensive temple system of ancient Rome, most of their worship is conducted on home altars called Laraiums, and family deities are especially revered. Any festivals to the gods are held on days dictated by the ancient Roman calendar. Some Roman Pagans also attempt to re-create the ancient mystery rites of the old religion based on what is known about them today.

The practice of magic is rare among Roman Pagans because it wasn't widely practiced by the ancient Romans. Instead of magic, Roman Pagans rely on offerings and prayer to help them receive assistance from the gods. Divination, on the other hand, is very common, as it was in ancient Rome, although the methods have been updated to fit the modern world.

Do I have to be Italian to practice Religio Romano?
No. None of the reconstructionist religions require that their adherents be of a specific ethnic descent. Having a personal or spiritual connection to a region is more important than having blood ties to its culture.

Thelema Faith

Thelema is not a re-creation of any ancient religion, but is instead based on the writings of Aleister Crowley, who is considered their prophet. Beginning in 1904, Crowley wrote a series of holy books while in a trance state and said he had received them from the spirit Aiwass. The central book is called *The Book of the Law*. The other books explain the text as well as the grades (or levels of spiritual ability and enlightenment) Thelemites can achieve.

The two most common Thelemic groups are the Ordo Templis Orientis (OTO) and the Argenteum Astrum (AA). The AA was founded by Crowley and he later became the leader of the OTO. Following his death, both groups suffered upheavals, but were revived in the 1960s and '70s.

Thelemic Beliefs

The governing principles of Thelema can be summed up as "Do what thou wilt shall be the whole of the law" and "Love is the law, love under will." Both phrases are credited to Crowley and are interpreted to mean that the goal of a Thelemite is determining his or her True Will, or life purpose, and living according to it. Interfering in the True Will of another person is taboo, and will result in a personal karmic backlash.

Thelemites also believe that each person has a soul and a guardian angel spirit. The soul reincarnates, its knowledge and wisdom evolving with each incarnation. Death is merely a transition, not the end of life.

Time is not counted according to the civil system. Thelemites believe that time consists of several epochs, which they call *aeons* (eons). Each aeon lasts up to 2,000 years and the spiritual and societal focus for each is different. The system is similar to the zodiacal ages. According to the zodiac, the earth is now entering the Age of Aquarius, a more peaceful and loving age than the previous age of Pisces. In Thelema, the New Aeon of Horus began in 1904 and has a similar nature to the Age of Aquarius.

Thelemic Practices

Because Thelemites believe that all religions ultimately derive from the same truths, they draw their practices from a variety of belief systems. All of their practices are designed to help Thelemites accomplish their life purposes. Some of the practices include meditation, prayer, astral projection, divination by I Ching and tarot, ritual, yoga, numerology, and tantric sex magic. Certain practices, such as higher levels of astral projection, are restricted to those who have achieved higher grades.

Thelemites honor the natural cycles of the sun, moon, and stars. Meditations and sun devotions are performed four times a day, along with twice-daily purification rituals. They pay homage to the star that was rising when they were born, and are aware of the lunar cycle, especially the new and full moon. Equinoxes and solstices are celebrated as holy days and some also honor the Celtic cross-quarter days.

In addition to natural holidays and observances, there are certain feasts unique to Thelema. The First Night of the Prophet and His Bride recognizes the marriage of Aleister Crowley and his wife with a feast on August 12. The Writing of the Book of the Law is celebrated with feasts on August 8, 9, and 10. The Supreme Ritual, commemorated with a feast on March 20, honors the invocation of the Aeon of Horus on that date in 1904 and marks the beginning of the Thelemic year.

Do-It-Yourself Paganism

Some Pagans don't adhere to any specific tradition, but instead refer to themselves simply as Pagans. They cobble together something that works for them by drawing on a variety of practices from various traditions. If you use Wiccan magic and shamanic meditation, but celebrate Kemetic holidays, you would be a DIY Pagan, and might identify yourself as an eclectic Pagan.

If you choose to borrow from various Pagan and Neo-Pagan faiths, it's important to respect the traditions you take from. For example, if you celebrate the Kemetic holidays, use Kemetic rituals during these celebrations. That doesn't mean you can't still celebrate the Wiccan sabbats, as long as you do so with Wiccan rituals.

> As with any religion, there are rigid traditionalists within Paganism who frown on new traditions. If you are attempting to establish a new tradition, don't claim a false lineage or purport that your beliefs and practices have descended intact for 1,000 years. Pagans respect historical honesty, even if you created your tradition yesterday.

Some DIY Pagans may be subjected to harsh criticism from people within the Pagan community. Unless you are making false claims, this shouldn't bother you. You are doing what is spiritually right for you, and that's all that matters. Besides, most modern traditions are in some way a blend or modification of older traditions. It would be impossible to practice the old religions exactly as they existed thousands of years ago because modern people don't have access to the same materials, and some practices are now forbidden by law.

Native American Traditions

Native Americans are most definitely not Neo-Pagan. A useful definition for their faiths is Paleo-Paganism, which means that their beliefs and practices descend directly from older ways and are indigenous to the people. Beliefs vary among the various tribes, but Native American beliefs are generally polytheistic and earth-centered.

As Neo-Paganism has evolved in the United States and Canada, some of the practices of Native Americans have been adopted by Neo-Pagans. It's not meant as an affront to Native Americans and is not an attempt to co-opt their beliefs. Instead it is intended as a sign of respect for the land spirits and related practices indigenous to the American continents.

Pagans can be grouped into three categories: Paleo-Pagan, Meso-Pagan, and Neo-Pagan. Some Wiccans, Druids, and Asatruar prefer to be called Meso-Pagans, while others accept the Neo-Pagan label. Santeríans and Vodounsis are properly considered Meso-Pagans. African Paganism, as practiced in Africa today, would be a Paleo-Pagan faith.

While some Native American practices work well within Neo-Paganism, others are best left to Native Americans, who have been raised with the traditions and know how to use them properly. Federal law in the United States also restricts certain practices to Native Americans. If you're unsure about a certain practice, and whether or not it's appropriate for your use as a non–Native American, contact a local tribe elder for advice.

Native American rituals are examples of practices that should be left to their people. If you attend a Native American ritual, you should fully participate in it, but don't try to re-create it later. Native American rituals are sacred acts and you won't be able to perform them properly if you haven't received the right training.

The U.S. government restricts the use of peyote, a hallucinogenic plant, and the ownership of feathers from birds of prey like eagles. Peyote may only be used within a religious context, and its use is usually limited to Native Americans. Many birds of prey are endangered, and restricting the ownership of their feathers reduces the temptation to hunt these beautiful birds to extinction. Native Americans, however, can use them in their traditional headdresses and garb because it is a part of their religion and they respect the great power of the birds.

Chapter 16

Neo-Pagan Ethics

Pagans in the movies and on television are sometimes depicted with questionable ethics, but these portrayals couldn't be farther from the truth. While Pagans lack a concept of sin, most do live their lives according to a code of ethics taught within their faith. And all Pagans recognize that they need to take personal responsibility for all their actions and the outcomes. Some Pagans have also adopted the concept of karma, the idea that each person's actions are part of a cause-and-effect system that will affect the future.

Personal Responsibility

Pagans do not have the option of confession to remove their spiritual or societal errors, nor do they believe that forgiveness should automatically follow a certain amount of penance. The rallying cry for Pagan ethics is personal responsibility. Whether you're acting to help or to harm, you must carefully consider all the effects of your actions, and be prepared to accept the consequences. Personal responsibility isn't all bad, though. It also means you get to accept the credit for good deeds. A reasonable amount of pride is a virtue among Pagans.

Every action you take affects others and yourself. Sometimes it's as simple as hurting someone's feelings, and a sincere apology will repair the damage. The first step is admitting that you were wrong. Then you can best decide how to proceed.

Most of the time you're aware that you're causing someone harm, but occasions do arise when you think you're helping someone, but really you're making things worse. It can be difficult to admit that you did more harm than good, but you must accept the reality of the situation. Once you acknowledge your error, you can get to work making up for it.

Most Pagans are aware of the Golden Rule, which states that you should do unto others as you would have them do unto you. The Golden Rule is often credited to the Christian Bible, but strains of it are found in nearly every culture and belief system, including Hindu, Confucian, and Greek. It seems to be a universal theory governing proper human relations, and it has been effective for millennia.

Karmic Consequences

Karma is a Hindu concept that has been adopted by many Westerners, especially those in the New Age and Pagan communities. While many people talk about karma, not everyone fully understands it. Its effects over several lifetimes are also often misunderstood.

What Is Karma?

Karma is the Hindu law of cause and effect. For every action you take, there is a reaction, although it's not equal and opposite. When you take beneficial action, you receive a beneficial effect. When you take baneful action, that will come back to you, too.

Your karma is a part of your soul, and it determines, in part, how your life will play out. If you live a just life, you will receive more just benefits. If something negative befalls you, look to your history and see what might have caused it.

Leftover Karma from Past Lives

The karmic backlash or reward for your actions is not always immediate. Sometimes it takes years to feel the full karmic effects of any action. The span of time between an action and its karmic effect can actually stretch over more than one lifetime. The actions you took in your past lives affect your current life to some degree. They might decide your role in this life, or how your life is lived. You can rest assured that really evil people will receive appropriate punishments in their future lives. Hopefully, you weren't a terrible person in your past life, but if you can't see any reason why so many things in your life seem to be going wrong, you might be dealing with retribution for mistakes you made in a previous life.

The Hindu concept of time is not strictly linear, so there can also be a karmic influence for an action you've not yet taken. Living the best life you can in order to balance out the negative weight on your karma is the best solution for dealing with karmic effects you had no role in creating in this life. A Hindu's goal in life is to carry out his dharma (duty). If you attempt to serve your life purpose, it will benefit your karma and counterbalance the mistakes of the past or future.

Wiccan Ethics

When discussing Pagan ethics, you will often hear people refer to the Law of Three and the Wiccan Rede. The Law of Three explains the results of actions, while the Wiccan Rede is a guide for taking correct action. It's important to know that these two rules apply mainly to Wiccans, although the original version of the Rede is also followed by Thelemites.

Law of Three

The Law of Three, also called the Rule of Three, is the concept that everything you put out returns to you threefold. This applies to physical action, magical action, and energy, and the effects are usually felt immediately.

Many Wiccans also consider the karmic effects of their actions. While the Law of Three has immediate effects, they dissipate quickly. Karma has longer-lasting effects, and most Wiccans believe that the two concepts together create a real picture of the effects of your actions on your soul.

According to the law, if you tell a lie, people will lie to you. If you cast a spell to make someone sprain her ankle, you'll probably break your ankle and be in a cast for three times as long. If you tend to be a sunny, positive person, you will attract three times as much positive energy. If you tend to be pessimistic and expect the worst, what you dread will come to pass, and it'll probably be three times as bad as you expected.

There are some exceptions to the rule. For example, if you bind someone to prevent him or her from causing you harm, you won't be harmed. You won't be able to cause that person harm, though, and that's not necessarily a bad thing. If you unintentionally cause harm, the effect won't be as intense as if you'd caused the harm on purpose.

Wiccan Rede

The Rede states, "An it harm none, do what thou wilt." While the language is archaic, the concept is not. First, it is important to define harm. Causing harm is not the same as causing hurt. Sometimes hurting someone is necessary to prevent him from coming to greater harm. For example, if you are in a relationship that's not working, you need to end it. While the person you're breaking up with will be hurt, not ending the relationship would ultimately cause both of you more harm because you would be miserable, and you wouldn't be able to start new, better relationships.

Where does the Wiccan Rede come from?
The Rede is taken from the works of Aleister Crowley. He originally phrased it as "Do what thou wilt shall be the whole of the law" and "Love is the law, love under will." Thelemites adhere to both rules when making ethical decisions.

While you should avoid harming others, it's not possible to completely avoid it. You probably kill a few flies every time you drive in your car. The key is to avoid causing intentional harm, or serious unintentional harm. If you are aware of your actions, you should be safe.

The Rede seems simple, but it gets tricky because harm doesn't only apply to others. "An it harm none" includes you. You can choose to bring yourself harm, for example, by smoking, but it's not wise. Try to avoid actions and activities that have the potential to bring you mental, emotional, or physical harm. At the same time, remember that life is full of risks and you can't live in a bubble just in case something might happen. If you use caution when necessary, and take risks when appropriate, you will manage to avoid harming yourself and others.

Asatruar Ethics

Asatruar have an extensive ethical system based on the Nine Noble Virtues, discussed in Chapter 7. The Virtues are courage, truth, honor, fidelity, discipline, hospitality, industriousness, self-reliance, and perseverance. They are drawn from one of the Eddas, the *Hávamál*.

When considering an action, Asatruar check to see how it lines up with the Nine Noble Virtues. Is the action courageous or meek? Is it honest? Will it detract from one's honor? Will an oath be broken as a result? Will the action be lazy or inhospitable? Do more creative solutions exist? And so on.

Not all nine virtues will apply to every possible action, but consider each point carefully. Sometimes two of the virtues might seem to be at odds; for example, if someone offers to help you with something, then you're not being self-reliant. But it might be more industrious to get help. And, if it's a task you thought you'd be able to do on your own, it takes courage to admit you need help and to accept it.

You should also remember the importance of oaths. Breaking an oath is the worst thing an Asatruar can do. Think carefully before making one so you don't have to break it.

If you're in doubt about the correctness of a certain action, go with your first instinct. Ethics can be black and white, but sometimes there are shades of gray and your intuition and the Nine Noble Virtues can guide you onto the correct path.

When studying the Nine Noble Virtues, read the *Hávamál* for greater insight into how they should be applied. If you can't decide how to proceed, you might find the answer there. You could also ask the runes if some action is correct and what the outcome will be. The runes may reveal the will of the gods, or they might reveal your subconscious leanings. Your subconscious usually knows the right answer, even if your conscious mind doesn't.

Druidic Ethics

Aside from the central concepts of respect and tolerance, Druids subscribe to several other ethical guidelines. The Universal Druid Prayer can be seen as a guideline for life. Druids have also developed several Celtic virtues based on ancient lore. You may also hear Druids refer to the triads when making ethical choices.

The concept of harmony is the central component of all Druidic ethics. Harmony and balance maintain the interconnection of everything.

Each element in the natural world cannot exist without the other elements. Druids honor the sacredness of the natural world and humans when making ethical considerations.

Universal Druid Prayer

The Universal Druid Prayer, originally written by Iolo Morgannwg states:

Grant, O God, Thy protection;
And in protection, strength;
And in strength, understanding;
And in understanding, knowledge;
And in knowledge, the knowledge of justice;
And in the knowledge of justice, the love of it;
And in that love, the love of all existences;
And in the love of all existences, the love of God.
God and all goodness.

*Some groves substitute "God and Goddess" or "Goddess" in the first, eighth, and ninth lines.

From this prayer, you can extract several important characteristics every person should practice: strength, understanding, knowledge, justice, and love. When considering whether or not an action is ethical, think about those five traits and see if your action adheres to them. Are you drawing on your inner strength and the strength of the gods? Do you understand all the implications of the actions? Do you have all the necessary knowledge to render a proper decision? Is the action just? Is it an act of love? Ultimately all correct actions are acts of love.

Celtic Virtues

The Celtic Virtues are strength, truth, and generosity. Many Druids expand on these and recognize six Celtic Virtues: honor, loyalty, hospitality, honesty, justice, and courage. Wisdom is often added as the seventh.

Strength encompasses courage, as well as physical strength. Courage is mental and emotional strength, and this is often more important than physical strength. Strength in your heart and in your correct intent are vital to ethical action.

Members of Ár nDraíocht Féin (ADF) have additional ethical guidelines in the form of nine virtues: wisdom, piety, vision, courage, integrity, perseverance, hospitality, moderation, and fertility. You may notice similarities between the ADF virtues and the Asatru virtues. The nine ADF virtues are also considered an expansion of the six Celtic Virtues.

Truth includes honor, loyalty, honesty, and justice. You must speak the truth, know the truth, understand the truth, and remain loyal to the truth. By doing all this, you maintain your honor. Without knowledge of the truth, there can be no justice. Be true to yourself, and also be true to your friends, relatives, and other grove members. If you make a promise, stick to it.

Hospitality and generosity are closely connected. By being generous with guests, you are showing them hospitality. You should also be generous of spirit when dealing with other people. Allow them room to be who they are. Hospitality is shown to the gods and other spirits by honoring the elements and the earth, and by doing what you can to prevent harm from coming to either.

Wisdom develops over time and comprises a deep understanding of all the virtues and how they should be applied. When you have wisdom, you usually know the correct action automatically. Wisdom also brings with it a certain degree of humility.

Celtic Triads

Celtic lore is filled with triads, which are simple statements that can act as ethical guidelines or statements of Celtic values and tradition. You often see triads stitched onto samplers or hear them repeated by Irish people. A typical triad reads: "Three words of counsel: know thy power, know thy wisdom, know thy time."

Here is another Celtic Triad that you should keep in mind when deciding if you are acting wisely: "Three things that ruin wisdom: ignorance, inaccurate knowledge, forgetfulness."

There are hundreds of triads, and if you need help determining whether or not an action is correct, look to them for advice. While the statements are simple, they contain deep wisdom. Usually it is basic common sense, but when facing a difficult question, common sense sometimes gets tossed out the window.

Ethics of Other Traditions

Other types of Pagan faith have their own ethical guidelines. Vodoun and Santería ethics are somewhat related to Catholic concepts about sin. The only ethical consideration for shamanism is respect for the earth and the spirit realm. Kemeticism, Hellenism, and the Religio Romano all offer their followers a slightly different take on ethics.

Kemetic Ethics

Kemetics are governed by the concept of ma'at, the same concept that also governed the lives of the ancient Egyptians. *Ma'at* means "right order" or "balance." Ma'at is also the name of the Goddess who judges your soul at death. If you have lived your life with balance and sought to maintain order and do what was right, then you will be rewarded.

Guidelines for what is right are hard to come by, but your intuition is a powerful tool. You should also look to how the ancient people lived, and adjust those concepts to modern needs. You don't need to give a certain amount of your harvest to the pharaoh, but making offerings to the gods will help you maintain ma'at. Recognizing the source of all things and living in honor of those who created life will help you live in balance.

Hellenic Ethics

Hellenes adhere to the virtues of reciprocity, hospitality, and moderation. Reciprocity is similar to the Golden Rule, and Hellenes generally approach other people as they expect to be approached. They also treat people the way others treat them. If you treat a Hellene with generosity, he or she will be generous with you. If you are shifty or dishonest, Hellenes see no problem with acting in kind.

Hospitality was very important to the Greeks. Many legends tell of the generosity of the Greek people toward strangers, who sometimes turned out to be gods. It is appropriate Hellene conduct to welcome guests with food and drink and to do your best to make them comfortable.

While Senistrognata (Celtic Reconstructionists) don't agree with all modern Druidic beliefs and practices, they do adhere to the same six Celtic Virtues as the Druids. Some also expand the virtues out to nine, and may call them the Nine Noble Virtues.

Moderation is another Hellenic virtue, but it is one that can become confusing. Self-control and balance are both a part of moderation, but Hellenes also celebrate some holidays that are antithetical to self-control and balance. Use your own judgment in deciding when and how moderation is appropriate.

Religio Romano

Roman Pagans adopt numerous virtues, some of which are private, some of which are public. Piety is in some ways both public and private. Pious Roman Pagans show respect and honor for the gods as well as their nation. When being pious to your nation, you should act according to the prevailing laws, but at the same time you should work to ensure that those laws are just. Other Roman virtues relate to ideals that benefit others, such as generosity and hospitality, and ideals that benefit the self, such as frugality and dignity.

The Matter of Hexes

There is some debate about hexes, and whether or not they are appropriate for Neo-Pagan use. It's important to understand what a hex actually is before deciding whether or not it is appropriate or determining if you've been hexed.

What Is a Hex?

A hex is usually defined as a spell or charm designed to harm a specific person. Fairy-tale witches often use hexes to turn people into toads or cause fair maidens to fall into a deathly slumber after biting an apple or pricking her finger on a spindle. Hexes in the modern world are more likely to take the form of a spell to puncture someone's tire or to cause them to break out with hives or acne.

A hex can be cast from afar, or it may require close contact with the actual victim. In some instances, the hex works due to the ingestion of harmful substances. In other cases, the hex works because the victim believes it will. Sometimes a hex works because karma or the Law of Three has kicked in.

Are Hexes Ever Okay?

Whether or not a hex is okay depends on your path and your purpose. If you belong to Wicca, Asatru, or Druidry, hexes are unlikely to be acceptable or advisable. Traditional witches, ceremonial magicians, and Hellenes do not abide by similar restrictions and are willing to use hexes to gain retribution. Vodounsis and Santeríans also have specific beliefs relating to hexes. Generally Santeríans are not allowed to use hexes, but there is a related black magic practice called Palo Mayombe that does rely on hexes. Vodounsis are sometimes willing to use hexes for personal gain or retribution.

What should you do if you are tempted to use a hex? Consider why it's necessary. Did another woman steal your man? Let her guilt do the dirty work and don't sully your own hands with a curse. Did someone you know bust out all the windows on your car? Call the cops. Once again, no curse necessary. But what if you don't know who broke your windows? In that case, you might want to cast a spell asking that he be caught and brought to justice. It's not a hex, because you're not stipulating the form of punishment, and justice is not an incorrect motive.

You might hear the term Hexcraft used in conjunction with Asatruar or practitioners of American folk magic. Hexcraft refers to the creation and posting of certain symbols that serve as wards against evil or negative energy and people. You might see these symbols hanging on country barns and over doors and windows.

There might also be times when you're tempted to hex someone in the heat of the moment. For example, if you've been stabbed, you might yell out a curse so a similar fate will befall your attacker. That is a hex, but if the attacker does receive a similar injury, it's also probably due to karma and not your heated words.

What If I've Been Cursed?

Curses and hexes are not common among Neo-Pagans, and their use is decreasing among Vodounsis and Santeríans, so it's unlikely that you've really been cursed. If everything in your life seems to be going wrong, take a long look at your choices and attitudes. Are you doing something to draw all this negativity to you? If that's the case, change your attitudes and things will get better.

If you really have been cursed—for example, if someone has cast a spell to make you love her—then you should do a counterspell. A binding to prevent that person from harming you any further is the best option, and then it should be followed by a firm dumping and orders to never contact you again.

Chapter 17

The Role of Magic

Magic is a tool used by members of most Pagan faiths. Unfortunately, magic is misunderstood and often feared by many outside the Pagan community, sometimes because they believe the depictions in movies and TV shows, and sometimes because they aren't aware of the rules regarding its use. Pagans don't use magic frivolously. Before attempting to use magic, it's important to understand what it is and how to use it properly.

What Is Magic?

The lure of magic attracts many to Paganism. It seems spooky and fantastic, the thing that will get you everything you want without any serious effort, but you probably wonder how you can acquire the "supernatural powers" necessary for doing magic. Here's a news flash: Magic is not supernatural, and you don't need special abilities. Anyone can do magic; all it takes is the will and the skill.

Magic is a tool for change. In order to create change, you manipulate the natural elements of earth, air, fire, water, and spirit and ask the gods or the universe for help. Any time you do magic, you are causing change. If you cast a spell to attract love, your goal is to change from your current single state. If you do a spell to prevent change, your goal is to alter the chain of events that would have caused it.

When you read metaphysical books, you'll notice that some authors use the alternative spelling *magick*. They do this to differentiate magic performed by Pagans from the magic performed by illusionists like Penn and Teller. Many Pagan authors are shifting back to the original spelling, magic, because they feel most people can recognize the difference without the extra letter.

Two of the most common forms of magic are prayers and spells. Prayers are magic when you make a request for change, such as asking the goddess to quell your urge to toss your computer out the window when it crashes for the fourth time in an hour. Spells are the more common form of magic, but usually require advance planning. Spells can also be done off-the-cuff, but it's best to wait until you have a lot of experience with them. Once you've learned the color correspondences and moon phase associations and mastered meditation or visualization, you can grab a candle and go. With practice, magic becomes second nature, just one more tool in your life-changing arsenal.

"Hollywood" Magic

Magic has always been a popular topic for movies and television shows. Most of the time, what you see in the popular media has little to do with real magic. Real magic is actually very boring to watch. Streams of light won't shoot from your wand, and you can't fly on your household broom unless you jump off the roof with it, and even then the ride will only last the few seconds between launch and smacking into the ground. Despite what you might have seen on TV, witches can't teleport or throw people across the room with a flick of the hand.

Then there are all those fantastic scenes with fires blazing under cauldrons and candles left burning unattended. Very poor fire safety. If you do a spell that involves fire of any kind, always be careful. Fire is powerful when used properly, but you're unlikely to be able to continue your spell after you've set your carpet on fire.

On rare occasions, you will see magic in the media that is almost factually correct, or at least humanly possible. Some shows also follow proper magical ethics, but again, this is rare. Don't assume something is okay, or forbidden, just because you saw it on TV, and consult a nonfiction book or a person who knows what she's doing before attempting a spell you saw on TV, because TV shows and movies often skip important steps.

Even though it's clearly fantasy, the classic TV show *Bewitched* offers good lessons on the appropriate uses of magic and what can go wrong when you use it incorrectly. Unfortunately, Dr. Bombay can't fix your mistakes if you make them in the real world.

Types of Magic

Over the years, several types of magic have proven to be especially effective: sympathetic, natural, ceremonial, and sexual. All are useful for spells, but some require more preparation or skill than others. Elements from one type can sometimes be used with other types.

Both natural and sympathetic magic could also be termed *folk magic,* and are used by Wiccans and Asatruar. Wiccans may occasionally use ceremonial magic or use tools from ceremonial magic with natural magic, but it's more popular among Thelemites and members of orders like Ordo Templis Orientis and the Golden Dawn. Sex magic is practiced mostly by Wiccans.

A glamour is a spell to alter the appearance of something, but it does not cause a physical change. Instead the change is in how others perceive it. For example, if an attacker was approaching you, you could cast a glamour to make yourself vanish from his field of vision, but you wouldn't really be invisible.

Sympathetic Magic

Sympathetic magic is the oldest form of magic, the form used by prehistoric peoples. This type of magic uses objects or actions to represent the desired objects or actions. For example, if you want it to rain, sprinkle water or run your shower.

Sympathetic magic seems simple, but in reality it can be difficult. Effecting change by example and will alone requires a deep connection to nature and the gods. The ancient hunters who re-enacted the hunt were using sympathetic magic, but they had a much stronger connection to the earth than modern people who live in homes with electricity and buy food in stores.

Natural Magic

Natural magic uses many of the tools and techniques mentioned in the chapters on Wicca to effect change. An effective natural magic spell will include the right colors and should be held during a propitious moon phase, day of the week, or within the right astrological sign. Candles are especially useful for directing and focusing energy. Drumming, dancing, and chanting are powerful methods for raising energy.

Natural magic is suitable for any purpose. For example, if you have received an unexpected bill and have trouble coming up with the funds, you could burn a green candle, mark a copy of the bill with money oil, ask the gods to help you pay it, visualize yourself paying it, and then burn it to send your request to the universe. If you want to add sympathetic magic to this spell, you could write "paid" on the bill as a symbol of your intention.

Ceremonial Magic

Ceremonial magic is the most complicated type of magic. A ceremonial magician attempts to gain control over other nonhuman entities and instruct them to do his or her will. Control is acquired via strict and elaborate sets of steps that vary according to the practitioner's purpose.

While ceremonial magic relies on some of the tools of natural magic, such as colored cords, oils, or candles, each of the tools adheres to specific requirements. In natural magic, practitioners can change the words to suit their own purposes or use a different colored cord in a pinch. Ceremonial magic doesn't allow for such variations.

In 1531, Henry Cornelius Agrippa published *Three Books of Occult Philosophy,* a compendium of natural and ceremonial magic techniques and theory. It has since been reprinted, with notes to help you understand the old terms and associations.

Sex Magic

Sex magic is commonly used with natural magic, but it can be used exclusively. During sex magic, the magician's arousal raises and focuses energy. That energy is released at orgasm and from there it merges with the energy of the universe to bring the practitioner's desire to fruition. Sex magic can be done solo, or with a partner. When performing sex magic with a partner, it is best to reach simultaneous orgasm, but it's not necessary.

Sex magic can be used for a sex-related goal like the conception of a child, but it can also be used for any other purpose, like buying a house. If you are doing sex magic with a partner, your goal should be something you both desire. If you're working toward a personal goal, masturbation would be a better option. Be aware that the energy raised and released during sex magic is very potent. Use an additional method of birth control if you and your partner don't want to conceive.

If you want to combine sex magic and natural magic, burn colored candles associated with your goal and do the spell during the appropriate moon phase and on the right day of the week. You can also burn incenses or anoint each other with oils suited to your goal. Unless you invoke your matron and patron deities, any gods you call should be related to your purpose.

Witch's Pyramid

The witch's pyramid is the key to successful magic. Each concept at the bottom of the pyramid—to know, to will, to dare, and to keep silent—is necessary for a spell to achieve the best outcome. Ignoring one of the concepts can prevent the practitioner's spell from working as well as it could, or could cancel its effects altogether.

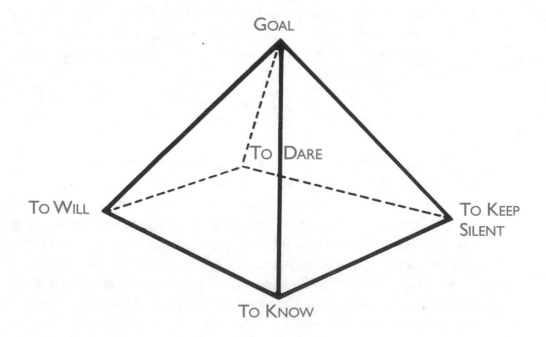

▲ Using the concepts of the Witch's Pyramid will help your spell be successful.

To Know

To know means that you have a clear objective. Before doing a spell, you need to be able to easily and fully visualize your goal. Items to visualize include what your goal will look like (if it's an object) and how you will feel once you've achieved your goal. You can also visualize yourself completing the steps necessary for acquiring it. For example, if you are doing a spell for a new job, you would visualize yourself finding good leads, sending out the perfect resume, going on a fantastic interview, and accepting the perfect offer. You could then go another step and visualize yourself happily working at your new job.

To Will

To will means to deeply want to achieve your goal, so that your desire will be clear in your spell. Doubts may weaken your will and the results of the spell. For example, if you're doing a spell for that new job, but you're scared that your spell might not work right, or a part of you worries about whether or not you'll be able to handle the new responsibilities, then your fears will interfere with your intent and the spell won't work.

Once you do a spell, it is very important that you also take the necessary real-world steps to help you achieve your goal. If you cast a new job spell but don't check the want ads and send out resumes, it's going to take a lot longer for your spell to work, if it works at all.

To Dare

To dare means you have the courage to do the spell. You have the inner strength to handle any unexpected consequences, as well as the courage to do what needs to be done in the material world to achieve your desired result. It also means that you won't refuse to accept what you've asked for once it's been offered. For example, if you cast a spell for a new job that's a bit of a reach, you must have the courage to apply for those jobs and the ability to step up to the plate once your desire is fulfilled.

To Keep Silent

To keep silent means that you can't talk about the spell or think too much about it once it's completed. You almost have to forget about it entirely. Once your spell is done, do something completely unrelated. Go see a movie, clean your bathroom, or read a book. Get your mind off the spell so you don't analyze it, looking for anything you did wrong or allowing doubts to creep up on you. If you start to doubt your spell, you'll weaken its energy. If you tell people about the spell, their doubts could also corrupt it.

Magical Ethics

Magic itself is neither negative nor positive; it is simply energy. People often refer to negative or positive magic, but what they actually mean is that the intention of the person doing the magic is negative or positive—the terms positive and negative magic are a shorthand way of speaking. Black magic is another term for magic performed with a negative intent, and white magic is often used to describe magic performed with a beneficial intent. Both forms of magic have ethical considerations that can shift a seemingly positive spell into the realm of negative magic. Manipulation, permission, and personal benefit are all elements of magical ethics.

Avoid Manipulation Magic

Manipulation should be avoided for two reasons. First, manipulating people with magic interferes with their free will. If the desired action isn't something she would do without being under the influence of magic, making her do it through the use of magic is akin to rape. Second, there is an element of "do unto others as you would have done to you" in magic. If you wouldn't want someone to use a certain spell on you, don't use it on another person.

It might be tempting to use magic to halt a friend's self-destructive activities, but unfortunately, it's not a good idea. Even though you see it as beneficial to him, it's still manipulation. And it's possible that he's in the middle of an important life lesson. Interfering might halt the lesson, which means he'll have to learn some other way later, and the second lesson could be worse.

Manipulation is a consideration for all those who practice pagan faiths, but it is an important concern for Wiccans. According to Wiccan rules, magic should never be used to intentionally manipulate the will of another person, even if it seems like the right thing to do.

Unintended manipulation should also be avoided. For example, if you are trying to buy a house, you could visualize yourself finding the house of your dreams, but you shouldn't visualize the owner of a specific house putting a "For Sale" sign on the front lawn. The best way to avoid unintended manipulation is to say "I do this for the good of all" at the end of every spell. That way, if you made an error in your spell, the effect of it will be mitigated.

Get Permission First

It is generally unwise to do spells for the benefit of others, but sometimes it's necessary. Whenever possible, get permission to do the spell first. For example, if your friend has cancer, ask if you can send him healing energy or do a healing spell. If he says no, don't do it. He has his reasons. If he's unconscious, you can send the energy or do the spell, but include a statement that allows his higher spirit to reject the energy or spell if he doesn't need or want it.

Permission gets complicated when children are involved. If they're your children and they're under the age of twelve, then the choice is up to you. If they're someone else's children, then you should ask their parents for permission. Child abuse is the exception. In this case, you probably won't be able to get permission from the child to act on her behalf. You also won't be able to get permission from the abuser. Even without permission, you should cast a protection spell on the child, and then call the authorities.

Personal Benefit

Contrary to what you might have seen on TV, it is perfectly acceptable to use magic for personal gain. Magic for personal gain is usually called "low magic," as opposed to "high magic," which is a spell for something on a greater scale, like world peace. Both types of magic have places in your life.

It's a good idea to balance your use of high magic and low magic. Always acting for the benefit of the world will deplete your energy. Always acting for the benefit of yourself makes you seem greedy and the gods will force balance on you. It's also good to make an offering to thank the gods after you've received a personal benefit from the spell.

Take Precautions

Before doing a spell, consider your actions carefully. Ask yourself several questions to make sure your spell is necessary, correct, avoids manipulation, and has a clear goal. You should also use your preferred divination method to confirm that it will have the desired outcome and see if there are any warnings against doing the spell. If the cards or runes warn against the spell, don't do it! Go back and check the spell for anything you missed, then rewrite it and check again.

Is It Necessary?

Before you do a spell, ask yourself if it's necessary. Is it something trivial, or is it something you really need? Is there another way to get what you want? For example, if you want to lose weight, you could cast a spell to make your pounds melt away, but what's the use of being thin if you're too tired to do anything because you don't exercise and your diet is poor? A better option would be to eat better and exercise regularly. Then you wouldn't need to do a spell.

Is It the Correct Action?

Sometimes a spell seems necessary, but doing it might not be the correct action. For example, if your job is in trouble, you could do a spell to secure it, but what if the company you work for isn't financially sound? You'll still have your job, but you might not get paid for doing it.

Carefully consider the correctness of any magical action before you take it. List any other possible goals or ways of wording your goal that might be better. In the previous example, you could ask for a new job that's similar to your old job, but with a financially stable company. If your job is in trouble because of something you did, do a spell to help you correct the problem. If it isn't clear whether or not an action is correct, it's better to wait until you've come up with a goal that is clearly correct than to risk taking the wrong action.

Love spells are one of the trickiest types of magic. If you cast a love spell on a specific person, you might get what you want, but the gods will make you pay for it, and it won't be fun. It's better to cast a spell to draw love into your life and allow the gods to bring the right person to you.

Am I Manipulating Anyone?

When considering a spell, make sure it won't manipulate anyone else. Avoiding manipulation also ties in to making sure it's the correct action and it's necessary. For example, if your relationship is in trouble and you suspect it's because your partner is cheating, you could cast a spell to keep him from straying, but this spell raises two problems. First, you're interfering with his free will. Second, even if he stops cheating, you still haven't solved the problem that caused him to cheat in the first place. It would be better to do a spell to help you heal your relationship, and then talk to your partner.

If you're being careful to take the correct action, and to ensure that it's necessary, it's much easier to avoid manipulating someone. If there is no way to avoid manipulating someone by doing the spell, then maybe you shouldn't do it. (An exception to the manipulation rule applies when someone is causing you personal harm. In this case, you can bind her from harming you further.)

Am I Clear on the Desired Outcome?

Finally, before you cast a spell, make sure your desired outcome is crystal clear. For example, you need money to pay your bills and several people owe you money, but instead of casting a spell specifically to bring back the money owed you, you cast a general spell to draw money to you. You'll get the money, but it might come in the form of a lump-sum severance check. Before doing a spell, make sure you've made it specific enough without making it too specific. You could write "All loans I've made to others will be repaid in the next month," but not, "Bob will pay me back Tuesday." By being specific but not too specific, you leave room for the gods to choose the best way to bring you your desire. And sometimes, it's not what you expected. Someone might repay a loan you'd forgotten about.

Chapter 18

Neo-Pagan Sexuality

At the mere mention of Neo-Pagan sexuality, most people conjure images of wild orgies in forests and drunken, drugged-out sex parties. While Pagans are more sexually open-minded than the average person, that doesn't mean they lack sexual morals and don't form long-term relationships. Pagans are very tolerant of homosexuality, BDSM, polyamory, and other forms of alternative sexuality, but they are still moral and are just as interested in finding love as non-Pagans.

The Neo-Pagan Nymphomaniac

The myth of the Neo-Pagan nymphomaniac is one of the many misconceptions about paganism and pagan women. Male Pagans are subjected to this stereotype less often, but they might receive questions about how often they have sex with all those wild Pagan women. Unfortunately, men who get involved with Neo-Paganism in order to get laid are soon disappointed to learn that the Neo-Pagan nymphomaniac myth is just that—a myth.

While it is true that some Pagans are more open to sexual experimentation than non-Pagans, and Pagans are certainly very tolerant of alternative sexualities, wild Pagan orgies are not nightly occurrences. Most Pagans were raised by non-Pagans and grew up in sexually restrictive societies, so they have to deal with all the same issues as non-Pagans. They also have to deal with the same concerns about safe sex, consensual sex, and appropriate sexual activity as everyone else in modern society.

This chapter focuses on Neo-Pagan sexuality in the United States. Western Europe and the United States have very different attitudes toward sex, with Western Europe being much more progressive.

This is not to say that Pagans don't enjoy sex. They certainly do. But even though some Neo-Pagan holidays celebrate sexuality, the religion isn't about sex. If you encounter a Neo-Pagan group that requires sexual initiation or seems to have been formed so the leader can have sex with nubile young women, run far, run fast. That's not Neo-Paganism. That's a sex club, and a not very balanced one at that.

Neo-Pagan Sexual Mores

Due to centuries of sexual oppression and negative sexual attitudes, as well as the more recent exploitive representations in the media, many Pagans were raised with conflicting messages about sex. On the one hand, sex is a sin. On the other hand, sex is fun and everyone is doing it. You have to respect everyone's sexual freedom, but not if it's outside the norm. Huh?

Pagans take a different approach to sexuality. The first hurdle most Pagans face is overcoming all the sexual stereotypes and judgmental attitudes society has spoon-fed them, but because Pagans are outside-the-box thinkers to begin with, it's not a difficult hurdle to jump. Instead of judgment and criticism, when it comes to sexuality Pagans promote respect and tolerance.

Respect Yourself and Others

The goddess plays an important role in Neo-Paganism, and because of that, most Pagan men are very respectful of women. It also helps that many Pagan men and women either were part of the 1970s feminist movement or were raised by parents who respected its goals.

Neo-Pagan sexuality centers around respect: respect for physical needs, physical health, and the gods who gave us our body. Masturbation has no negative associations, because Pagans understand that each person is a sexual being with sexual needs. Sublimating them because of outdated ideas about sin is not emotionally, mentally, or physically healthy.

Sex can be a sacred act. It's important to understand that while the gods want you to enjoy your sexual nature, they don't want you to endanger your health or do something you're not comfortable with just because you're Pagan and other Pagans are doing it. Respect your own comfort levels, and others will, too.

Practice Tolerance

Neo-Paganism is an alternative religion, albeit a large and growing one, and therefore attracts many people interested in alternative sexuality. Monogamy, homosexuality, bisexuality, BDSM, and polyamory all have a place within Neo-Paganism.

Tolerance, or acceptance without judgment, is the rule in Neo-

Paganism. Pagans understand that just because you might not be drawn to certain sexual activities conducted between adults, that doesn't mean it's wrong or immoral. At the same time, it's not expected that just because you're Pagan, you have to experiment with your own sexuality.

> Transgendered people are welcome members of Neo-Pagan society, whether they are preop, postop, or still trying to decide whether or not to undergo the operation. They are not discussed in this chapter because transsexuality is a gender identity issue rather than a sexuality issue.

Marriage and Divorce

Pagans get married and divorced, just like non-Pagans. Like other religions, Pagans have developed ceremonies to celebrate their unions, but they have also created ceremonies to recognize separations. Many Pagans choose to marry non-Pagans, or are already married to non-Pagans when they come to the faith, and both situations present special challenges and concerns.

Wedding Ceremony

When Pagans decide to form a permanent union, they do so with as much—or as little—fanfare as everyone else. Some get a quickie marriage or a civil union document from the courthouse, while others spend months planning a wedding and reception to be attended by friends and family. The difference is not in how they do it, but in what is said at the ceremony.

Unlike most major religions, there is no standard Neo-Pagan wedding ceremony. You can find books and Web sites that provide a framework, and each tradition within Neo-Paganism has certain wedding customs that are a part of the ceremony or reception, but Pagans usually write most of their wedding ceremonies and ask their group leaders or other friends to officiate for them. There are Pagan ministers licensed to perform ceremonies, but it's a legal designation and doesn't necessarily connote religious ordination. State laws governing who can and can't officiate a wedding vary, so check with your state's marriage license office before choosing someone to officiate your wedding.

Another difference between Pagan weddings and non-Pagan weddings is the length of the commitment. If you and your partner don't want to get legally married, you have the option of making an informal marriage lasting a year or more. You could also have a religious wedding ceremony, and then later get legally married at city hall. If you're gay, you can celebrate your commitment with a Pagan wedding ceremony and Pagans recognize the marriage as valid.

Wiccans and Druids sometimes refer to their weddings as handfastings, and being married as handfasted, because the couple's hands are ritually bound during the ceremony. It is believed to be an old Irish custom restored to modern day. You might also see it in Irish Catholic wedding ceremonies. A handparting ends a handfasting.

Separating Ceremony

As with marriages between non-Pagans, sometimes Pagan marriages don't work out. Pagans have the same separation options as non-Pagans. They recognize that ending a marriage is as serious an undertaking as getting married, and some choose to hold a separation ceremony to formally end their spiritual union.

Separation ceremonies are also usually written by the couple, but they don't need to be presided over by a legally recognized officiant even if the couple is receiving a legal divorce. The ceremonies are sometimes performed before the couple's coven, kindred, or grove, or before friends and families, but can also be performed in private. The ceremonies are designed to help couples amicably end their relationship and ease the emotional pain that accompanies breakups.

Marriage Between Pagans and Non-Pagans

Interfaith marriages are becoming more common. There are many more female than male Pagans, so finding a Pagan mate can be difficult for women. If you can't find a mate who is a member of your faith, look for one who accepts it. You may not be able to fully share your spirituality, but it's important to respect each other's beliefs. You can attend each other's religious ceremonies, and even have a mixed wedding ceremony.

If you're already married, becoming Pagan together is easy, but if your partner doesn't share your devotion, it poses a challenge for you. First, make sure becoming Pagan is what you really want to do. Second, explain your new beliefs to your partner clearly. Emphasize that it doesn't change your feelings toward your partner or your marriage. Give your partner time to get used to the idea. You might invite your partner to attend a ritual with you so he or she can get a better understanding of it.

Sometimes non-Pagans simply can't accept that their partners have joined a new religion that they don't understand. If you've given your partner ample time to accept your beliefs and he or she refuses, you have to decide whether your marriage or your faith is more important to you. Give yourself time to choose with your head and avoid making an emotional outburst or giving an ultimatum. There's no right or wrong here, only what is right for you, your marriage, and your family.

Homosexuality and Bisexuality

Alternative sexuality is not a new practice. It has been found in many ancient cultures. The Greeks were especially notable for their fluid sexuality. Homosexuals are as welcome in Neo-Paganism as heterosexuals. Homosexuality is not considered a sin, nor an aberrant choice, but simply a part of who you are. No heterosexual Pagan will ever try to "fix" a homosexual. There's also no concept of "love the sinner, hate the sin." Homosexuals are accepted totally and without judgment.

Because Pagans embrace homosexuality as a valid lifestyle, homosexuals are a growing segment of the community. Some homosexuals, whether lesbian or gay, form their own worship and study groups within the various traditions. At the same time, homosexuals aren't steered toward, or excluded from, specific traditions, with the possible exception of certain Wiccan groups that emphasize gender polarity.

Groups that are exclusively homosexual, or have homosexual members, either don't stress gender polarity or recognize that all people have both masculine and feminine sides. Both men and women produce estrogen, progesterone, and testosterone. In an exclusively lesbian group, one of you could adopt the masculine role for the duration of a ritual if you were invoking a god.

Some Neo-Pagan mythology might present you with a challenge if you're gay because much of it is based on heterosexual gender roles and interaction. A few pantheons, such as the Hindu pantheon, have gods that have no gender and sexually interact with both genders. There are also gods who switch genders or encompass both genders at once.

Keeping in mind the gods that switch genders or are portrayed as bisexual, bisexuality is also accepted within Neo-Paganism. Like homosexuals, bisexuals are a growing segment of the Neo-Pagan community. It is simply one more facet of the multi-sexual Neo-Pagan culture.

Neo-Paganism and BDSM

BDSM is an acronym for three interrelated types of alternative sexuality. These types are domination/submission, bondage/discipline, and sadism/masochism. Some Pagans use the latter two in ritual to raise energy or achieve an ecstatic trance state similar to the one created by sex in sex magic. It could be said to be another form of sex magic, but sex is not always a part of BDSM.

BDSM may seem confusing or strange to those who don't participate in it, but it works for those who do. People who enjoy BDSM can be found in all walks of life, and are not exclusively Pagan. BDSM may be one aspect of a Pagan's spirituality, but it is not always tied to spirituality.

BDSM is very subjective, and attitudes and beliefs about it and how to practice it vary from community to community. If the BDSM community you find doesn't mesh with your own preferences, keep looking until you find one that does.

Domination and Submission

Domination and submission, usually called D/s, is not always sexual in nature, and may or may not involve pain or restraints. D/s usually refers to the actual relationship, as opposed to the actions within that relationship. In a D/s relationship, you willingly give control over your body and your choices to another person, with prearranged limits, or you accept control over another person and all the coincident responsibilities. One party becomes the submissive, and the other the dominant. It is always a choice, and the choice to end a D/s relationship, or to refuse to do something, is yours.

D/s is about control, and submissives are often people who have a great deal of power or control in the day-to-day world. Submissives enjoy the feeling of not having to make choices or decisions, of being subject to the will of another. For many it is a release from their "real world" mindset.

Bondage and Domination

Bondage and Domination, usually called B&D, is often more sexual or physical in nature. In B&D, a dominant physically restrains a submissive. These restraints may simply be a form of deprivation or mental restraints or control, or they may be a precursor to spankings, whippings, or another form of physical punishment. Degradation and humiliation are other forms of control. It's important to know that control/punishment is not an excuse for physical abuse and should never be carried out in anger. When used in magic, the deprivation or pain from the control/punishment produces excitement and endorphins that raise large amounts of energy that can then be channeled into magical purposes.

Sadism and Masochism

Sadism and Masochism is usually called S&M. Pain is the goal of S&M. The sadist enjoys giving pain, and the masochist enjoys receiving pain. Aspects of B&D may also play a part in the experience. As with D/s and B&D, the choice to begin or end the experience lies in the receiver. Once again, the pain produced by S&M can induce powerful energy that can be channeled in magic.

Some people choose to enter into a full-time Master/slave relationship. The choice to become a slave is made freely, and can be rescinded at the end of a specified length of time, or in whatever way is mutually agreed upon.

Safe BDSM

BDSM requires a vast amount of trust. You are placing your physical, mental, and emotional well-being in the hands of another person, or accepting responsibility for the well-being of someone else. Safe, sane, and consensual BDSM is the key to ensuring well-being, whether you are dominant or submissive. Some important guidelines to remember:

- Know who you're playing with. Get to know the person outside of play before agreeing to play. Get references from others in the community if you can.
- Establish "safe words" that indicate you want to stop. It should be an uncommon word, but not difficult to remember. The most accepted safe word at public playhouses is "red."
- Use caution if any body fluids will be exchanged. Be especially careful with any play that draws blood.
- Become a part of a BDSM community or club. The other members watch out for new members and help them find safe people to play with. Pagan BDSM communities are beginning to evolve within the larger communities.

- Don't attempt to resolve relationship issues during BDSM play. Don't bring your anger or fear into play if you're the dominant.
- Always remember that BDSM is about consent and you are responsible for your own well-being. Think before you enter into any agreement.

Relationships with Multiple Partners

Polyamory, the practice of having many romantic partners, is becoming more prevalent in Neo-Paganism. People who engage in polyamory may establish a stable primary relationship first and then bring others into the mix, but this isn't always the case.

Polyamory is not the same as "swinging." Some polyamorists join in long-term group marriages, which is often called polyfidelity. Polyamory is not simply about sex; it is about love. Polyamorous people recognize that they are capable of loving more than one person at a time, and they don't want to limit their romantic experience to a single person. The romantic relationship may or may not also be sexual. These romantic relationships usually involve some level of commitment.

While polyamory and other alternative sexualities are becoming more common within Neo-Paganism, monogamous heterosexual relationships are still the most prevalent form of romantic connections. If you don't feel the need to explore your sexuality beyond traditional relationships, that is a perfectly valid choice. When it comes to sexuality, the key is to go with what works for you.

Adding Polyamory to Your Relationship

Polyamory is not an excuse for cheating on your partner. Monogamous couples who decide to become polyamorous discuss their decision before they become involved with other people. Both partners agree to the arrangement, and may set ground rules. If you violate one of the rules you've agreed to, it's still considered cheating. For example, if you and your partner have agreed to form one additional relationship each, and then you have a one-night stand with a third person, that would be a violation of your agreement.

Communication is the key to a successful polyamorous relationship. If you and your partner decide to become polyamorous, you should first decide what that means to each of you. Does it mean that you will each find someone to bring into a group marriage? Does it mean that the two of you will find a third person to share? Will one or both of you have same-sex partners?

Once you've started to form polyamorous relationships, you have to learn how to deal with any jealousy that may arise. Try to find the source of the jealousy. It's probably rooted in fear or insecurity. If you are a member of the primary relationship and start to feel neglected by your primary partner, talk to your partner and explain that your needs have changed. You can then decide together how to proceed.

What about Swinging?

Swinging has no connection to polyamory. Couples who swing engage in sexual activity outside of their primary relationship. These sexual interactions don't involve love, and the couple doesn't establish romantic relationships with other people.

If you feel sexually, but not romantically, limited by monogamy, then swinging might be a solution to the problem. Before either of you seeks sex outside the relationship, you and your partner have to agree to swing. Having sex with someone other than your partner without your partner's prior consent is cheating, no matter how you rationalize it.

Group Marriage

A group marriage consists of three or more polyamorous people who agree to form a long-term relationship. Usually they all move into a single home. Sometimes the members of the marriage agree to be faithful to each other and don't become involved with other people outside the marriage. Other groups still allow relationships outside the marriage. In a group marriage, any partners that aren't legally married to each other are called co-wives or co-husbands.

An example of a group marriage might begin with a legally married couple who decide to become polyamorous. The wife brings another man to the relationship while the husband finds another woman. The new couple might also decide to get legally married, or they might not. All four could engage in same-sex or opposite-sex activity, depending on the arrangement. The more people you add, the more complicated the arrangement becomes.

Group marriages are fraught with all the same difficulties as traditional marriages. There are ebbs and flows in sex and love. Child-rearing and financial issues arise. Once again, clear communication and an ability to transcend jealousy are the keys to a successful group marriage.

Pagans come from all walks of life, and may have a variety of sexual persuasions or interests. All sexual and romantic choices are treated with respect and tolerance, whether it's a traditional marriage or a group marriage.

How is polyamory different from polygamy?
In polyamory, both men and women are free to have multiple partners and all involved parties agree upon acceptable behavior. Polygamy, and its converse polyandry, means one person has multiple spouses of the opposite sex, but those spouses may not also have additional partners.

Chapter 19

Living as a Neo-Pagan

Regardless of your chosen branch of Neo-Paganism, being Pagan is more than a religion; it is a way of life. Most Pagans are devout, and their faith is a daily experience. Many meet with their study group on a regular basis or communicate in online forums and via e-mail. Practices like initiation, taking a Pagan name, daily rites, meeting and communing with deities frequently, displaying your faith externally, and honoring important rites of passage help Pagans form a deeper connection to their faith.

Declaring Yourself a Pagan

The first step to honoring your Pagan beliefs is declaring yourself a member of the religion or one of its branches. Before you can explain your beliefs to others, you must understand them yourself. You also need to recognize this change in your life, and you may find the transition to Neo-Paganism a long and hard road to walk, especially if you were raised in a particularly conservative religious or cultural tradition.

Initiation is a good way to recognize and declare your beliefs both internally and externally. If you choose self-initiation, you make the declaration to yourself, the elements, and the gods. If you choose a formal initiation with a coven, kindred, or grove, then the declaration is public as well as private.

For some time, the concept of self-initiation was controversial in the Pagan community. Members of formal traditions didn't consider self-initiations valid and only recognized those that came from covens, groves, or elders with a verifiable lineage. With the rise of solitary practitioners, self-initiation has become more accepted within the larger community.

Self-Initiation

Self-initiation, also known as self-dedication, is the act of declaring yourself a Pagan in some sort of ceremony without the assistance of a teacher or elder. Your self-initiation can take place whenever you are ready. It might follow a period of personal study, or you can dedicate yourself to your new path before you embark on your studies.

Before you initiate or dedicate yourself, make sure that you are fully committed to becoming a Pagan. Once you are ready, create a self-initiation ritual. You can find one in a book, but you might find it more powerful if you write it yourself and use the rituals in books as templates. The ritual can be as long or as short, as formal or informal, as you like. As you plan your self-initiation ceremony, consider the following elements:

- **Location:** Choose a location that is sacred to you, whether it's a beach or a meadow. You can also hold the ceremony before a specially decorated altar in your home.
- **Date:** The new moon, full moon, or Imbolc are most ideal.
- **Declaration:** Your ritual should include your intent—accepting a new faith.
- **Personal Deities:** You should announce your decision to your personal deities, or the gods in general.
- **New Name:** If you wish to take a new Pagan name, you should announce it during the initiation.
- **Anointment:** Anoint yourself with oil as a sign of your conversion.
- **Oath:** Promise to honor your new beliefs regularly.

If you are particularly poetic, you can write beautiful words to accompany each declaration. If you can't even rhyme two words together, then speak from the heart, saying whatever feels appropriate to you. You could also burn incense or anointed candles, or cast a circle and call the quarters if you feel so moved and it fits with the tradition you've chosen.

If you've formed a working group of uninitiated friends, you could perform a round-robin initiation. Standing in a circle, each member initiates the member to his or her right until all are initiated. This ritual can also be used to formally dedicate a new working group.

Formal Initiation

A formal initiation is one you receive through a coven, grove, or kindred once you've been accepted into it. Initiation usually follows some period of training and study based on the group's recommended materials and methods. The initiation takes place on a formal occasion and follows the traditional framework established by the group. A formal initiation usually includes the following elements:

- A challenge

- Introduction to the group
- Vows to uphold the group's traditions and beliefs
- A vow of secrecy (optional)
- Being anointed
- Being welcomed to the group

In some traditions, the challenge consists of physical binding and presentation to the group, followed by a vocal challenge asking if you fully understand what you're doing and come to the group with pure intent and of your free will. Other groups may offer some sort of challenge in meditation.

Taking a Pagan Name

Some Pagans choose to take a new name during their initiation, or sometime around that period. Those who use a Pagan name—sometimes called a magical name or a craft name—usually use it when dealing with other Pagans, but don't have their legal or given name changed.

Think carefully when choosing a name. It should have a personal meaning for you and be in some way connected to your personal path. When choosing a name, you can draw on several tools, including numerology and association.

Adopting a Pagan name is similar to the practice of adopting a new name at Catholic confirmation. The name is a method of affirming your faith, declaring a new path in life, and in some ways becoming a new person. Some Pagans use their name only with the gods and never reveal it to anyone else.

There are pros and cons to taking a Pagan name. On the pro side, it hides your legal identity in case you feel the need to remain closeted. On the con side, some people may know you by your legal name while others know you by your Pagan name, and keeping track of who knows which name may become difficult.

Using Numerology

You can use numerology to help you choose your pagan name. In numerology, each letter is associated with a number. By taking the numbers that correspond to letters in the name you usually use, you can discover your name number, and then create a new name with the same number. You can use just your first name, your first and last name, or your entire birth name. You can also total the numbers in your birth date and match that number to your new name.

Numerical Correspondences of Each Letter								
A	B	C	D	E	F	G	H	I
J	K	L	M	N	O	P	Q	R
S	T	U	V	W	X	Y	Z	
1	2	3	4	5	6	7	8	9

For example, let's say your name is JOE PAGAN: first, add the numerical equivalents of each letter together: $1 + 6 + 5 + 7 + 1 + 7 + 1 + 5 = 33$. Next, add the two digits together, and keep adding until you end up with a one-digit number: $3 + 3 = 6$. This means a good Pagan name for you would also have the numerological value of 6. If you were born on 6/5/1970, you would add $6 + 5 + 1 + 9 + 7 + 0 = 28$, then add $2 + 8 = 10$, and add $1 + 0 = 1$. So if you choose to have your new name correspond to your date of birth, this name should have the numerical value of 1.

Some people add numbers from the top down and then across to get their birth numbers. For example, to get the value for 6/5/1970, you'd add up $6 + 5 + 1970 = 1981$, then add up all the digits: $1 + 9 + 8 + 1 = 19$, $1 + 9 = 10$, $1 + 0 = 1$. This method is as valid as the "add across" method, but note that you won't always get the same result.

Using Associations

As you are thinking about possible names, think about your favorite things and the images they conjure up for you. For example, if your favorite month is December, do you think of winter storms, pinecones, whistling trees, and silver wind? Perhaps your new name will contain an element of that, like IceMoon.

Animals are commonly found in Pagan names. You could take your name from a power animal, your familiar, or just an animal you happen to like. For example, if you feel the need to bring wisdom into your life, you could name yourself after the owl.

Names of gods and heroes are also popular choices (heroes are especially popular among Asatruar). If you feel called by a certain goddess, what does her name mean? For example, if you are dedicated to Arianrhod, your name could be Ariane. If you haven't been called, what do you enjoy doing or what are your skills? Are you a skilled craftsman? Perhaps you should choose a legendary hero who was also a craftsman and take that as your name.

When taking your name from a deity, choose wisely. Loki or Kali might not be good choices, unless you want to draw the forces of chaos and destruction into your life. Luckily, if you later discover you chose poorly or your name no longer applies, you can change it.

Names connected with crystals, minerals, plants, stones, colors, and trees are other possible choices. Names like Amber, Rose, and Willow are commonly found among Wiccans. Druids often take the name of the tree they feel most connected to.

Regular Religious Practices

Most Pagans incorporate regular religious practices into their lives. These practices may be held daily, weekly, or monthly—or whenever the mood strikes. When you are just starting on your new Pagan path, you may find that a daily practice helps you deepen your connection with your deities, the elements, and the earth.

Your practice doesn't need to be long or complicated. It can be as simple as putting fresh water in your offering bowl or greeting the elements. Over time, you may include new practices that allow you to strengthen your bonds with other energies. You might want to spend a month attuning to one element, and the next month to another, until you finally create a practice that honors all of the elements together.

Your regular practice can take place any time of day, but morning and evening are the most popular times. You could also opt to make an offering whenever you happen to walk by your altar or whatever other time is convenient for you. There are no rules governing your daily rites.

Morning Rites

If you're a morning person, you could perform a small rite every day at dawn. Thelemites and Asatruar both have rituals to greet the sun, and the practice is also known among Druids. If you're not a morning person, it might be interesting to get up early and experience the sun at dawn to see how the energy is different from the energy of noon.

To perform a morning rite, it is best to go outdoors or face a window through which you can see the sun rise. At the first peek of the orange crescent, raise your arms and hail the sun, perform the hammer rite, or make another physical gesture. You could simply stand with arms spread and soak up the energy of the new light. Extend your greetings to the sun and thank it for bringing you its light once again. Draw in any energy you need, then ground what you don't need and continue with your usual morning routine.

An alternative morning rite can take place after your usual rising time. If your gods or guides have requested morning meetings, go to your altar and make an offering. You could pray or ask if they have any messages for you. Some people perform a morning divination to see what the lesson of the day is or check for warnings of possible challenges during the day.

Evening Rites

Evening rites can be held to honor the sun, the moon, or it might simply be a good time to hold your daily rites. If you honor the sun, hold your rite at sunset. You could also honor the moon with an evening rite, but only during the two weeks that it rises at night. During the dark moon, the moon is actually up during the day, but you can't see it because the sun blocks its light.

Some Pagans don't establish regular practices, but instead consider everything they do an experience of faith. You might go through phases when you want to meditate at your altar daily, and phases when you don't meditate for months on end.

If you're an evening person, you might find that an evening meditation before going to bed is a good way to close the day. It can help you process the day's events and allows you more time for connecting with your gods or the elements. You can also make offerings in the evening, or use divination methods that require fire or candlelight.

Working with Your Personal Deities

Working with your personal deities and spirit guides should be a regular, if not daily, occurrence. It's important to treat the relationship with your god, goddess, or power animal as you would a marriage. Once you establish a strong relationship, your gods will help you, and you will need to meet their requests as well as you can. It's a give-and-take situation. The first step in working with your deities is to meet them; then you can decide on how best to commune with them.

Meeting Your Deities

Reading about gods and goddesses, asking who your matron and patron deities are in meditation, or being struck by a name in ritual are all ways of discovering the gods that have claimed you, but they are not the only ways. You can simply pick one. If you've chosen one for yourself, you should meditate on the deity and ask if he or she is willing to accept your service. Most will agree; if not, you should choose another deity.

If a deity has chosen you, you should speak to your matron or patron to establish the relationship. You may find that he or she visits you unbidden, and that's fine, but sometimes you have to go looking. Meditation is the best way to meet your matron or patron. Focus on any images of the god or goddess you came across in your research, or go on a journey through one of his or her legends. When you find your deity, introduce yourself, acknowledge that you have been chosen, and express your willingness to be in his or her service.

Communing with Your Deity

As you begin to work regularly with your deities and spirit guides, they may make certain requests of you, and you should agree to fulfill them, as long as they are reasonable. If your goddess asks for something impossible, like a daily one-hour prayer at 3:15 in the afternoon, when you're at work, explain that you can't accommodate the request, but offer something else in exchange. You could say a one-minute prayer at 3:15, and then pray for one hour either before or after work.

If your deities and power animals require less of you, you should still make an effort to honor them regularly. Perhaps you could make a regular offering to your goddess on your altar. You could also build a special altar in honor of a specific deity and maintain it regularly by changing the seasonal decorations.

It's important to connect with your deities outside of the spirit realm as well. You could visit the woods to commune with your spirit guides once a week. You could volunteer to plant trees or clean up a local wilderness area as a gift to the spirit realm. The human realm and the spirit realm used to be closely tied together, but as the human world became more intellectual and mechanized, the two realms drifted apart. It pains the gods to see what humans have done to their beautiful work. By helping take care of the environment, you re-establish and strengthen the ties between the two worlds, and please the gods.

Outward Signs of Faith

Most Pagans choose to display some outward sign of their faith. These displays often take the form of a piece of jewelry or a tattoo. Most New Age/metaphysical stores carry a variety of moon, pentacle, Celtic knot work, and hammer pendants. You could get one piece to wear every day and additional pieces to wear for ritual. You could also buy several pieces and rotate your collection. Silver is the most popular metal for Pagan jewelry, and crystal decorations are common.

Not all Pagans are tattooed, but those who are often have multiple tattoos. Before getting one, carefully research possible images and spend some time with your chosen image to make sure you really like it before being permanently marked with it. When deciding where on your body to put your tattoo, consider your career. A giant pentacle on the back of your hand might not be the best choice if you plan on a corporate career. You should also ask other people with tattoos for tattoo parlor recommendations to ensure that your design will come out the way you intended and that the parlor adheres to health codes.

Most pendants come with a leather cord, but if you plan to wear the pendant on a regular basis, consider putting it on a silver chain so you don't lose it. A silver chain also looks more professional when worn with office attire.

Rites of Passage

Most major religions have ceremonies to mark the important rites of passage you undergo during your life. While your culture might not recognize all of these important moments, your religion should. The most common rites of passage honored by Pagans are birth, puberty, marriage, and death.

Birth Rites

Births are celebrated in most cultures, and most religions do so with a special ceremony. Neo-Paganism is no different. The birth or naming ceremony is usually held within the first year of the child's life. Wiccans sometimes call the naming ceremony a Wiccaning.

During a naming ceremony, the child is officially introduced to the gods and given a name. Godparents, sometimes called the godfather and goddessmother, are also announced. The guests offer the child blessings, and the gods are also asked for blessings.

The naming ceremony is usually held at your home, a friend's home, or a traditional ritual space for your group. The ceremony should be presided over by your teacher, elder, or another Pagan friend. Whether or not you include non-Pagan family and friends in the ceremony is up to you. People may bring gifts, but it's not required. The ceremony is followed by a party.

Puberty Rites

Aside from Jewish and Native American traditions, most people in the United States don't undergo any form of a formal celebration or ritual at the onset of puberty. Most Pagans feel this is unfortunate and have developed rituals to honor the transition from child to adult. The ceremonies aren't set in stone, and each parent and teen decides how best to conduct the rite if their working group doesn't have a traditional ritual. The womanhood ceremony is held when a girl has her first period. It's a little more difficult to pinpoint the change for a boy, but some people hold the manhood ceremony when a boy's voice changes or his pubic, chest, or facial hair first appears.

It is traditional for adulthood ceremonies to be unisex. For a girl, her mother, her Pagan friends who have also reached puberty, her mother's female friends or members of her working group, and possibly female relatives hold a ceremony to welcome the new woman into the sisterhood. It is a joyous occasion featuring discussions of what it means to be a woman, celebrations of women's roles and power, a ritual welcoming the girl to womanhood, and lots of comfort food like chocolate and other sweets. The girl receives gifts appropriate to her new role.

For a boy, his father, his Pagan friends who have also reached puberty, his father's male friends or members of his working group, and possibly male relatives hold a ceremony to welcome the new man into the brotherhood. Men usually take a more "masculine" approach to the ceremony and make it a camping trip complete with feasting, toasting, and drumming. The boy also receives gifts appropriate to his new role.

The ceremonies don't necessarily have to be unisex, but many young teens find that it's the most comfortable way for them to begin to understand the changes their bodies are undergoing. Puberty rituals also make the whole process seem less scary and isolating. Most are excited to receive special rituals honoring this major shift in their lives and should be included in the planning, but if he or she doesn't want a fuss made, that's okay, too.

Marriage Rites

Marriages are honored with celebrations and feasts in nearly every culture that engages in the practice, and Pagans are no different. Pagan attitudes toward marriage are discussed in Chapter 18, but those who do get married usually hold some kind of a feast or ceremony to honor the occasion.

Whether it's your first or your fourth, a marriage is a long-term, formal commitment to another person and it should be celebrated as a major change in your life. Very few other changes alter every aspect of your life as dramatically as marriage. Your marriage also has an impact on the lives of your friends, family members, and children, if you have them, and everyone will want a chance to share your joy.

Whether you get married in an elaborate ceremony or in a Las Vegas chapel, the rite of marriage has a small ceremony built in, and that alone honors the change and the powerful commitment you have just made. You might also want to hold a party to commemorate your choice and start your new life with joy and merriment that will hopefully continue through the rest of your married life.

Death Rites

For most Pagans, death is a transition to a new stage of life rather than the end of the soul's cycle. Most Pagans believe in some form of reincarnation. After death, your soul goes to the Summerlands, or another spirit plane, to process the lessons of your previous life. When your soul is ready, it will reincarnate in a new body. Some people believe that babies hold memories of their previous lives, but those memories are soon pushed out by all the new information they must assimilate. Even though you forget your past life, your soul retains the lessons it's learned so far. This is why some people are called "old souls"; they seem to have a great deal of wisdom and knowledge that can only have been gained through several lifetimes on earth.

Are Pagans buried or cremated?
Most Pagans prefer to be cremated, for several reasons. First, there isn't enough room on earth to bury everyone. Second, ashes can be scattered at a favorite natural location, which allows the person to become a part of nature. Third, Pagans believe that the body is just a vessel, and it won't be needed again.

Most Pagans don't fear death, but it's still not an easy process, especially when it involves a great deal of suffering. If you are terminally ill, you could hold a releasing ceremony to honor your willingness to sever your current ties to the earthly plane. If you are well, but approaching an age when death becomes likely at any time, you could hold a ceremony to celebrate everything you have accomplished in your life.

Although they focus on the deceased, funerals and memorials are not about death, they are about life. Funerals allow your friends and family members to celebrate your life. They also help your survivors cope with your loss and how it impacts their lives. While you should leave instructions for your memorial and burial, allow room in the plans for your friends and family members to meet their own spiritual needs.

Chapter 20

Explaining and Protecting Your Beliefs

Once you've decided to become Pagan, you have to make some important decisions about how to proceed, such as whether or not you should share the truth about your new faith with others. You may also be confused about how to explain your new beliefs. As a Pagan, you may have some privacy and safety issues to deal with. You may also face religious discrimination, so you need to be aware of your legal rights.

Pagans "in the Closet"

The first question most new Pagans face is whether or not they should hide their beliefs from others. For some, this is an issue of privacy. For others, the desire to be closeted is due to a fear of discrimination or familial rejection.

Although Paganism is becoming more acceptable in some regions, and understanding of the faith is increasing, there are still many people who hate Pagans. When deciding whether or not to remain in the closet, you must first consider how public you are with other aspects of your life. Is everything in your life an open book? Then you'll probably want to be a public Pagan. You should also determine if you want to fight for the rights of Pagans, or if you prefer to live under the radar. Either choice is valid.

For some Pagans, the experience of informing people about their faith is similar to the experience of gay people faced with coming out. If you wouldn't tell someone you were gay, you probably shouldn't tell them you're Pagan.

The area where you live should play a role in your decision. A Los Angeles Pagan is unlikely to face serious discrimination even if he walks around with a giant pentacle tattooed on his chest, but a Pagan in a rural section of the Bible belt might have problems displaying so much as a tiny pentacle pendant.

It's unfortunate that all Pagans aren't able to practice their religion as openly as members of other faiths, but the world is rapidly changing. Someday there may be acceptance for all people of all faiths. Until then, you need to decide how public you want to be with your religion.

People Who Need to Know

Even if you choose to keep your pagan faith private, there are people you will need to tell about your religion. Family members and friends are the most likely people to notice a change in you. Your spouse or significant other is one person who definitely needs to know. You should tell him or her soon after deciding you want to be Pagan. Hiding your beliefs is not healthy for your relationship.

Family Members

At some point, many Pagans decide to reveal their beliefs to close family members. Whom and when you tell largely depends on how open-minded the individual members are. If you are lucky enough to come from a very accepting family, you can be completely open about your new beliefs. If you come from a very conservative family, you may not be able to tell anyone. In most cases, you'll be able to tell some people.

Friends and Coworkers

Some friends will want to know about your new beliefs, and some won't. You should tell friends that were aware of your previous religious beliefs. If religion isn't something you previously discussed, there's no need to start now. Pagans don't proselytize, so you don't need to start recruiting. You'll find that most of your true friends won't care that you're Pagan, but if you belong to a very conservative circle, becoming Pagan might cost you a few friendships. If this is the case, they weren't your true friends to begin with.

You definitely need to reveal your beliefs to people you're dating. It's best to mention them early on in the relationship, preferably within the first few dates. It might not be necessary to launch into a full explanation on the first date, but if someone isn't going to understand, then you don't want to develop strong feelings for him or her.

It's not always necessary to tell coworkers that you're Pagan, but there are times when it might come up. If you plan on taking off holy days, then you're going to have to explain why. If you wear a piece of Pagan jewelry, someone may ask you what it means. It's best to have an answer ready. Even if you try to hide your jewelry, it might fall out or someone might ask you why you always wear your necklace under your shirt, so you should still have an explanation handy.

How to Explain Your Beliefs

When describing your beliefs to someone, it's not always necessary to explain everything. It's best to start with your personal beliefs, and then to segue into a longer explanation. It also helps to make connections between Neo-Pagan practices and the practices of other religions. Finally, you should be prepared to allay fears people have about magic and those wild Pagan orgies.

Share the Basics

When first explaining your beliefs, stick to a skeleton of your basic belief system. For a coworker, it's enough to say something like, "I follow a nature religion." You can answer further questions if you want to, but try to steer clear of talk about working skyclad. With friends, you can explain your beliefs a little more deeply. It's okay to mention the deities you follow, your holiday celebrations, or anything else that seems appropriate. Your friend may or may not ask questions. If she does, then explain further. For example, if you're asked if you believe in God, you can answer that you believe in a god and goddess. If you are asked if you worship Satan, you can explain that Satan is a Christian construct and that you don't worship anything that could be construed as evil.

Answer the Questions

Family members and people you have a romantic connection to will ask the most questions. Work slowly, starting from the basics. Allow the person time to digest your answers and then think of new questions. You might want to invite them to attend a ritual with you, or send them a copy of a ritual so they can see what it's like.

You will most likely be asked if you still celebrate the holidays of your original faith. Many Pagans choose to celebrate Christmas as a secular holiday and share the day with family and friends, just as they did before, but without the trip to church. Most Jewish Pagans find that their traditions work very well with Neo-Paganism and are able to honor both the Jewish and Pagan holidays. You can also explain that you honor the cycles of the sun and earth, or adhere to a holiday calendar that predates Christianity. You can point out that many of these celebrations continue in the regions where they originated.

> Some Christians don't know that Christ's actual birth date is unknown. Christmas was first moved to December 25 in the fourth century, and was later set by Pope Gregory. The new date coincided with Pagan celebrations of Saturnalia, the winter solstice, and the birth of the sun god Mithras.

If you are asked specifically what you do, then give a very basic rundown of an average ritual. You will most likely be asked if you use magic. If you do use magic, you can explain that you don't practice black magic or sacrifice animals during your rituals (unless you're Santerían). Magic can be likened to prayer because both are tools for asking the gods for help.

The tools, especially ritual knives, usually arouse the most curiosity. Explain as much of it as you feel comfortable with. For example, you could explain that your athame is a symbol of the element of fire because steel is forged from fire. You don't need to get into its relation to male energy and the symbolic Great Rite unless you already explained Beltane.

Make Connections Between Religions

When explaining your faith, it also helps to make connections to more familiar religions and holidays. For example, you can liken the goddess to Mary, mother of Jesus Christ, whom many Pagans honor as a goddess. When asked about Yule, explain that you celebrate the return of the light in the form of the sun god, spelled *Sun*. You can point out that the Christmas tree, holiday wreaths, and decorations are all pre-Christian practices.

If you use other practices, such as shamanic journeying or meditation, compare your practices to those of Native Americans or Buddhists. Other practices, like wearing a Celtic Cross pendant or hanging a Witch Ball in your window for protection, can be related to the folk traditions of Europe and the British Isles.

Allay Fears

When people hear the words *heathen, Pagan,* and *Witch,* all sorts of scary images are conjured up. Your family members may worry that you've joined a cult or gone off the deep end. You should clarify that you are not a sorcerer or the Wicked Witch of the West. You should explain that Pagans have no single leader, you're not required to give all your money to anyone, and there is no strict dogma, so it would be difficult for you to be a member of a Pagan cult.

If a friend or family member insists on trying to "save" you, gently but firmly explain that you believe differently, but you appreciate theconcern. You might want to give him a copy ofa beginner's book on your chosen path or direct him to an explanatory Web site.

Once you've explained your personal beliefs, your friends and family members may be less worried but might still have a few concerns. You may be asked if you have orgies in the forest. Even if you do, that might not be the right thing to tell your mom. You might be asked if you hex people. Again answer with a simple "no," unless you want to get into a long conversation about magical ethics.

The most common fear is that you'll become a different person. Reassure them that you are the same person you always were, and you just have a different religion. Chances are you had Pagan leanings before you made the conversion, and once they recognize that, they will be better able to accept your religious choices.

Concerns about Privacy and Safety

Being a Pagan raises additional concerns about privacy that you might not have otherwise faced. Unfortunately, there are people who hate Pagans and are bent on harassing them. You need to take certain steps to protect your privacy. If you are very concerned about privacy, adopting a Pagan name will help, but there are also other things you can do.

If you are a public Pagan, don't use your home address on any official documents like park reservation requests. You should acquire a P.O. box, and mark the "personal use" box so people can't get your home address from the postal service. If you go by your legal name, consider getting an unlisted phone number or just using your first initial and last name, with no address listed.

If you have a Web site, or post a message on a public Pagan forum, you may find yourself the subject of harassing e-mails designed to "save" you. Don't bother replying. There is no talking to these people, and they're likely to publicly post your replies. Your best option is to report the harasser to his or her ISP.

You should have the greatest concerns for your privacy if you live in a small, conservative community. If you live in a big city, you will face less harassment, and possibly none. Either way you should still take appropriate precautions if you are public with your beliefs.

Google.com has a phone number search that provides home addresses, and a map to that location. If you're a public Pagan, follow Google's instructions for removing that link. People have been known to track down Pagans and vandalize their homes or send death threats.

Your First Amendment Rights

The First Amendment of the United States Constitution states, "Congress shall make no law respecting an establishment of religion, or prohibiting the free exercise thereof . . . " The government can't formally recognize any religion, Pagan or otherwise. You might hear people say that the government recognizes their religion, but this usually refers to a description of the faith in the *U.S. Military Chaplain's Handbook* or a letter from the IRS granting a Pagan organization nonprofit status as a religious group. For example, your community can't stop you from opening a Pagan church unless you are somehow violating health requirements or trying to build it in an area zoned for homes.

The First Amendment also means that the government can't reasonably limit how you practice your religion. If you wanted to jump off a three-story building straddling a broom, your local government could tell you "no" because it is a public safety issue. However, if you try to rent park space for a ritual and the permit agency rejects you solely on the basis of your religion, but allows other religious groups to hold services at the site, they are violating your First Amendment rights to free expression and equal treatment under the law, as guaranteed by several laws passed as a result of the Civil Rights movement.

Free Expression of Religion at Home

The right to freely express your religion at home ties into your privacy rights. Certain aspects of your faith are strictly protected, such as the values you instill in your children or the decorations in your home.

However, some regulations do apply, like construction codes for buildings and outdoor structures. In order to ensure that you are within your rights, check the building codes before erecting a permanent ritual structure.

Free Expression of Religion at Work

The Civil Rights movement also extended the First Amendment protections to private sector discrimination. If your employer permits religious observances for some employees, they should be permitted for all employees. For example, if the person in the cubicle next door can wear a cross, but you can't wear your pentacle, your rights are being infringed. If your Jewish coworker is allowed to take off Rosh Hashanah as a holiday but you can't take off Samhain, that's a violation.

Employers are required to treat all employees equally, so long as it doesn't cause them undue hardship. For example, if you're in a three-person office, it might not be feasible to take off all of your holy days unless you use up your vacation time to do so. Or, if you work in a church rectory, you might want to remove your pentacle out of respect. Sure, they can't ask you to do it, but making the parishioners uncomfortable isn't good for you or your employers.

Just as you have a right to freely express your religion, so do others. Pagans don't try to convert others. Apply the Golden Rule and approach the religions of your friends and coworkers the way you want them to approach yours. A little bit of courtesy goes a long way in gaining acceptance for your beliefs.

Legal Concerns

Discrimination is a common fear among Pagans, as is the possibility that someone will attempt to distort their beliefs and use that against them. It is very common to hear stories of spouses using misrepresentations of Paganism as a divorce tactic. On-the-job discrimination and harassment are also not uncommon. The biggest fear among Pagans is that their children will be taken away from them because of their beliefs.

A Reason for Divorce

Divorces are always difficult, but they can become even more complicated when one spouse is Pagan and the other is not, and the non-Pagan spouse attempts to use that as a weapon by exaggerating or fabricating information. It's unlikely that your religion will come up in your divorce proceedings if you don't have children, but it may if you do, especially if your religion is the reason you're getting the divorce in the first place.

Custody fights are known for turning nasty, and some spouses hurl any accusation they can in an attempt to win. Your first concern—and the concern of the judge—should be the well-being of your child. You should educate your lawyer about your faith so he or she can educate a judge who is not aware of the truth about Neo-Paganism. You should also be prepared to disprove any false claims made by your ex-spouse.

Usually, your religion doesn't become a factor in deciding child custody unless the judge believes your specific practices pose a danger to the child. If you practice skyclad with others, you may be precluded from bringing your child to these events, but it shouldn't be a consideration for whether or not you're a fit parent. If your religion does become a factor, and it's very clear that you otherwise should have had custody of your children, contact the ACLU. They may be able to help.

Job Discrimination

The Federal government has enacted several guidelines and rules regarding religious discrimination in the workplace. It is quite simply illegal. Some bills have been proposed that would allow certain groups to discriminate on the basis of religion, but they've not yet passed. As of now, you can't be denied employment or a promotion because of your faith. You can't be cited for expressions of faith if others are allowed to make them.

Don't let discrimination fears discourage you from practicing your religion. Most people never face challenges to their faiths. At some point, you may choose to fight for your religious rights, but that's your choice to make. If you're confused about how to explain your faith or want more information about your rights, many Pagan gatherings offer workshops on these topics.

If you think you're being discriminated against, you have several options. First, you can file a complaint with the human resources department, if your company has one. This is most likely to be helpful if other employees are harassing you, trying to convert you to Christianity either verbally or by leaving tracts on your desk, or are otherwise making you uncomfortable because of your religion.

If you were fired, and you think it is solely because of your religion, you can file a complaint with your state's employment agency or the EEOC. You can also contact the ACLU for help. Both groups also deal with cases where you believe you weren't hired because of your religion, but it's illegal to ask about your religion in an interview, so this doesn't come up often.

Child Protective Services

It's rare, but there are stories of Child Protective Services removing children from Pagan homes. Usually other factors are involved, and being Pagan has very little to do with the case. Still, there are situations where a well-meaning, but misinformed, teacher, relative, or neighbor contacts Child Protective Services. At this point, most agencies are well versed in religious freedom and won't investigate unless they suspect that you're also putting your child in danger.

If an investigation is launched, be prepared to explain your faith. You may want to download some basic information from the Internet or copy pages from your books that explain your beliefs. You should also contact an attorney and educate him or her about your beliefs. Your children can't be removed from your home just because you're Pagan. That is yet another protection offered by the First Amendment and Civil Rights laws.

Chapter 21

Pagan Gatherings

If there's one thing that can safely be said about all Pagans, it's that they like to party. In addition to feasts that accompany their major rituals and holiday celebrations, numerous larger gatherings take place throughout the year. Regardless of your specific path, there's a gathering out there for you. General Pagan gatherings usually offer a little something for every-one. Wiccans, Asatruar, and Druids also host gatherings for members of their own traditions.

Benefits of Attending a Gathering

Attending a large Pagan gathering is an experience like no other. Imagine being surrounded by hundreds of people just like you. Imagine a weekend, or even a week, of activities geared toward exploring your religion. Imagine reveling in an atmosphere of acceptance and joy. That is what you get at large Pagan gatherings, which are about networking, celebration, education, and powerful rituals.

Networking and Community

If you're new to the Pagan community, you might wonder just where all these other Pagans are. You've attended rituals at stores, and met a few people, but where are the thousands that claim to be living in your area? Attend a large Pagan gathering and you'll find them by the bucketful. Even better, most of the people there will want to meet new people like you.

In addition to merchants from your area and beyond vending wares of all kinds, you'll also see booths and information tables for Pagan groups and organizations. Some groups hold mixers, hospitality suites, or "meet and greets" at these events. There's no need to be shy. Find a group you're interested in and introduce yourself. Usually there's someone on hand who can answer your questions.

Education and Connections

Pagans love to learn. Because most weren't born into the faith, there are scores of books on a range of possible topics, but sometimes a book isn't enough. That's where workshops come in. Every large Pagan gathering offers a slew of workshops for nearly every interest.

If you're particularly interested in a topic and want to learn more after a workshop, the presenters usually stay afterward and are easily approachable. For example, if you attended an introductory Asatru workshop and were interested in joining a kindred but didn't know how to go about it, you could talk to the workshop leader afterward and he or she would probably be able to give you some pointers or contacts.

Ritual Experience

Beginning Pagans usually start by doing rituals at home, following the instructions in a book. Next up, you might attend a holiday celebration hosted by a local group. If you're really lucky, you might even find one that draws a large crowd. But there's nothing quite like the ritual energy created at large gatherings.

If it's your first large ritual, you might become overwhelmed by the energy raised. If you do, go to one of the watchers stationed just outside the circle. They are there to help you.

Most large gatherings feature several rituals. Some smaller rituals are held during the day, but others are huge and held at night. At camping gatherings, these rituals often feature drumming and a bonfire, and sometimes that bonfire lasts until morning. Rituals at large gatherings usually have a specific theme like healing, follow the traditions of a specific path like Druidry, or honor a specific deity, like Aphrodite.

It's Fun

The last but certainly not least important reason to attend Pagan gatherings is that they're just plain fun. There is always something entertaining going on. If you don't feel like attending a workshop, just hang out in a central area and the fun will come to you. Discussion groups will spring up in the middle of the hotel bar. Someone will wander through your campsite offering to paint your face. Another person will offer to read your tarot cards for you, even though you don't know each other.

Pagans are friendly and welcoming, and a Pagan gathering is a good place to make new friends. It's also a good place to try something different with your old ones. Finally, it's a chance to get gussied up in your best Pagan attire and receive not a single odd look. In fact, you'll probably get lots of compliments.

Minding Your Manners

While you're busy networking, celebrating, learning, experiencing, and having fun, there are also a few etiquette matters to keep in mind. Different rules apply at different types of gatherings, so if you're unsure, check with the organizers. It's probably not a good idea to challenge the rules that have been established. The organizers have established them for reasons you may not be aware of.

Appropriate Attire

Acceptable attire at Pagan gatherings varies from ritual costumes and street clothes to nothing at all. Pagans tend to be comfortable with their bodies and many enjoy being nude when possible. At the same time, it is also important to remember that there are laws governing public nudity. Some of the larger Pagan gatherings held on private or reserved property like private campgrounds or a private, secluded area of a public campground are clothing-optional. It's always a choice, and some events have limits on nudity. A few allow complete nudity; others require you to cover your genitals.

Pagan events are good places to buy new ritual attire. There are always a few vendors offering unique items. You can find everything from full Renaissance regalia to ritual robes and belly-dancing outfits. Jewelry and things to hang from a belt are also popular items.

Regardless of the rules, clothing is always required off-site, and gatherings held in public places like parks or hotels are never clothing-optional. Some events also offer guidelines for dressing. For example, Pantheacon asks that guests wearing revealing outfits to dances or rituals cover up in the elevators and other public areas of the hotel.

When you attend a gathering, you should always dress comfortably. If it's clothing-optional, only remove as much as you feel comfortable with, and of course, apply extra sunscreen to those parts that rarely see the sun. If you're a "jeans and a T-shirt" kind of person, don't feel obligated to wear a ritual robe or a wild costume just because it's a Pagan event. No one cares what you wear as long as you're comfortable.

> Always practice safe sex when hooking up with anyone new, even at Pagan gatherings. Pagans are usually careful, but you can become intoxicated by the energy at a Pagan gathering and lose your head.

Sexual Manners

Good Pagans recognize the importance of respecting boundaries, but sometimes it's easy to get sexual signals crossed after spending a day with a new friend in such a welcoming setting. Be clear on where you and your friend stand before making an advance. By the same token, other people should respect your boundaries, and if someone pushes them, speak up about what you're comfortable with. Don't feel pressured just because you're at a Pagan event and it seems to be the norm.

If you do hook up with someone who is of like mind, there is no reason that you shouldn't go for it as long as you practice safe sex. No one will think any differently of you! It doesn't matter if you're gay, straight, bisexual, or transsexual; no one at a Pagan gathering will think less of you or even care who you're with.

Food and Drink

Larger Pagan events sometimes offer meal plans, but most of the time you're on your own. Some events hold a communal feast, so check the info sheet to see if you need to bring anything. If you'd like to host a meal in your campsite, post a notice and people will come. Because some Pagans are vegetarian, event organizers are careful to offer those options if they, or their location, provide food. If you're at an event near restaurants, usually the organizers can provide a list of places nearby that have vegetarian dishes.

As with attire, alcohol rules may be dictated by the site. If you're at an event where alcohol is allowed, don't go overboard. If you're camping in hot weather, drinking too much could be downright dangerous. You shouldn't feel obligated to get stinking drunk, or to drink at all, just because you're at a Pagan gathering. At a gathering, treat alcohol just as you would treat it anywhere else.

Potlucks are the rule when it comes to Pagan feasts. If you are invited to visit another campsite for a meal, always bring something with you. It might not be needed, but it's a nice gesture. Even a few bottles of beer or a box of cookies will be appreciated.

Photography

Pagans are an odd mix of public and private. Some Pagans are totally out there, willing to reveal their religion to anyone. Others, fearing repercussions at work or home, choose to keep their faith private. Both types attend Pagan gatherings, and for this reason, certain photography etiquette has evolved.

Some gatherings have banned cameras. Others allow cameras but ask that you only take pictures of your group, or receive permission from others before taking their pictures. If someone doesn't want his or her picture taken, respect that. You also have the right to say no if someone asks you. If your picture is taken without your knowledge and it shows up on a Web site, just drop the Web master an e-mail and it'll come right down.

If you're very concerned about having your picture taken, face paint works wonders for disguising your appearance! It also helps to dress plainly rather than in full belly-dance attire or faerie wings. People who stand out the most will obviously get the most attention from the cameras.

This rule holds true for gatherings in very public places like city parks. Some events invite the media, but usually ask the photographers to receive permission before photographing anyone. Most reporters and photographers are respectful of your preferences.

General Pagan Gatherings

The largest Pagan gatherings are designed to appeal to Pagans from all traditions and offer a wide range of activities. These gatherings take the form of conventions, camping trips, and one-day events in public parks. Most of these events are great places to meet prominent Pagan personalities or discover new musical groups. A few of the major events will be covered here, but this list is by no means comprehensive. The attendance figures are as of the publication date of this book, and all are growing rapidly.

Conventions

Pagan conventions are usually held in the winter months when it's too cold to be outside. They are often weekend events, or go from Friday to Monday for an extended weekend. Regardless of length, they are packed with workshops, vendors, rituals, concerts, and general revelry. Four of the best-known conventions are Pantheacon, Ecumenicon, Invocation, and Convocation.

- **Pantheacon** was established in 1994 in the San Francisco Bay Area by Ancient Ways, a local store. The four-day convention attracts around 1,500 people. It is held on President's Day weekend.
- **Ecumenicon** is usually held in Washington, D.C. It is hosted by the Ecumenicon Fellowship, which is an interfaith church. The church was established in 1988 and has links to interfaith organizations in other areas.
- **Invocation** was first held in 1998. It is hosted by the Midwest Pagan Council. The convention is usually held in Illinois in October.
- **Convocation** is held in February (usually the weekend after Pantheacon) in Troy, Michigan. It is sponsored by the Magical Education Council.

Camping Events

Camp-outs usually take place in late spring, summer, and early fall, depending on the weather of the specific region. July and August are especially popular because good weather is almost guaranteed. These events range from several days to over a week and are attended by hundreds. Here are three of the best-known events:

- **Starwood** was established in 1981 and is one of the clothing-optional family camp-outs. It lasts six days and is held in late July in upstate New York. With over 1,800 people, the event is so large that it's practically a village. The Association for Consciousness Exploration is responsible for the main event and several other events throughout the year.
- **Pagan Spirit Gathering** was also created in 1980. It is sponsored by Circle Sanctuary and takes place in Ohio. It is not a clothing-optional event, and families are welcome. Because it's closer to the middle of the country, PSG attracts Pagans from all over the United States.
- **Pan Pagan Festival** is hosted by the Midwest Pagan Council. The event was established in 1976. It is held each August in a campground in Indiana. The event is targeted at families, and pets are welcome.

Out of the Dark, Inc., offers two events, the Spring and Fall Gathering of the Tribes in Virginia. The events range in attendance from 500 to 800 people, and take place on the Memorial Day and Labor Day weekends. Out of the Dark took over the events in 1994. It had previously been arranged by a chapter of the Covenant of the Unitarian Universalist Pagans, beginning around 1987.

Children are welcome at all of these events—and at most other Pagan gatherings. Some events even offer child-care services. Because most of these children have been raised as Pagans, they are well versed in ritual etiquette.

Pagan Pride Day

Pagan Pride Day is not actually one event, but rather over 100 events on almost every continent. The bulk of the events are held in the United States between late August and early October. Most are one-day events, but some are two days. They feature at the very least a picnic and ritual, but the larger events also have vendors, workshops, and entertainment.

Each event is organized locally with guidance from the International Pagan Pride Project, which was established in 1998. The events range in size from fifty people to a few thousand. Unlike other Pagan gatherings, these events are free and the general public is invited, as well as the media. The goal of the event is to encourage tolerance and understanding of Pagans, but most of the activities are aimed at Pagans, and are mostly attended by Pagans.

Wiccan Gatherings

Wiccan gatherings are popping up all over the place. They are targeted at Wiccans, rather than the general community, and offer training and a chance to deepen the sense of community. The most well known gatherings are Merry Meet and the various WitchCamps.

Merry Meet

Merry Meet is an annual event hosted by the Covenant of the Goddess. It is first and foremost their annual meeting, which is called the Grand Council. The event has grown into a gathering of several days that also features workshops of interest to Wiccans as well as non-Wiccans interested in learning more about the faith. The gathering is attended by upwards of 120 people and was established in 1976 when the first Grand Council was held. It is held in rotating locations depending on which local council has opted to plan and host the event each year. It usually takes place around Labor Day weekend, but is sometimes a week or two earlier.

WitchCamp

WitchCamp is not one event, but is instead several intensive training retreats based on the teachings of the Reclaiming Tradition. Attendance at WitchCamps vary depending on the capacity of the location. Each four- to seven-day camp is offered once per year. As of the publication of this book, there were twelve WitchCamps in existence in the United States, Canada, and Europe.

Asatruar Gatherings

Gatherings specific to Asatruar are usually smaller than general Pagan gatherings. Some Asatru gatherings are held within larger Pagan gatherings, but individual groups hold smaller, local gatherings as well.

Trothmoot is a Pagan festival sponsored by the Troth. It's not limited to Troth members, but the organization does hold its annual meeting at the event. All rituals and activities focus on topics of interest to Asatruar. The location rotates between the East Coast, West Coast, and middle of the country, but it is always the first weekend of June. The average attendance is 80 to 100 people.

California's Hammer of Thor Kindred holds two annual festivals, usually along the coast. The first event is held the same week as Easter, so the date varies. The fall festival, the Feast of Aegir, is held close to the fall equinox. Both gatherings were established in 1997. The spring gathering hosts 80 to 105 people, and the fall gathering hosts 95 to 120 people.

Several groups host annual AlThings. These events serve as networking opportunities and the annual meeting of those groups registered as nonprofits. Their attendance depends largely on the number of members.

Druidic Gatherings

Druidic gatherings are held in the United States and the United Kingdom. Ár nDraíocht Féin (ADF) groves host several regional gatherings throughout the year in addition to their annual meeting. The Order of Bards, Ovates, and Druids (OBOD) hosts a conference in the United Kingdom. Some British groves also present rituals at the more prominent sacred sites like Stonehenge. Their summer solstice rituals at Stonehenge frequently make the news in the United States.

Neo-Pagan gatherings are wonderful opportunities for networking and learning. They are also joyous occasions. Once you've attended a large Pagan gathering, you'll want to repeat the experience year after year.

Several groves in the United States hold local rituals or weekend camp-outs. Contact a grove in your region for more information about gatherings in your area. You may also be able to attend public rituals throughout the year.

Chapter 22

Networking
and Community

Community is very important to Pagans. Even those who choose to practice their faith alone the majority of the time enjoy visiting with Pagan friends and occasionally participating in group activities. For some, finding other Pagans can be daunting—especially in places where many people are keeping their Pagan faith private. That doesn't mean that you shouldn't look, but carefully consider any group you'd like to join and show proper respect once you're received.

Finding Online Groups

In the age of the Internet, the best place to find other Pagans is online. In addition to taking online classes, you can also chat with other Pagans and learn about upcoming events. Some people have even attempted to hold online rituals, but these endeavors have largely been unsuccessful.

There are several ways to find online groups. The first is to visit a large mailing list service like YahooGroups, Topica, or SmartGroups and run a search. If you're looking for people who follow a specific path, you could enter "Celtic Shamans" or "Dianic Wiccans." If you're looking for general Pagan groups local to you, try entering a search term that mentions your area.

In addition to joining a mailing list, you could try a newsgroup, which is sort of a message board that you read online or download to your computer, or an IRC chat, which offers real-time online chatting. Both require that you install special software on your computer.

Most Pagans are very comfortable with technology, so you'll find that many groups are quite active. Once you've joined or been accepted into an online group, your first order of business is an introduction. Your intro should include your name, path, and any other pertinent stats like age, experience, and what you hope to gain from the group. Please, be real and show a little humility. Announcing yourself with a message like, "Hi, I'm Lady Buffy Snowfeather Dawn Aradia, Grand High Priestess of the Enchanted Unicorns of Avalon Coven. I'm nineteen and I've been studying Wicca for two months and did a spell in the park. I'm here to share my vast wisdom with everyone" is a surefire way to get mocked mercilessly.

Finding Offline Groups

Of course, when it comes to human contanct, nothing can replace joining a real group, such as a kindred, coven, circle, grove, or just a general working group. Offline groups usually hold regular meetings, often for purposes of study or ritual planning. Offline groups also hold holiday or other rituals, some of which may be open to the general public.

> Get-togethers for online groups are common. Some groups have regular monthly gatherings, while others may just agree to meet at a bar some Friday night. An in-person get-together is a great way to put a face with an e-mail address and strengthen your friendship.

As with online groups, there are several ways to find offline groups. First, visit one of the main Web sites for the path you'd like to follow, such as the Asatru Alliance's site or Witchvox. These offer local listings for groups open to new members. You can then visit a specific group's Web site, or call or e-mail the listed contact person for information about attending an upcoming ritual or joining the group.

Second, check at local metaphysical stores for groups holding introductory classes. Attend a class and if you like it, speak to the teacher about your interest in joining the group. You could also ask the owner of the store for leads or introductions. The owner might offer a beginner's class, after which you could start your own group with your fellow classmates. If you can't locate an offline group in your area, ask an online group for help. In some areas, groups are very secretive and don't advertise for new members, but might respond to an online request.

Meeting Other Pagans in Person

Meeting other Pagans in person for the first time can be intimidating for a new Pagan. Remember: If you follow certain guidelines and etiquette rules, you should be fine. The guidelines vary depending on whether or not you're meeting an online group in person, meeting a new offline group, or attending a large gathering.

Meeting your online group in an offline setting is the easiest type of meeting. If your online personality is the same as your offline personality, then these people are already your friends. Your only concern should be about judging the appearance of your online friends. Sometimes people don't look the way we expect them to, but you shouldn't let that interfere with your fun.

If you're interested in joining a new offline group and you don't know any of the members, you'll usually be asked to either attend one of their open rituals or to meet one or more of the members in a public place. If someone asks you to come to his or her house before you've met in person, you should be alarmed. Ask to meet in public instead. Go to the meeting with a set of questions about the group to make sure it is actually what you're looking for. Expect to be asked questions about yourself, your background, and your interest in Paganism. If you're under eighteen, don't be surprised if the group leader wants to talk to your parents before allowing you to join.

If you're attending a large group ritual for the first time, try to arrive early. If you can, find a member of the group and introduce yourself. Let him or her know that you're new and ask if there is anything you need to be aware of. If you see someone else standing alone, go up and introduce yourself. Now you're not alone anymore, and you may have just made a new Pagan friend.

Is the first meeting with a Pagan group an interview?
Sort of. You should do your best to make a good impression, but you should also be honest about your background and your degree of experience. No one is going to ask you to be the high priestess at the first meeting.

Participate in Rituals

Most Pagan rituals are participatory. While some events might be willing to allow bystanders to observe from outside sacred space, for the most part it's expected that you'll join in the ritual. Now, don't fret that someone is going to ask you, the newbie, to invoke the goddess your first time out. Participation means standing in the circle and following along with the leader while keeping your attention focused on the ritual.

Most public rituals are extensively planned and rehearsed, but sometimes the leader of a small group ritual will ask for volunteers. If you feel comfortable taking on a larger role, go for it. You could be asked to pass around the ritual beverage, or to call one of the directions. If you don't feel comfortable volunteering, no one will think less of you.

Potluck Contributions

Most Pagan rituals are potluck, and will say so on the announcement or flier. At very large rituals, you'll also be asked to bring your own cup, plate, and utensils to reduce costs and save the earth from another 100 paper plates tossed in a landfill. Bring your potluck contribution in a container you don't mind losing, and bring enough to serve five to ten people.

At small, private rituals bring food for three to four people. If you're not sure what to bring, ask the ritual leader for advice. A few bottles of juice or soda are always appreciated because most people bring food.

Most potlucks have something for everyone, but it's best to bring something you know you like. Potluck dishes are usually in keeping with the season, such as deviled eggs at Ostara or a Yule log cake at Yule.

If you're at a group meeting, the leader may provide munchies, members may rotate snack duty, or everyone might bring something every time. Follow the lead of the other members. Meeting munchies are usually simple, like cheese and crackers or a bowl of grapes.

To Pay or Not to Pay?

Hosting rituals or running a group can get expensive, but the question of payment is controversial in the Pagan community. Some people believe you shouldn't have to pay to participate in your religion, but others think it's unfair to ask one person to shoulder the cost all the time. At some point you'll be faced with this quandary, and here are a few pointers:

·   If the class or ritual is held in rented space, a sliding-scale fee is a reasonable request.
·   If the ritual is at a member's home, bring a potluck item.
·   If the teacher provides many handouts or craft materials, reimbursement is a reasonable request.
·   If someone provides you with a professional service, expect to pay accordingly.
·   If you can't afford the fees, offer a work-trade.

Generally, covens, kindreds, and groves don't charge students who will become initiates. Most other classes, like aromatherapy workshops or drum-making classes, do charge fees. If a fee seems exorbitant, which is more likely with a class aimed at New Agers than a class aimed at Pagans, then skip the class.

Know Your Place

When you join a group or participate in ritual, show respect for the older members or event planners—no one likes a showoff newbie. If the ritual leader uses a tool in a different way than you do, go along with it. The person who says, "That's cool, but here's how *I* do it," is never popular.

When choosing a group or class, look for a leader or teacher who has been following the path for several years. The wisdom carried by elders is enormously beneficial to your learning process. If you want to lead a group eventually, having a good teacher will make you a better leader.

When you're new to a group, feel free to contribute, but follow the guidance of the group. For example, if your group is deciding on a new topic or book to study and there's one you're itching to delve into, suggest it. If your suggestion is voted down, don't hold a grudge about it. Your topic may be picked next, or you may discover that the chosen topic is even better than yours.

Before You Join

Once you've managed to locate a group, it's tempting to just jump right in. This is perfectly fine if the group is online. You can subscribe and unsubscribe from online groups quickly and easily with little risk of hurt feelings. Offline groups involve real people in the real world, and require a greater commitment from you. Pagan groups become small families, and changing families is not always an easy or painless process.

Approach joining an offline group like you would buying a new car. You don't necessarily buy the first car you see on the lot. First you take it for a test drive. Use the questions here to help you take your potential new group out for a spin.

Do My Beliefs Mesh with the Group's?

This should be the first question you ask. If you're interested in Asatru and you find a Wiccan group, that obviously won't be a good fit, but there are divisions even within the main branches that you should consider. For example, are you interested in working with a specific pantheon, like the Greek gods, or do you enjoy a more eclectic approach? If the group is at odds with your personal preferences, you might find rituals and meetings tense instead of enlightening.

Does the group work skyclad and are you comfortable with that? Do they meet monthly, weekly, or on full and new moons and can you make the same commitment? Do they stress magic over religion, or vice versa? What sorts of topics do they study?

Make a list of the beliefs and practices that are important to you. You may even want to rank them by priority in case you find a group that coincides with some, but not all, of your preferences. Once you know what you can and can't live with, it will be easier to choose a working group that's right for you.

Do I Like the Leader?

Some groups have a specific leader all the time. This could be the person who formed the group, but it could also be a trained priest or priestess. Other groups have leaders elected for a specific length of time. Still other groups have no leaders and work by consensus.

It's especially important to make sure you're comfortable with permanent leaders. While temporary leaders usually step aside at the end of their term, some permanent leaders view their groups as personal fiefdoms. Be wary of power trips or extreme demands and restrictions. Also be wary of disorganization or an unwillingness to really lead. There should be some give and take within a group, but if the group has a leader, at some point he or she has to be willing to take charge. At the same time, the leader should know when to concede to the desires of the rest of the group.

Do I Like the Group's Structure?

In addition to determining whether or not you are comfortable with a specific group's leader, you should also decide how comfortable you are with the group's structure. Groups that operate by consensus often work without a leader, which can be tricky if members have trouble with communication. In groups with leaders, the members hold discussions and votes, with the leaders casting the tie-breaking votes. Groups based on Gardner's model, Druid groves, and Asatru kindreds may have a hierarchy consisting of several officers with specific duties in addition to a degreed training system. Groups that are organized as tax-exempt churches may also have certain offices in keeping with the requirements of the tax code.

Do I Meet the Group's Requirements?

Finally, decide just how serious you are about joining a new group and how able or willing you are to meet its requirements. If you're looking for a casual study group, don't join a hierarchal group with a degreed training program. If you are looking for a group with a longer lineage or like things organized and structured with prescribed training materials and requirements, then a hierarchal group is for you.

Also consider where you are in your life and how easy it will be for you to meet the requirements. Are you going to school and working full-time? Then you probably shouldn't embark on a first-degree Gardnerian training program just yet. Are you a full-time student who will soon be graduating and beginning a job hunt that could take you out of state? You might want to wait until you're settled before finding a group. Are you just working to pay the bills and want more meaning in your life? This is the perfect time to join a group that requires a lot from you.

Covens, groves, and kindreds require varying levels of commitment from new members. Study groups and other working groups outside of an organized coven, grove, or kindred may be more casual about meetings. They also tend to have a greater fluctuation of membership and may fall apart quickly or continue for years.

If Someone Makes You Uncomfortable

So, now you've found a group and it seems to be a good fit, but then someone in the group starts to make you uncomfortable. Whether it's the person's behavior, or just a general weird vibe, you don't have to accept it. No group is perfect and you do have options for dealing with it.

Pagan Predators

It's sad to say, but as with any community, there are predators within the Pagan community. These predators often roam from community to community preying sexually, emotionally, and mentally on young people new to Paganism. These people often use the same methods, which makes them easy to spot and avoid. For example, a predator new to the community might introduce himself by announcing the formation of a coven for young women that requires a sexual initiation.

Unfortunately, there are predators who know how to blend in. They may find their way into groups before their true colors show. If someone in a group does something to make you uncomfortable, speak to the group leader. If you have no leader, pull someone aside and ask if he or she has noticed anything strange, then keep an eye out for odd or inappropriate behavior. If your suspicions are confirmed, you can decide whether to call the police, magically bind the predator, or boot him from the group.

Pagan Antagonists

Antagonists pose a less cut-and-dried challenge than predators. There are certain people who enjoy causing trouble or challenging authority. If someone in your group becomes antagonistic toward you, speak to the leader. The leader can then ask the person to quit it or leave the group. If you have no leader, speak to the person privately. If the behavior continues, discuss it with other members and decide what to do as a group. If you have to ask the person to leave, it will be difficult, but it's better than having your whole group disband because of the behavior of one person.

How to Leave a Group

At some point in your Pagan life, you will probably have to leave a group. It could be because the group no longer meets your needs. It could be that you're moving far away. Maybe you need some time off. Or maybe the permanent leader of your group has decided to disband it.

The proper etiquette for leaving a group that no longer meets your needs depends on how the group is structured. If you're moving away, well, that's simple enough. Everyone can understand that.

If it's a coven with a large membership and you're ready to become a leader, speak to the current leader about hiving off a new group. If you want to join a new, unrelated group, simply tell your current group that your path has shifted and you don't want your new interests to interfere with the rest of the group.

If you need time off, that's also understandable. Most religions offer their priests sabbaticals, and your Pagan group should be no different. Just make sure not to burn any bridges in case you want to return to the group eventually.

Being disbanded by your leader is a little more difficult. You may feel lost without your group. Just because the leader doesn't want to meet, that doesn't mean that you and several other former group members can't form a new group. This could also be an opportunity for you to join a different group altogether.

There are cases where several members of a group decide to form a new group and the leader takes it personally. The situation can quickly become fractious and devolve into a witch war. Do your best to avoid sinking to the lowest level. It's important that you do what's right for you, but be civil about it.

Many Pagans start out as solitaries, but there is much to be gained from becoming a part of the larger Pagan community. Once you've decided it's time to join a group, you'll find that your faith evolves in new ways. You might stick with your group for life, or you might transition to new paths or practices within Neo-Pagansim. This book can help you decide where to start, and the resources in the back can help you learn more about every aspect of Neo-Paganism.

Appendices

Appendix A

Pagan Deities

Appendix B

Additional Resources

Appendix A

Pagan Deities

Goddesses and Their Attributes		
Name	**Culture**	**Attribute**
Amaterasu	Japanese	sun
Aphrodite	Greek	love
Arianrhod	British	stars, time, birth, initiation
Artemis	Greek	hunt, animals
Athena	Mycenaean	warrior goddess
Branwen	British	love, death
Brighid	Irish	smithcraft, poetry, healing, fire, learning, fertility
Cerridwen	British	corn, inspiration, rebirth
Danu	Irish	mother of all, rivers
Demeter	Greek	earth, winter, spring
Eostre	Teutonic	spring
Epona	Gallic	horses
Flora	Roman	flowers, spring
Freya	Norse	magic, sex, love, health
Frigga	Norse	marriage, childbirth
Gaea	Greek	earth
Hathor	Egyptian	motherhood, love, sex
Hecate	Greek	guardian of the crossroads
Hera	Greek	marriage
Hestia	Greek	hearth
Inanna	Sumerian	mother goddess, childbirth
Juno	Roman	marriage, childbirth, women
Kali	Hindu	creation, destruction
Kore	Greek	spring, underworld
Lilith	Hebrew	pregnant women, death
Macha	Irish	death
Maia	Greek	plants

Name	Culture	Attribute (continued)
Morrigan	Irish	war, death
Oshún	Yoruban	beauty, sensuality, pregnancy, rivers
Oyá	Yoruban	storms
Rhiannon	British	horses
Shakti	Hindu	divine mother
Sunna	Norse	sun
Yemayá	Yoruban	mother goddess, oceans

Gods and Their Attributes		
Name	Culture	Attribute
Angus Og	Irish	love
Anubis	Egyptian	cemeteries, funerals
Apollo	Greek	music, poetry
Arawn	British	underworld
Ares	Greek	war
Balder	Norse	sun
Belenos	British	fire
Bran	British	war, land
Cernunnos	Gallic	fertility, animals
Chango	Yoruban	lightning, thunder
Crom-Dubh	Irish	harvest, sacred bull
Dagda	Irish	knowledge, father god
Dionysus	Greek	wine
Eleggua	Yoruban	crossroads, future
Esus	Gallic	trees, cranes
Frey	Norse	fertility, erotic love
Gwydion	British	sky, magic, poetry
Hades	Greek	underworld
Helios	Greek	sun
Hephaestus	Greek	fire, smithcraft
Hermes	Greek	messenger

Name	Culture	Attribute
Herne	British	hunt
Jupiter	Roman	sky, property
Loki	Norse	trickster, wildfires
Lug	Irish	skills, light
Mabon	Gallic	light
Manannan Mac Lir	Irish	sea
Mithras	Persian	sun
Njord	Norse	sea, peace
Obatalá	Yoruban	purity, patience, intelligence
Ochossi	Yoruban	plants
Odin	Norse	magic, poetry, runemasters
Ogún	Yoruban	iron
Orunmila	Yoruban	wisdom
Osiris	Egyptian	death
Pan	Greek	forest
Poseidon	Greek	sea
Ra	Egyptian	sun
Shiva	Hindu	supreme god
Taranis	Gallic	thunder, wheel, oak tree
Teutates	Gallic	warrior
Thor	Norse	warrior, loyalty
Tyr	Norse	law, justice, oaths
Vali	Norse	vengeance, rebirth
Zeus	Greek	sky

Additional Resources

Recommended Reading

History

Ancient Egyptian Religion, by Stephen Quirke. New York: Dover Publications, 1992; reprint, 1995.

Drawing Down the Moon: Witches, Druids, Goddess-Worshippers, and Other Pagans in America Today, by Margot Adler. New York: Viking, 1979; reprint, Beacon, 1986; Penguin, 1997.

Gods and Myths of Ancient Greece: The Archaeology and Mythology of Ancient Peoples, by Mary Barnett. New York: Smithmark, 1996.

A History of Pagan Europe, by Prudence Jones and Nigel Pennick. London: Routledge, 1995.

The Sacred World of the Celts, by Nigel Pennick. Rochester, VT: Inner Traditions International, 1997.

The Triumph of the Moon: A History of Modern Pagan Witchcraft, by Ronald Hutton. Oxford: Oxford University Press, 1999.

Witches and Neighbors: The Social and Cultural Context of European Witchcraft, by Robin Briggs. New York: Penguin Books, 1996; reprint 1998.

Wicca and Witchcraft

Ancient Ways: Reclaiming Pagan Traditions, by Pauline Campanelli. St. Paul, MN: Llewellyn, 1991.

Buckland's Complete Book of Witchcraft, by Raymond Buckland. St. Paul, MN: Llewellyn Publications, 1975; reprint, 1986.

Circle of Isis: Ancient Egyptian Magic for Modern Witches, by Ellen Cannon Reed. Franklin Lakes, NJ: New Page Books, 2002.

Circle Round: Raising Children in the Goddess Tradition, by Starhawk, Diane Baker, and Anne Hill. New York: Bantam Books, 1998.

The Craft: A Witch's Book of Shadows, by Dorothy Morrison. St. Paul, MN: Llewellyn Publications, 2001.

The Everything® Wicca and Witchcraft Book, by Marian Singer. Avon, MA: Adams Media Corporation, 2002.

Italian Witchcraft: The Old Religion of Southern Europe, by Raven Grimassi. St. Paul, MN: Llewellyn Publications, 2000.

To Ride a Silver Broomstick: New Generation Witchcraft, by Silver Ravenwolf. St. Paul, MN: Llewellyn Publications, 1998.

The Spiral Dance: A Rebirth of the Ancient Religion of the Goddess, by Starhawk. New York: HarperSanFrancisco, 1979; reprint, 1999.

Wheel of the Year: Living the Magical Life, by Pauline Campanelli. St. Paul, MN: Llewellyn Publications, 1989.

Wicca: A Guide for the Solitary Practitioner, by Scott Cunningham. St. Paul, MN: Llewellyn Publications, 1988.

Asatruar Faith

Futhark: A Handbook of Rune Magic, by Edred Thorsson. York Beach, ME: Samuel Weiser, 1984.

Gods and Myths of Northern Europe, by H. R. Ellis Davidson. New York: Viking, 1990.

Leaves of Yggdrasil, by Freya Aswynn. St. Paul, MN: Llewellyn Publications, 1994.

Myths and Symbols in Pagan Europe: Early Scandinavian and Celtic Religions, by H. R. Ellis Davidson. Syracuse: Syracuse University Press, 1988.

Northern Magic: Rune Mysteries and Shamanism, by Edred Thorsson. St. Paul, MN: Llewellyn Publications, 1998.

Teutonic Magick: The Magical and Spiritual Practices of the Germanic People, by Kveldulf Gundarsson. United Kingdom: Freya Aswynn, 1990, 2002.

Teutonic Religion: Folk Beliefs and Practices of the Northern Tradition, by Kveldulf Gundarsson. United Kingdom: Freya Aswynn, 1993; reprint, 2002.

Druidry and Celtic Myths

The Book of Druidry, by Ross Nichols. London: Thorsons, 1975; reprint, 1990.

Celtic Gods, Celtic Goddesses, by R. J. Stewart. London: Blandford Press, 1990.

Celtic Myths, Celtic Legends, by R. J. Stewart. London: Blandford Press, 1994; reprint, 1996.

The Druids, by Peter Berresford Ellis. Grand Rapids, MI: William B. Eerdmans Publishing Company, 1994.

The Druid Source Book, compiled and edited by John Matthews. London: Blandford Press, 1997; reprint, 1998, 1999.

Encyclopedia of Celtic Wisdom: A Celtic Shaman's Source Book, by Caitlin and John Matthews. Dorset: Element Books, 1994.

Kindling the Celtic Spirit: Ancient Traditions to Illumine Your Life Throughout the Seasons, by Mara Freeman. New York: HarperSanFrancisco, 2000.

Ritual: A Guide to Life, Love and Inspiration, by Emma Restall Orr. London: Thorsons, 2000.

Thorsons Principles of Druidry, by Emma Restall Orr. London: Thorsons, 1998.

The World of the Druids, by Miranda J. Green. London: Thames and Hudson, 1997.

Vodoun and Santería

The Altar of My Soul: The Living Traditions of Santería, by Marta Moreno Vega. New York: Ballantine Publishing Group, 2000.

Cuban Santeria: Walking with the Night, by Raul Conizares. Rochester, Vermont: Destiny Books, 1993; reprint, 1999.

Jambalaya: The Natural Woman's Book of Personal Charms and Practical Rituals by Luisah Teish. New York: HarperCollins Publishers, 1985.

Voodoo & Hoodoo: The Craft as Revealed by Traditional Practitioners, by Jim Haskins. Lanham, MD: Scarborough House, 1978; reprint, 1990.

Shamanism

Fire in the Head: Shamanism and the Celtic Spirit, by Tom Cowan. New York: HarperSanFrancisco, 1993.

Shamanism as a Spiritual Practice for Daily Life, by Tom Cowan. Freedom, CA: The Crossing Press, 1996.

The Way of the Shaman, by Michael Harner. New York: HarperSanFrancisco, 1980; reprint, 1990.

Neo-Pagan Magic

Dark Moon Mysteries: Wisdom, Power and Magic of the Shadow World, by Timothy Roderick. Watsonville, CA: New Brighton Books, 1993; reprint, 1996, 2003.

Grandmother Moon: Lunar Magic in Our Lives, by Zsuzsanna E. Budapest. New York: HarperSanFrancisco, 1991.

Three Books of Occult Philosophy, by Henry Cornelius Agrippa. Edited and annotated by Donald Tyson. Translated by James Freake. St. Paul, MN: Llewellyn Publications, 1995.

Neo-Pagan Sexuality

The Ethical Slut: A Guide to Infinite Sexual Possibilities, by Dossie Easton and Catherine A. Liszt. Oakland, CA: Greenery Press, 1998

Gay Witchcraft: Empowering the Tribe, by Christopher Penczak. York Beach, ME: Red Wheel/Weiser, 2003.

Modern Sex Magick: Secrets of Erotic Spirituality, by Donald Michael Kraig. St Paul, MN: Llewellyn Publications, 1999.

Polyamory: The New Love Without Limits: Secrets of Sustainable Intimate Relationships, by Dr. Deborah M. Anapol. San Rafael, CA: Intinet Resource Center, 1997.

Screw the Roses, Send Me the Thorns: The Romance and Sexual Sorcery of Sadomasochism, by Phillip Miller, Molly Devon, and William A. Granzig. Fairfield, CT: Mystic Rose Books, 1995.

Sexual Ecstasy and the Divine, by Yasmine Galenorn. Berkeley, CA: The Crossing Press, 2003.

SM 101: A Realistic Introduction, by Jay Wiseman. Oakland, CA: Greenery Press, 1998.

Explaining Your Beliefs and Protecting Your Rights

The Law Enforcement Guide to Wicca, by Kerr Cuhulain: Victoria, Canada: Horned Owl Publishing, 1997.

Pagans and the Law: Understand Your Rights, by Dana D. Eilers. Franklin Lakes, NJ: New Page Books, 2003.

The Truth About Witchcraft, by Scott Cunningham. St. Paul, MN: Llewellyn Publications, 1988; reprint, 1998.

Pagan Fiction

Aphrodite's Riddle, by Jennifer Reif. Niceville, FL: Spilled Candy Books, 2003.

Harm None: A Rowan Gant Investigation, by M. R. Sellars. St. Louis, MO: WillowTree Press, 2000.

Once Upon a Beltane Eve, by Selene Silverwind. Niceville, FL: Spilled Candy Books, 2001.

Quicksilver Moon, by Barbara Ardinger. Longview, TX: Three Moons Media, 2003.

Recommended Web Sites

General Pagan Information

About Guide to Alternative Religions: *http://altreligion.about.com* This site provides a collection of links concerned with nearly every alternative religion practiced today.

Beliefnet: *www.beliefnet.com* Online community for members of all religions. Its central feature is a group of message boards that foster religious debate. The site also contains columns and articles from prominent members of various faiths.

The Cauldron: A Pagan Forum: *www.ecauldron.com* A compendium of information useful to Pagans, it also has extensive links to information about reconstructionist faiths.

Ontario Consultants on Religious Tolerance: *www.religioustolerance.org* This site should be your first stop for accurate, unbiased information about almost every major and minor religion.

The Religious Movements Homepage at the University of Virginia: *http://religiousmovements.lib.virginia.edu/* Another site offering unbiased profiles of most of the world's religions and religious movements. They also offer religious rights and freedom information.

The Witches' Voice: *www.witchvox.com* This Web site is usually referred to as Witchvox. It is the largest single source of Pagan information and includes lists of stores, events, and groups in every state and around the world, message boards, and a newslink for Pagan rights issues or favorable media coverage.

Neo-Pagan History

National Geographic, Salem Witch-Hunt: *www.nationalgeographic.com/salem* This section of the National Geographic Web site allows you to experience the witch trials as one of the accused.

Salem Witchcraft, the Events and Causes of the Salem Witch Trials: *www.salemwitchtrials.com* An interesting history of the events and attitudes that led to the Salem witch trials.

The Salem Witch Museum: *www.salemwitchmuseum.com* The online version of the Salem Witch Museum in Salem, Massachusetts, provides information on the witch trials.

The Witching Hours: *www.shanmonster.com/witch/index.html* An extensive site documenting the people, beliefs, causes, and effects of the European Witch Craze.

Wicca and Witchcraft

Covenant of the Goddess:*www.cog.org* The online home of the Covenant of the Goddess contains information about their networking activities, the Merry Meet gathering, and an introduction to Wicca.

La Vecchia Religione, Home of Authentic Italian Witchcraft: *www.stregheria.com* This site is hosted by Raven Grimassi, the leading author on the topic of Italian witchcraft. It provides information on Stregheria, his books, and a link to his online store.

PanGaia: *www.pangaia.com PanGaia* is one of four magazines published by Blessed Bee, Inc. They also publish *SageWoman*, a magazine aimed at Pagan women, *newWitch*, a magazine for twentysomething Pagans, and *The Blessed Bee*, a Pagan parenting newsletter.

Reclaiming: *www.reclaiming.org* The online home of the Reclaiming tradition where you'll find networking information and links to the WitchCamps. You'll also find information about how this specific tradition is practiced and learn more about its political activities.

The Third Road:*www.well.com/~zthirdrd* Author Francesca De Grandis teaches her version of the Feri tradition through her books and intensive training courses. Information about her classes is available here.

Asatruar Faith

The Asatru Alliance: *www.asatru.org* The Asatru Alliance also hosts an annual AlThing gathering. Their site features information on Asatru holidays, a list of Asatru kindreds registered with the alliance, and links to other Asatru organizations.

Asatru Folk Assembly: *www.runestone.org* The Asatru Folk Assembly is one of the more prominent Asatru organizations. It includes informative FAQs, articles, and contact information for several kindreds.

Echoed Voices, Modern Asatru: *www.echoedvoices.org* A basic, introductory article on Asatru from the online *Echoed Voices* magazine.

Hrafnar: *www.hrafnar.org* The official site of the Hrafnar Kindred. It contains several useful articles about Asatru and information about upcoming Hrafnar events.

The Irminsul Aettir: *www.irminsul.org* This site hosts an annual AlThing gathering. It provides information about upcoming events, an extensive list of kindreds worldwide, and links to other Asatru sites and articles.

Islenka Ásatrúarfélagið, Asatru in Iceland: *www.asatru.is/english* This is the official site of the Pagan Assembly in Iceland. It's an interesting look at how the faith is practiced in the land in which it originated.

Raven Online, Your Homepage for Traditional Asatru: *www.webcom.com/~lstead* This Web site is hosted by the Raven Kindred and features information about the basics of Asatru as well as the specific practices of the kindred.

The Rune-Gild: *www.runegild.org* The Rune-Gild is dedicated to the study of runes and educating others in their use. Their member groups, called Halls, are found in the United States, England, and Australia.

Sacred Texts, the *Poetic Edda*: *www.sacred-texts.com/neu/poe* A public domain translation of the *Poetic Edda*. The *Prose Edda* is also available through the site's Legends and Sagas link.

The Troth: *www.thetroth.org* The official site of the Troth, a major Asatru organization, provides information on their clergy training program and Asatruar beliefs. Their entire 700-page book, *Our Troth*, is posted for free viewing.

Druidry and the Celts

Ár nDraíocht Féin, a Druid Fellowship:*www.adf.org* ADF explains their take on Druidry at this site. They offer several training courses, including one for clergy. The site also includes a list of affiliated groves and guilds.

Celtic Ogham: *www.csupomona.edu/~jcclark/ogham/index.html* This site provides an overview of the ogham alphabet. It also features a downloadable ogham font for Windows.

The Druid Grove, the Order of Ovates, Bards, and Druids: *www.druidry.org* OBOD's site focuses primarily on British Druidry, but includes information of use to American Druids, such as recommended reading lists and a review of the practices of Druids.

The Druid Network: *www.druidnetwork.org* This site offers networking information for Druids around the world. The group also hosts retreats in the United Kingdom.

Every Ogham Thing on the Web: *www.evertype.com/standards/og/ogmharc.html* Check here for a comprehensive list of ogham links. You can also download a Mac ogham font.

The Henge of Keltria: *www.keltria.org* The Henge of Keltria is another American Druid organization. Their site contains information specific to their approach to Druidry and their grove and training system.

Santería and Vodoun

The Ifa Foundation, the Home of American Ifa: *www.ifafoundation.org* This site offers a new perspective on African religions modified for modern American life.

Lucumi.com, Internet Religious Botanica: *www.lucumi.com* One-stop shopping for Santería supplies and information.

New Orleans Voodoo Spiritual Temple: *www.access.avernus.com/~rogue/temple* This site provides straightforward answers about Vodoun from a Vodoun priestess. They also offer consultations, rituals, and tours of New Orleans.

Voodoo Authentica: *www.voodooshop.com* An online botanica that also provides information about Vodoun and spiritual consultations.

Shamanism

Shamanism, Frequently Asked Questions: *www.faqs.org/faqs/shamanism/overview* This simple FAQ offers a clear explanation of shamanism and the various types of trance used by shamanic practitioners.

Shamanism, the Foundation for Shamanic Studies: *www.shamanism.org* Michael Harner founded this organization. You can learn more about shamanism and his upcoming lectures and workshops at this site. They also have an online store.

Other Pagan Traditions

Hellenion: *www.hellenion.org* This site, hosted by an organization dedicated to furthering Hellenism, offers clergy training and links to other Hellenic groups.

The International Network of Kemetics: *www.inkemetic.org* As the name says, this is mainly a networking site for Kemetics, but it also provides articles and information about the religion.

The Kemetic Orthodox Faith: *www.kemet.org* Kemetic Orthodoxy is an alternative version of the Kemetic faith, and this site provides an explanation of Kemetic Orthodox beliefs and practices.

Nova Roma, Rome Reborn: *www.novaroma.org* This site has an extensive collection of information about the Religio Romano in seven languages.

The Stele, Home Page of the Omphalos: *www.cs.utk.edu/~mclennan/OM/index.html* This site has a large collection of resources for Hellenism and Roman Paganism.

The Virtual Temple of Minerva: *www.3commando.org/minerva_index.htm* This site provides one view on the Religio Romano and how it is practiced. It is also a temple to the goddess Minerva.

Neo-Pagan Sexuality

alt.polyamory: *www.polyamory.org* alt.polyamory is a newsgroup that also hosts a Web site. The site offers a vast collection of links about polyamory.

Leather Pagans: *www.leatherpagans.com* This site features articles and information about BDSM for Pagans.

Loving More: *www.lovingmore.com* Loving More is aimed at polyamorous people. They host a message board through their Web site and provide links to other polyamory organizations.

Pagan Rights

American Civil Liberties Union: *www.aclu.org* The ACLU is not a Pagan organization, but they actively fight religious discrimination.

Pagan Educational Network: *www.paganednet.org* The Pagan Educational Network works toward religious tolerance by educating others about Pagan practices. It also publishes brochures that teach Pagans to be successful activists.

Pagan Unity Campaign: *www.paganunitycampaign.org* The Pagan Unity Campaign is a political action committee. Their goal is to increase awareness of Pagans among politicians and to encourage Pagans to become registered voters.

Neo-Pagan Gatherings

Starwood: *www.rosencomet.com* The Association for Consciousness Exploration hosts the Starwood gathering and several other gatherings throughout the year.

Gathering of the Tribes: *www.outofthedark.com* Out of the Dark, Inc., hosts the Fall and Spring Gathering of the Tribes as well as a few other gatherings during the year.

Hammer of Thor Kindred: *www.hammerofthorkindred.org* The Hammer of Thor Kindred hosts the Feast of Ostara and the Feast of Aegir, both of which are Asatru gatherings.

Ancient Ways of Knowing Foundation: *www.ancientways.org* Ancient Ways, a metaphysical store in Oakland, California, hosts Pantheacon and the Ancient Ways Festival.

ConVocation: *www.convocation.org* Visit this site to learn more about the ConVocation convention held in Michigan.

Ecumenicon: *www.ecumenicon.org* The Ecumenicon Fellowship is an interfaith church that also hosts the Ecumenicon conference in the Washington, D.C., area.

Pan Pagan Festival: *www.midwestpagancouncil.org* The Midwest Pagan Council hosts the Pan Pagan Festival in Indiana. They also host the Invocation convention.

Pagan Spirit Gathering: *www.circlesanctuary.org* Circle Sanctuary hosts the Pagan Spirit Gathering, but they are also very active in promoting and maintaining religious freedom in the United States. They publish a quarterly Pagan magazine that includes updates from the Lady Liberty League.

International Pagan Pride Project: *www.paganpride.org* This site lists all Pagan Pride events scheduled to take place around the world.

Index